"Jared Looney not only pulls together a wealth of data to explain what is happening all over the world, but also charts a course to engage our world today. He and his co-workers are charting a course for the rest of us in practice as well as theory. I heartily recommend this work but warn you to leave your preconceived notions about the world and the church behind. In days like these, the church needs guides like Jared."

Dan Bouchelle
President of Mission Resource Network

"Time is constant, but our world is changing faster than ever. It seems like the distance between the present and the future is shrinking rapidly so that we no longer have much time to prepare. I suggest you read this book as soon as possible if you want to be relevant for more than a day."

Neil Cole
Author of *Organic Church*, *Church 3.0* and *Primal Fire*

"Jared Looney successfully challenges the 21st-Century church to re-imagine both its character and mission in a world being transformed by the forces of globalization and urbanization. He also makes an invaluable contribution to the growing field of diaspora missiology by drawing attention to urban immigrant communities in North America where transnationalism is opening doors to fruitful Kingdom expansion around the world. Every church leader and disciple of Jesus Christ who desires to partner with God in his mission in North America must read this important book."

Daniel A. Rodriguez, Ph.D.
Professor of Religion and Hispanic Studies, Pepperdine University

Crossroads of the Nations

Diaspora, Globalization, and Evangelism

Jared Looney

Series Editors

Kendi Howells Douglas
Stephen Burris

Urban Loft Publishers | Portland, Oregon

Table of Contents

Series Preface / 9
Acknowledgements / 11
Foreword by Enoch Wan / 13

Chapter 1: Nations on the Move 17
Conclusion / 32
Reflection Questions / 34

Chapter 2: A World in Transition 35
Rise of the Church in the Global South / 36
Decline of the Church in the West / 39
Unreached Peoples and Creative Access / 44
Global Migration / 47
Acceleration of Urbanization / 52
Cities: Nodes in a Global Network / 57
Conclusion / 60
Reflection Questions / 61

Chapter 3: Loving Our Neighbor:
Foundations for Witness in a Pluralistic Society 63
Beginning With Our Own Hearts / 63
Welcoming the Foreigner / 68
The Blessings of Exiles / 70
Jesus the Refugee / 71
Embracing Samaritans / 73
The Good Samaritan: Embracing the "Other" / 73
Meeting at the Well: Pathways for the Gospel / 76
A Truly Great Commission / 78
International Encounters: Ethiopian Eunuch / 78
Fellowship with Pagans: Finding Cornelius / 80
Universal Access and a New Humanity / 82
Renewing Our Mind for Mission / 83
    Hospitality / 83
    Vulnerability / 85
    Boldness / 86
Conclusion / 87
Reflection Questions / 88

Chapter 4: Diaspora, Globalization, and Migration **89**

Globalization / 89

People on the Move / 94

Global Cities / 97

Diaspora Churches: Transplanted Witness / 105

Conclusion / 132

Reflection Questions / 134

Chapter 5: Evangelism Among the Nations **135**

Evangelism in Tension / 137

    Transcending the Dichotomy / 139

    Disciple Making as a Holistic Practice / 140

    Evangelism as a Ministry Vocation / 141

Evangelism in Contemporary Society / 142

Ministry, the City, and the Nations / 164

    Applying Multiplication Principles / 177

    Reaching Diaspora Communities / 180

    Subcultural Theory / 184

    Continuum of Assimilation / 187

    Contextualization / 192

    Citizens of the Diaspora / 196

Immigration and Identity / 199

Second-Generation Faith / 200

Conclusion / 204

Reflection Questions / 206

Chapter 6: Transnationalism and The Gospel:
Mission Without Borders **207**

People and Place / 208

Global Nomads: Understanding Transnationalism / 217

Global Evangelism: In the City and Through the City / 230

    Pioneer Church Planting / 234

    Just Passing Through: Reaching Internationals / 240

    A Missionary Life Uninterrupted / 245

    Movements Without Borders / 248

A New Kind of Short-Term Mission Trip? / 254

Sending Development Home / 260

    Grassroots Economics / 264

    Linking Communities at Home:

    Angel Reyes's Story / 270

The Church in Transnationalism / 275
Conclusion / 275
Reflection Questions / 277

Chapter 7: The New Context for Missions and Ministry Implications 279
The Church at Global Intersections / 279
Church Multiplication / 283
Creating Hospitable Space / 284
Exploring Business-as-Mission in
Diaspora Communities / 285
The New Playing Field:
The Importance of Cities as Global Nodes / 286
Evangelism in the Space of Global Flows:
Transnationalism and a Mobile World / 295
Adapting to a New World: Rethinking Structures / 301
Rediscovering Mutuality: Global Partnerships / 305
Mission at Cultural Intersections:
Western Cities, Post-Secular, and Post-Christendom / 308
Adaptable and Relational / 308
Becoming Aliens and Foreigners / 310
Encountering Nonbiblical Authority Structures / 311
Direct Evangelism / 312
Conclusion / 314
Reflection Questions / 316

Conclusion **317**

References / 321
About the Author / 329
About Urban Loft Publishers / 330

Series Preface

Urban Mission in the 21st Century is a series of monographs that addresses key issues facing those involved in urban ministry whether it be in the slums, squatter communities, *favelas*, or in immigrant neighborhoods. It is our goal to bring fresh ideas, a theological basis, and best practices in urban mission as we reflect on our changing urban world. The contributors to this series bring a wide-range of ideas, experiences, education, international perspectives, and insight into the study of the growing field of urban ministry. These contributions fall into four very general areas: 1—the biblical and theological basis for urban ministry; 2—best practices currently in use and anticipated in the future by urban scholar/activists who are living working and studying in the context of cities; 3—personal experiences and observations based on urban ministry as it is currently being practiced; and 4—a forward view toward where we are headed in the decades ahead in the expanding and developing field of urban mission. This series is intended for educators, graduate students, theologians, pastors, and serious students of urban ministry.

More than anything, these contributions are creative attempts to help Christians strategically and creatively think about how we can better reach our world that is now more urban than rural. We do not see theology and practice as separate and distinct. Rather, we see sound practice growing out of a healthy vibrant theology that seeks to understand God's world as it truly is as we move further into the twenty-first century. Contributors interact with the best scholarly literature available at the time of writing while making application to specific contexts in which they live and work.

Each book in the series is intended to be a thought-provoking work that represents the author's experience and perspective on urban ministry in a particular context. The editors have chosen those who bring this rich diversity of perspectives to this series. It is our hope and prayer that each book in this series will challenge, enrich, provoke, and cause the reader to dig deeper into subjects that bring the reader to a deeper understanding of our urban world and the ministry the church is called to perform in that new world.

Dr. Kendi Howells Douglas and Stephen Burris,
Urban Mission in the 21st Century Series Co-Editors

Acknowledgments

I deeply appreciate the support, encouragement, and patience of my wife, Hylma, and my daughter, Adalia. They have been my cheerleaders as I worked on this book. I cannot express how much I appreciate the moments they sacrificed while I was typing away at a keyboard.

I am thankful for our Global City Mission Initiative team, and I am grateful for our partners with NYC International Project and Global Gates. Together, we have been living these stories, and the adventures on the streets of New York City gave life to this book.

Mission Resource Network has been an exceptional partner, and I appreciate its role as champion of the ideas presented in this book.

Seth Bouchelle was a great help as he read an unfinished manuscript and offered input where I most needed it.

I am thrilled that Kendi Howells Douglas and Stephen Burris invited me to join this series. I have loved writing every page, and I pray this work will be a resource for the mission of God and truly help contribute to a Gospel movement in our urban world in the 21st century.

Foreword

Jared Looney and Aldous Huxley are both good story tellers but a century apart. Huxley's *Brave New World* was published in 1931 and *Crossroads of the Nations* in 2015. Huxley wrote a novel but Looney's book is a collection of real-life stories. Huxley creatively imagined a futuristic world, whereas Looney systematically compiled many cases of contemporary diaspora communities/congregations. Huxley wove together themes such as pharmacological conditioning, psychological manipulation, and sleep-teaching into his fictitious work. In this book, Looney calls contemporary Christians to "brave through the storm of the twin forces" of globalization and urbanization in the 21st century. Huxley warned of the world-to-come but Looney attempts to waken the Church to the present reality of a changed landscape that requires major adjustments when carrying out the Great Commission.

The city is the focus of both "urban missiology" and of this book. Looney's macro perspective of the "city" is refreshing and inspiring. His statement below is telling: "While processes of globalization and urbanization intersect and overlap in countless towns and cities, global cities—the primary global command centers in the global network—have been particularly challenging for Christian evangelism as well as gateways for vast opportunity." Looney's "urban missiology" is different from other authors in missiological literature because it is global in perspective, contemporary to the 21st century, complex in operation, and fluid in framework due to ongoing socio-cultural changes. Its distinctive is summarized as follows: "The rise of the processes of globalization is leading us to see 'the world as a single place' with greater and greater connectedness between once distant locations, and borders between nation-states are less and less of a barrier to religious, cultural, and commercial exchanges. Time and space are being compressed through information, communication, and travel technologies ..."

For more than a decade, one of the several areas of my research has been "diaspora missiology"—an emerging missiological paradigm with relatively few publications. This book will add to the limited pool of literature in a unique way, giving helpful illustrations to diaspora missiological theory by: (a) telling the "life story" of his own career development and family expansion; (b) providing "case study" of diaspora communities in global cities such as New York City, London, Tokyo, Paris, Toronto, Sao Paulo, etc.; (c) offering rich ministerial examples such as Global City Mission Initiative, New York City International Project, etc.

This book joins an ongoing conversation concerning missions and the global diaspora. It provides a wider framework of globalization's impact on world missions while focusing on mission *in* and *through* diaspora communities. It is a collection of tangible experiences currently playing out among those reaching out to diaspora communities, leading to the recognition of mission principles currently being explored and discovered within a global context.

The author's premise is that the "global city" is the "crossroads of the nations" where social currents of globalization and urbanization converse. Globalization is working symbiotically with urbanization to simultaneously transform the global context of Christian missions. Consequently, the missionary task of our time is "standing at a crossroads" due to the daunting challenge of adapting to a new global reality and strategizing accordingly.

In the new context of an urbanized and globalized society, missiologists are challenged to go beyond the traditional route of crossing cultures in a distant land. They are tasked "to train a Western and sometimes insulated church how to interact and engage with a pluralistic and international society that is both near and far."

In this book, many helpful descriptions and convincing arguments are offered to help readers grapple with the new reality that global cities are "nodes in a global network and are of strategic importance for the mission of the church. These are the centers of human activity that connect people and institutions through city-to-city and city-to-region interactions. This blurs the distinction of local and global." Consequently, the Church is faced with the challenge of reimagining ministry and revising strategy in "a mobile world in constant flux driven by the twin forces of globalization and urbanization."

One of the goals of the author is "to equip and enhance the evangelism of the church among diaspora communities as the body of Christ navigates its way through an age of globalization." Another goal is to offer a corrective to "the dichotomy between addressing primarily physical needs or exclusively addressing spiritual needs." Therefore, Looney insists that disciple-making is both holistic and relational in approach, contextual and flexible in practice, international and transnational in scope, dynamic and evolutionary in operation, fluid and adaptable in paradigmatic framework, and global and local simultaneously. In this book, the author manages to achieve these goals with impressive eloquence.

Throughout the book, the author aptly uses examples of real practices taking place in our contemporary context of world missions. I recommend this book because I agree that:

> "... there are trailblazers riding the waves of globalization and migration as missionary agents in our world. Through the stories flowing out of new ministry practices in and through diaspora networks, I hope we will continue to develop practices aligned with our new contexts for global missions and adjust the way we think about Christian missions."

Enoch Wan (www.enochwan.com)
Former president of Evangelical Missiological Society (2008-2014)
Director, Institute of Diaspora Studies, Western Seminary

Chapter 1
Nations on the Move

The world is changing, and that fact has gotten quite a lot of press in recent years. A simple Internet search along the themes of global trends, cultural changes affecting the church, and the like, will open up a Pandora's Box of blogs, books, articles, lectures, conference themes, and curriculum. Certainly this book is adding to that larger conversation. While the 20th century saw the rapid increase of urbanization, which is continuing its momentum today, our entrance into the 21st century is riding the wave of globalization. The twin forces of globalization and urbanization are changing everything right before our eyes. While conversations among church and mission leaders invoke the themes of engagement such as missional, organic, or incarnational as well as contextual themes such as postmodern, post-Christendom, or "glocal" (global and local considerations), the currents of globalization and urbanization have become the drivers of our societal transformation, and it is difficult to imagine that these social forces won't have a deep and lasting impact on how the church thinks about her participation in the global mission of God. Indeed, the ripple effects of a world that is both shrinking through its connectivity and growing through the rise of massive urban conglomerates is felt in personal ways in billions of individual stories. Each of our own stories is caught up in the drama of a world transforming.

The world in which I now live is quite different than the one I used to know. I grew up riding on a tractor, climbing trees, fishing in canals with not another soul in sight, and exploring the fields of brush, trees, and cactus that surrounded our trailer that sat just outside the city limits in the middle of the Rio Grande Valley of the United States. It was a great adventure to run with our dogs through wooded areas and chase rabbits while trying to avoid running into the piercing needles of a cactus growing side-by-side with thorny little mesquite trees. The other neighborhood boys and I would ride our bikes up and down what were then caliche roads, and we would momentarily pause for the occasional car rolling into the neighborhood in the days that preceded emerging suburban development. Parents could just yell—either in English or in Spanish—down the street that it was time for their child to come home for supper, and they often did. Not long after I left for college, the road was paved, new houses were built, and today my childhood neighborhood sits on the edge of expanding subdivisions within the city limits.

The rhythms of my life are now quite different. Immediately following my college graduation, I lived in downtown Houston, in the neighborhood known as the Sixth Ward, a few blocks from the towering high rises of the central business district. Living in a small one-bedroom apartment owned by my Spanish-speaking landlord, I once again lived on the edge of change as "the hood" was becoming increasingly gentrified. Eventually, I moved to New York City as a church planter, and I now live on the sixth floor of a mid-rise apartment building in the Bronx. Trains and buses run throughout the day and night. Cars never stop moving up and down our street—a main thoroughfare for the neighborhood. Our area is actually full of magnificent trees lining the streets, but I never see any children climbing them. There are rules here about where to ride bikes or play ball. Parks and community gardens bring nature into contact with the urban jungle of concrete and steel. Our lifestyles move at a quicker pace, and I'm convinced that time must be doing so as well.

My world is entirely multicultural. When I walk through my New York City communities, I may taste the spices of Bengali in the fast-growing Bangladeshi community in the Southeast Bronx, or I might meet up with a friend for Albanian burek and espresso at a Kosovar restaurant not far from my home. On any given day, I could be interacting with South Asians, Albanians, Latinos, Koreans, Russians, and the list of potential cross-cultural encounters could go on and on. I live in New York City, and it is a conglomeration of nations from around the globe. For me, living out the realities of a global, urban, and multicultural world is not limited to walking the streets of my city, but it is part of my own story. I met my wife while attending Manhattan Church of Christ on the Upper East Side, shortly after I had moved to New York as an urban missionary. She is of West Indian ancestry, and the citizenship of her birth is the United Kingdom. She holds passports from both the United States and the United Kingdom, and she is able to give our daughter dual citizenship as well. In addition, my sister and I went to the same college, Abilene Christian University, in West Texas. While there, she met an international student from Thailand. They eventually married, and they live and work as a family in a middle-class neighborhood in Bangkok on the other side of the planet. They are not on an extended short-term mission trip or vacation through Asia. In their Bangkok neighborhood, they are simply home. We've adapted to different rhythms and adjusted to cultural realities far more complex than the world as we understood it growing up as children.

The neighborhood in which I grew up keeps changing. I still remember how different things seemed when I visited from college and saw that our old caliche road was paved following the expansion of the city limits. Today, when I visit family, it is a completely different place. The woods and brush areas that I used to explore no longer exist. Instead, those spaces are now populated by city lots filled with brick houses, backyards, and swing sets. Subdivisions have been built where I used to run and hide in tall grass and small trees. Cars run up and down the street much more frequently, and plenty of malls, department stores, shopping centers, and restaurants are within walking distance or a very short drive. The reality, of course, is that these shifts in demography are only one reflection of greater and greater momentum in urbanization and globalization both in North America and around the world. Our little story is repeated over and over again by countless millions as the world becomes a place of cities.

My own journey simply reflects a multitude of personal stories that demonstrates a shift toward a new urban and globally connected world, but my adaptation is far less radical than the culture shock faced by a rural Fujianese villager arriving in Manhattan's old Chinatown and working seven days a week to pay off debts after being transported to the United States. Nor is it comparable to the adjustments that have to be made by a small child smuggled across a river outside of Matamoras, Mexico, in the hopes of being reunited with his father who's been laboring day and night hundreds of miles away in Chicago for his family's future. It's not nearly as traumatic as the deep loneliness felt by an African relocating from a family-based tribal culture to a Western city driven by autonomous individualism or the insecurity felt by a new Japanese immigrant navigating the different customs of Portuguese-speaking Sao Paulo. It cannot possibly compare to a Lybian escaping the violence of civil war to an Italian city across the Mediterranean. The stories of globalization are human narratives. It is the anthology of hundreds of thousands of unique stories of opportunities and hardships. They are families and individuals, courageous pioneers and desperate entrepreneurs. It is hundreds of migrant diaspora communities transforming the fabric of cities throughout both North America and around the world.

Attention to missions among diaspora communities has been increasing in recent years, and rightly so. We are living in the midst of the greatest international migration in the history of our planet. Examples that illustrate our global world could run on indefinitely. More than 1 million Japanese live in Sao Paulo, Brazil (Geromel, 2013), and Brazil is the location for the greatest Japanese diaspora outside of

Japan (Veselinovic, 2013). In Europe, more than 20 million people live in a country other than the one in which they were born (Claydon, 2004), and the United Kingdom is now home to more Muslims than it is to Methodists and Baptists combined (Crabtree, 2012). An estimated 20 million South Asians live in nations outside of the Indian subcontinent (Claydon, 2004). Significant numbers of Kurds are found in thirteen different countries outside of the region known as "Kurdistan" (an area including parts of northern Iraq, northwestern Iran, western Turkey, and northeastern Syria), and clusters of Uzbeks are reportedly located in 20 countries outside of Uzbekistan (Winter & Koch, 2009). It's been estimated that 37% of the Gross National Product of the Philippines comes from remittances sent home by members of the Filipino diaspora scattered around the globe (Claydon, 2004, p. 37). From 1996 to 2000, migration contributed to 75% of population growth in the United States, and at the conclusion of the 20th century the world's most developed nations saw migrant populations increase from 38 million to 110 million from 1980 to 2000 alone (Wan, 2010, p. 4). For the United States, minorities are expected to collectively outnumber the White majority by 2043 (Payne, 2013, p. 63), and if trends continue, by 2050, one in four people living in the United States will more than likely be Hispanic (Claydon, 2004, p. 8). This rundown of figures provides a hint of the societal transformation unfolding on our planet.

As a result of the phenomenon of international migration on a global scale, many in the social sciences have turned their attention to understanding the social trends, histories, and dynamics of ethnic diasporas. The term "diaspora" has most widely been used by academics to describe the Jewish experience of becoming scattered across the Mediterranean world, especially during the period of the Roman Empire. Of course, now the term has come to mean so much more as it is applied to ethnic groups throughout the world that are experiencing global relocation and establishing new ethnic communities (Cohen, 1997, pp. 21-22). Indeed, in recent years, diaspora missiology has arisen as a discipline within missiological studies. Meetings of mission leaders emphasizing discussions on globalization, migration, or urbanization—three themes underlying any discussion of diaspora missiology—are becoming increasingly common conversations for the church in North America and globally.

To identify the phenomenon of ethnic diasporas, we may summarize these movements as having three key characteristics: "people who (1) have migrated from a homeland and settled in a new place, (2) have taken the time and trouble to form a separate community there, and (3) still maintain connections with the homeland" (Rynkiewich, 2011, p. 207). For missiologists, gaining a clear understanding of the phenomenon of diaspora movements may at times be a moving target. In Robin Cohen's seminal work, *Global Diasporas*, he argues that diasporas are indeed dynamic and evolving. Therefore, "developing a taxonomy of the diasporas is an inexact science." Ethnic diasporas vary in the cause of relocation, and a single diaspora may have multiple causes that brought about the displacement and relocation (Cohen, 1997, pp. 179-180). Often motives are economic as people in rural areas or poorer countries seek better opportunities in cities (Fischer, 1984, p. 87). However, there may be a number of issues stimulating or impacting the existence of diasporas. Once ethnic diasporas emerge in the city of a host nation, they develop traits unique to that immigrant community and begin making a cultural impact on the societal dynamics of the city. Each immigrant community is unique and has its own story (or stories) to tell. However, there are key characteristics that are true for most diaspora communities, and Cohen highlights nine that may be true of most global diasporas. These characteristics include:

1. Dispersal from an original homeland, often traumatically
2. Alternatively, the expansion from a homeland in search of work, in pursuit of trade or to further colonial ambitions
3. A collective memory and myth about the homeland
4. An idealization of the supposed ancestral home
5. A return movement

6. A strong ethnic group consciousness sustained over a long
   time
7. A troubled relationship with host societies
8. A sense of solidarity with co-ethnic members in other
   countries
9. The possibility of distinctive, creative, enriching lives in
   tolerant host countries

All of these characteristics may not be true for every community, but many ethnic diasporas may exhibit an overlapping combination of many of these attributes (Cohen, 1997, pp. 180-187).

In recent years, a great deal of attention has begun to turn to developing a missiology for the current diaspora phenomenon. Of course, there is good reason for the increased attention to global migration on the part of missiologists, church leaders, and academics. Attention to global migration and urbanization is the result of these factors making a profound impact on nations around the world. In fact, due to the magnitude of current trends in global migration, these global shifts may change the whole fabric of how we think about and do missions. A missionary may arrive in a specific country to focus on a certain nation of people only to discover that a considerable portion of the population lives outside of its homeland. An agency may send a missionary worker to an unreached people group to then discover that the leaders of that society are not physically present but are conducting business and managing their household affairs from an American or European city. A church in the United States may send a mission team to the other side of the world to start a church-planting movement while gradually coming to the realization that immigrants from the same city where their missionaries now live have moved in next door to their church building. In fact, it may be their new neighbors who will have some of the most significant influence back in their homeland where the missionary is being sponsored to serve. Western missionaries may return home and have the option of continuing to serve with the same ethnic group that are now living in increasing numbers in an American city. While development agencies pass millions of dollars through massive administrative infrastructures, the size of their investments are surpassed by remittances transferred by migrants to their home countries with little to no overhead involved beyond perhaps a bank transfer or currency conversion fee. Bible institutes designed to train indigenous leaders for local church leadership in their country may find themselves training soon-to-be migrants who, in some cases, will end up immigrating to the missionaries' country of origin. Just last year, a former African missionary working with one of our organization's ministry partners put me in contact with a Christian leader from Rwanda who was studying for his PhD in New England; he had been the missionary's translator many years ago in Rwanda. Also, during two different summers, our organization hosted a summer ministry intern from a Bible institute in Quito, Ecuador. He was raised by his grandparents in Ecuador while his parents lived and worked in Queens, New York. After being trained by American missionaries in Ecuador, following graduation from Bible college, he and his wife and their son have migrated to the United States.

The reality of diaspora movements will lead to a transformation of the way we think about Christian missions. Missiologists have at times focused the missionary task on targeted regions or nations, and at other times, missionaries have concentrated their efforts among a specific tribe, language, or people sometimes spread out across a larger geographic distance. Similarly, urban missiologists, with their devotion to the city, are often anchored in their concern for development and reconciliation in specific neighborhoods or with larger city-reaching projects. While our missiological strategies have lived in the tension of people groups and geographic regions or urban neighborhoods in the past as well as in the present, emerging global trends point toward a missiology that must identify with the global dynamics of mobility and networking. In many respects our contemporary global context has begun to transcend our traditional missiological categories. In this book, I will seek to push us beyond these static categories. Many cultures are no longer a monolithic ethnic community, but rather a network being transformed by their stories of migration. With the rise of numerous diaspora movements, the emergence of a diaspora missiology is of real importance to the overall mission of the church. Developing a diaspora missiology likely represents a step toward wrestling through new frameworks of contextualization in a globalized world. Indeed, seeking to understand mission among diaspora populations is not simply a subdiscipline on the edges of missiology. Rather, as globalization touches nearly every corner of the planet and global migration sends ripple effects throughout the world, a missiological emphasis on diaspora is extremely important for the overall study of missions in our new global context. Ironically, despite the historical desire for isolationism that has permeated American culture, diaspora missiology is of extreme importance for the American church since the number of immigrants arriving from the majority world to Americans cities eclipses all other receiving nations. While migration is impacting nearly every nation of the world, the United States continues to be the recipient of an overwhelmingly large migration movement. Therefore, it is exceedingly important for both missiologists and Christian leaders of the American church to grapple with the emerging discipline of diaspora missiology.

This book joins an ongoing conversation concerning missions and the global diaspora. While much work is being done to advance the church's insight into diaspora missiology, it is my objective to address the wider framework of globalization's impact on world missions while focusing on missions in and through diaspora communities. I hope to reflect on tangible experiences currently playing out among those reaching out to diaspora communities in order to recognize missions principles currently being explored and discovered in this global context.

Diaspora missiology is essentially "a missiological framework for understanding and participating in God's redemptive mission among people living outside their place of origin" (Tira, 2011, p. 1). Enoch Wan cites the late Ralph Winter, considered a leading voice of the modern church-growth movement, expressing the importance of diaspora missiology for contemporary missions: "[Diaspora Missiology] may well be the most important undigested reality in missions thinking today. We simply have not caught up with the fact that most of the world's people can no longer be defined geographically" (2010, p. 11). Much of our missiological paradigms of the past were focused on static geographic realities, but today people groups are often constantly in motion, developing new ethnic neighborhoods in host cities, sustaining global networks, and moving through stages of adaptation to new places and cultures.

The inherent meaning of diaspora movements for mission is rooted in its underlying complexities. There are a variety of circumstances associated with various individuals, households, and ethnic groups on the move around the world. To assume that every migrant community mirrors all others would be misguided. Each situation is unique. In some cases, we are seeing large numbers of Muslims or Hindus developing new enclaves in Western cities. At other times, churches may experience revitalization accompanying a wave of new Christian members arriving from churches overseas. Some migrant groups develop expansive ethnic enclaves taking up several city blocks while others spread out into multiethnic neighborhoods while maintaining ties through businesses, ethnic associations, or family networks. Missiologists are confronted with an increasing need to focus church planting and cross-cultural evangelism efforts as well as other urban missions strategies on a variety of ethnic communities and unreached people groups in North American or European cities as mosques and temples spring up seemingly everywhere. Simultaneously researchers are running to keep up with tracking new ethnic churches dotting the urban landscape of many American cities and the accompanying change this shift in cultural tides brings to Christianity in the West. The movement of diaspora peoples is diverse and multidirectional.

Underlying the diversity of global migration, there is a diversity of opportunities related to the phenomenon of so many people on the move from so many places. As many in the Western church are presently wrestling with potential decline, stagnation, or division, simultaneously there are unprecedented opportunities for evangelistic engagement, new church planting, and global missions brought within close proximity of what is still a sizable collection of Christian witnesses. Both hospitality and pastoral care for Christians just arriving in our cities as well as loving evangelism and new missionary efforts among the unreached stand as proposals for vibrant ministry at the urban intersection of local and global. "Some of these people on the move are Christians and essentially take their churches with them. Others are not Christians, but have been cut loose from their family, clan, and caste ties that might impede their conversion. Others are at a crisis point in their lives, in special need of a new community and a new worldview. They may be more open to Christ, but they are also vulnerable to competing new ideologies and temptations" (Rynkiewich, 2013, pp. 105-106). Indeed, ethnic diaspora movements are transforming the makeup of our cities, and furthermore, there is not one description that can universally describe every diaspora community. While there are many Christians that are in exile in the West in an attempt to escape persecution, there are many more coming from a variety of non-Christian backgrounds as well as many newly secularized believers who remain absolutely nominal in their faith, lacking any sign of authentic discipleship.

We have typically approached missions contexts as either local or global. It's been an either-or scenario within our current missions paradigms, and this is reflected in the way we structure congregational or denominational missions programs, conference themes, and seminary education. However, in a globalized world, new considerations are needed. Does a strict duality of local or global, foreign or domestic, still make sense in a globalized and interconnected world? Missiological understandings that remain exclusively centered on a foreign versus domestic framework are bound to face new challenges in the world that is currently emerging. Missions organizations supporting these historical categories are going to be confronted with new contextual realities that remain fluid. As people groups move across continents and from city to city, "overall this begins to diminish the singular importance agencies have traditionally given to a specific geographic location in reaching a particular people. It pushes mission agencies out of their more sedentary focus to a more mobile focus on peoples" (Baxter, 2013, p. 119). "Bob," an evangelist to West African Muslims, explained that when he lived in West Africa he had no contact with a single homeowner in his neighborhood. He made contact with the poor of his city and with servants, but despite his efforts he had no access to the leaders and influencers of his African community.

It was when he moved to New York City that he encountered homeowners and community leaders from the very neighborhood where he once lived in West Africa. To find the influencers of his community, he had to cross an ocean and live among the global citizens of the African diaspora. Utilizing New York City as a platform for reaching out to an unreached people group, he has returned to this African country several times to visit the families of his New York friends who had originally migrated from Africa. He has stayed in their homes and received their hospitality. In fact, he has stayed in some of the same houses that he had no previous access to when he lived in the same neighborhood as a missionary. Now, due to his relationships with West African immigrants in New York City, he has unprecedented access to the leaders of a nation far beyond what he was able to do when he lived in West Africa. He has visited their homeland, stayed in the houses, and even spoken on state-run television sharing the Gospel of Jesus Christ. He has said on many occasions that he feels as if he is more of a pioneer church planter reaching out to unreached peoples living in New York City than when he lived in a Muslim country. His story ought to give us pause to evaluate our approach to global missions. What if our evangelistic focus on people groups implies that the importance of international cities as strategic mission fields are now more important than ever?

While geographic concerns don't simply go away, the context for world missions is clearly shifting. "The phenomenon of diaspora provides a new intermediate state between 'local' and 'global.'" Current missiology may be challenged to discover a new paradigm for evangelistic engagement in a constantly shifting world (Wan, 2011, pp. 6-7). Certainly, as people groups become geographically dispersed and international migration causes people to move in and through cities as centers for local and global activity, missiology, as a Christian discipline, is facing a new contextual framework. Our patterns of thinking should be challenged by these global currents. What if we have been asking the wrong questions? Rather than direct our evangelistic efforts around the dual choice of geographic focus versus the focus on a specific people group, what if a geographic orientation around specific urban spaces is equally important for the very purpose of targeting a people group for evangelism? Rather than missiological emphases on evangelism being defined as dueling options between place or people, geographic orientations are both less important and more important at the same time. In our tendency toward compartmentalization, we have often made "urban" a separate, if not minor, branch in the field of missiology despite the fact that urbanization and a pervasive culture of urbanism affects nearly every corner of the planet and is making a lasting impact on missions and ministry both near and far. In a world that is now a majority urban, rural missions—a necessary and important discipline— might be thought of as a specialization while missiological study of urban phenomenon should be an essential discipline of missiology. In the same way, we are wise if we recognize that global migration represents shifting cultural tides that may actually transform our approach to ministry. At the very least, our local churches will need to adjust to new demographics.

As most migration activity flows toward and through urban centers, we should be particularly interested in diaspora missiology as it interplays with urban mission. In large measure, diaspora missiology cannot be separated from urban mission as cities are essentially the nodal centers for migrant activity on a local and global scale. As cities represent mosaics of international cultures and diverse subcultures, the emergence of diaspora missiology reflects the importance of reimagining missiology for a new interconnected world. Much of our missions training has been focused on entering traditional tribal cultures, and there is of course a continuing need for this type of work as the existence of isolated people groups and traditional cultures has not completely disappeared. However, as the world shifts toward increasingly becoming a planet of cities connected through economic, political, cultural, and religious networks, new considerations are needed as we work out strategies for engaging the nations streaming through our cities. "Urban neighborhoods are now infinitely more complex than tribal cultures" (Bakke, 1999, p. 9), and new ways of thinking about missions must accompany a transition of this magnitude. A new global context will call for new strategic considerations and missiological paradigms. Migration leading to the formation of diaspora communities occurs as a result of varying circumstances (Wan, 2011, p. 6); the need for a missiological framework prepared to engage the fluid nature of diaspora communities is needed in order to participate in God's mission in an age of globalization. Adaptation is the much needed ministry skill of the 21st century.

Diaspora missiology, particularly in the West, leads us to a dynamic and timely intersection. Missions for churches in North America has overwhelmingly been focused on overseas contexts, and while missionary efforts to advance the Gospel in hard-to-reach places should in no way be diminished, diaspora movements bring those same people groups that have been the focus of numerous missions efforts to the doorstep of faith communities who were previously sending missionaries to their land. At the same time, many Christian leaders have awakened to the reality that the American church has been in an overall state of decline. As a result, there has seemingly been a renewed response to North American culture as a mission field. "The American church has held a prominent place in missions from the nineteenth to the early twenty-first century. This has changed as the church in the United States and Canada continues to witness a decline in membership and impact. This consequence stems from a misconception of mission as God intended it to be. Traditional missions had concentrated on foreign lands while leaving the home turf unattended. This thinking was so pervasive in the age of Christendom when there was the assumption that Europe, North America, and the West were already Christian in culture, thought, policy, and government, without need of evangelism and mission" (Gwamzhi, 2013, pp. 2-3). As many Christians leaders have been reframing Western cities as mission fields for the local church, new arrivals from the majority world are filling those same cities. Fortunately, such a dynamic cultural and demographic intersection may force the Western church to finally dissolve the dichotomy of "home" and "mission field." As Samuel Escobar so simply and purposefully said, missions is "everyone going everywhere" (Escobar, 2003). In an age of globalization and migration, the old binary of home and mission field or the more recent and well-intentioned dualism of domestic missions and foreign missions is being challenged by contemporary realities.

Encountering our new neighbors provides us with a number of opportunities to "live as Christ." We may incarnate an evangelistic presence among people from any number of nations, and we may also greatly benefit from partnerships with disciples of Christ who bring perspectives and experiences radically different from our own. The opportunity to "sit at the feet" of Christian leaders coming from radically different societies and cultures from our own should not be overlooked. As followers of Jesus, we are called to live as citizens of God's Kingdom while concurrently engaging the culture with the transforming hope of Christ. Participating in God's mission and living in fellowship with him, we often live in tension between culture and Kingdom. Many of us whose cultural roots are in what has been the dominant culture in the West may struggle to fully live "in the world but not of the world." We have been accustomed to a society where Christianity had a dominant voice, and we built large institutions to preserve and protect our religious culture. However, many Christian migrants come from contexts that are clearly defined as non-Christian where they have been accustomed to living in a dominant culture without completely identifying with it. In many respects, Christian migrants may have much to teach the church in Western society about living transcendent of a mainstream culture that cannot be mistaken for being Christian (Adeney, 2011, p. 6). We may learn that we have some blind spots in determining our own cultural accommodation to ideological worldviews or values that seek to undermine the Gospel. We may at times be blind to them due to our immersion in our home culture even when that culture has compromised the Gospel of Christ. However, we live on the edge of an opportune time to refine our vision of Kingdom life through the experiences of brothers and sisters who come from foreign lands and teach us once again how to live as aliens and foreigners in our own country, as citizens of the Kingdom of Heaven.

Conclusion

The discipline of diaspora missiology is continuing to emerge as researchers and missionary practitioners alike explore the phenomenon of global migration and its impact on the mission of the church. Much good work contributing to this missiological conversation has made valuable suggestions for taking advantage of evangelistic opportunities in and through diaspora communities. In this book, I hope to offer additional thinking that furthers the conversation among missiologists and church leaders. Also, I will draw from what is happening in missionary work in and through diaspora communities in specific urban settings in order to give some flesh to theory. Mission in and through diaspora communities is indeed taking place beyond the boundaries of academics. What do current narratives that are unfolding through evangelistic work in diaspora networks have to teach us moving forward? Indeed, we have much to learn from what is already taking place through pioneering missionary efforts unfolding today among migrant communities. I am not citing every missionary effort among migrants taking place in the United States, much less around the world. On a regular basis, I hear new reports of evangelism efforts taking place in diaspora communities—Hindus coming to faith in Houston, Muslims in Florida, Chinese in San Francisco, Latin Americans in Dallas. The good news of the Kingdom of God continues to break down walls and connect with people on the move who are coming from around the world and taking up residence in nearby cities .

Furthermore, diaspora missiology represents more than a new ethnic ministry niche. It is largely representative of significant global shifts as people across the planet are on the move, once distant places are now connected with the push of a few buttons, and previous orientations of religious demographics are shifting. While much of the historical approaches to missions will likely persist, the contours of missions are changing. Migrant churches represent a new wave of the Christian faith in Western contexts, access to unreached people groups is within reach of average believers, and global connectivity through modern transportation and communication technologies generates the emergence of a new wave of dynamic transnationalism. In the chapters that follow, I aim to contribute to actual missiological practice in diaspora communities and through the reach of diaspora networks. I will attempt to demonstrate the significant impact of globalization on missiology as a Christian practice, and I will argue that the current global shifts taking place on our planet will transform much of our understanding of the practice of Christian missions. The world is changing; our missiological practices must change, too.

Reflection Questions

1. To what extent have the average members of your church interacted with new migrants arriving in your city from majority-world nations?
2. What are the most important cities in your region?
3. What are some of the major immigrant groups living in your area?
4. Have you noticed the influx of any new ethnic groups moving into your city?
5. How has international migration impacted your local community or the ministry of your local church?

Chapter 2
A World in Transition

A little over a decade ago, I was asked to teach a workshop at a Christian university reflecting upon my experiences as a practicing missionary in New York City. Discussing my experiences in Gotham while standing in front of a class in Texas, I thought of a clever introduction that started out like this: "Hello, my name is Jared, and I am from the future." I then went on to explain how I was living in the midst of urbanism and in a city that reflects the increasing trends of globalization and pluralism that, as far as I could detect, were beginning to pick up significant momentum across the country. I explained that the local cultures of New York and the northeastern United States don't necessarily represent the future in terms of their own unique cultural character. The extension of those unique cultural characteristics would be unlikely. However, I argued that postmodernism, secularization, and cultural and religious pluralism, in addition to urbanization and globalization that typify places like New York or Los Angeles, would soon become normative even in cities in regions like Texas, the Midwest, and the Deep South. If I were to use what I thought at the time was a clever little introduction again today, I would have to say something more like, "The future is here." At the time, such societal shifts were already well underway when I gave my well-meaning introduction, and these trends were already recognized by many

Christian leaders, missiologists, and virtually any social scientists who were paying attention. Nevertheless, they remained unrecognized by a number of Americans. Now I would assume that the average church member recognizes the magnitude of these changes taking place around him or her as well. Indeed, we simply need to turn on the television or radio or skim through the Internet to listen to political anxiety over race, immigration, and the impact of globalization on local settings. Anxiety is filling the airwaves—left, right, and center. Today, these shifts are being felt in practically every corner of our society, and not only studied in academic halls or discussed in boardrooms but increasingly recognized by those sitting in church pews. Globalization is a mainstream reality, and it is increasingly being felt on a daily basis by the average person.

There can be little doubt that the world has been undergoing tremendous cultural and societal shifts. This chapter will review a few of the significant cultural patterns currently unfolding in our world. These factors have an impact upon the church, and they raise exceptional implications for missiology in general and evangelistic strategies in particular. These issues and trends are important themes in a discussion concerning diaspora missiology. "If one should desire to contextualize the understanding and practice of Christian missions for the 21st century, it is imperative to note the changing sociocultural landscape due to multiple factors such as demographic trends, globalization, postmodernist orientation, religious pluralism, etc." (Wan, 2010, p. 1). For the church to make a real and lasting impact on our world, Christians will need to adapt to an emerging set of cultural factors quite different than even 50 years ago.

Rise of the Church in the Global South

"In twenty centuries the church has moved from being a sect of Judaism to becoming an immense global family of diverse peoples, cultures, and languages who confess Jesus Christ as Savior and Lord" (Escobar, 2003, p. 53). The vision for the church was always to be a movement among all the nations of the earth, and in our time that vision is being realized perhaps to a degree greater than at any point in history. The fabric of the Christian faith has been undergoing an enormous transformation leaving behind the period of European domination to becoming a multicentered faith with the vast majority of adherents in the majority world. The face of world Christianity is no longer White. Rather, the face of the global Christian church is now from the South or East and may be Chinese, Indian, African, or Brazilian.

"We are living in the midst of one of the most dramatic demographic changes in the history of Christianity" (Kalu, Vethanayagamony, & Chia, 2010, p. 59). Following World War II, the process of decolonization and forging independent nations gave rise to grassroots forms of Christianity. Where the rise of the church in the majority world may have begun in many locations through initial missionary efforts during the second half of the 20th century, a new tide of local leadership has emerged. Indigenous non-Western churches began to flourish and spread in a new cultural environment where Western leadership once held exclusive managerial control (Chilcote & Warner, 2008, pp. 124-125). Despite whatever shortcomings may have been true of previous missionary eras, the result has been a vibrant and growing Christianity embodied by indigenous churches. Around 1990, Christianity saw the balance tip from the majority of its adherents originating in the West to a new majority of Christians living in the non-Western world, and at the turn of the millennium nearly 60% of the planet's Christians were living in nations of the majority world (Pocock, Rheenen, & McConnell, 2005, p. 134). Christianity and its associated missionary movement is no longer a Eurocentric or Americancentric faith. This dramatic shift in Christianity's center has taken shape over the course of the 20th century. The change to a multicentered global faith has evolved at an increasingly rapid pace. Centuries of missionary labor have recently found momentum in a wave of growth across the majority world of a truly global Christian church during the most recent century. What many previously imagined as the average Christian will surely need some rethinking in the decades that follow. "By the year 2050 only one in five Christians will be non-Latino and White" (Wan, 2010, p. 2). On the one hand, some could argue that it simply represents overall population growth among majority-world peoples while population growth has slowed among those of European decent, but on the other hand it most certainly demonstrates the rapid growth of the church in areas previously not associated with the presence of a strong and vibrant Christian church. The church has grown and multiplied in places where she previously did not exist. "The number of believers in what used to be 'mission fields' now surpasses the number of believers in countries from which missionaries were originally sent. In fact, more missionaries are now sent from non-Western churches than from traditional mission-sending bases in the West" (Winter & Koch, 2009, p. 1). Such a shift from a European or American center for Christianity to a multicentered global faith is likely challenging for many American leaders accustomed to maintaining the prominent or authoritarian position within the global church. One of the very real challenges for the Western church is to make the intellectual jump from the position of the faith's geographic and cultural center to realizing that the gravitational forces of Christianity are now non-Western (Kalu, et al., 2010, p. 68). The majority of passports of Christian leaders and church planters are not from the United States or a European nation but are likely to bear the symbols of China, Nigeria, South Korea, or a number of other nations typically thought of as traditional mission fields. Of course, with the rise of the church in the global South, a church that is no longer centered in Western culture reflects the historical roots of the church as a non-Western faith. Of course, the earliest church movement that we read about in Acts grew out of community bases in Israel, Syria, and Turkey.

Yet, these shifts back to a majority non-Western Christianity are not unfolding in a straight line. Changes in the demographics of the global church are less about a changing center—at least for the moment —but truly reflect a multicentered faith. Despite its new minority status, the Western church remains tied to Western economic powers, and many non-Western churches or ministries remain entrenched in a weight of dependence upon Western leadership. The global realities of the rise of the church of the global South remain complex and full of paradoxes (Hanciles, 2008, pp. 385-386). The Western church is likely to play a strong role in the missionary enterprise both in sending workers and in resourcing missionary efforts, but her minority status ought to become an encouragement for the church in North America and Europe to learn mutually from the majority of the church. Some ministries have critically addressed the need for mutuality in ministry partnerships between East and West, but others struggle with how to restructure for the new world in which they have found themselves. The rise of the church of the global South and East will continue to profoundly impact contemporary Christianity and the practice of missions, but it is not simply the passing of one and the rising of another. Rather it is the emergence of a greater mutuality. The Western church remains engaged in the missionary task along with the efforts of a dynamic and expanding majority-world church.

Decline of Church in the West

While the church in the global South rises and new streams of missions emerge from this global demographic shift, the centers of historic Christendom have been undergoing a significant transformation in the West as well. "Perhaps the big surprise for many classical Christian structures centered in the North is that the immigrant communities are now carriers of the leading energy for missions and religious transformation" (Garcia-Johnson, 2012, p. 119). The institution of a cultural Christendom as a dominating force in Western society appears, at least at present, to be largely fading into the pages of history. Christian leaders and institutions are certainly not without their voice in North American and European cultures, but they no longer hold the dominant center of power and influence. "One of the ironic features of the major shift taking place in world Christianity is the sudden and dramatic collapse of Christian faith among Western Europeans" (Kalu, et al., 2010, p. 61). For example, at the start of the 20th century, 80% of Christians worldwide were White, with most of that population living in Europe and North America; however, just 100 years later at the beginning of the 21st century, that same population only accounts for 45% of global Christianity (Barrett & Johnson, 2001, p. 3). Such a change within a single century is astounding. If these downward trends continue aggressively, White Europeans may need to be officially classified as an unreached people group!

As a sign of increased secularization in North America, the Pew Research Forum reported in 2012 that one of the fastest growing religious constituencies in the United States are the "nones." That is, those with no religious affiliation. In just a five-year period, the self-identified irreligious and unaffiliated in the United States grew from 15% of the population to 20%, indicating a fast-paced statistical climb (*"Nones" on the Rise*, 2012, p. 9). Although that leaves a large percentage of Americans as self-proclaimed adherents of one faith or another, the trend is striking. Studies such as these seem to substantiate the suspicions by many that the United States is heading in the same direction religiously as contemporary Europe. However, in a phone conversation with one European missions leader, he pointed out that while the United States is likely going to resemble European trends in some ways, he also drew the distinction that the United States has a unique cultural and religious history. Therefore, while religious life— and non-religious life—in the U.S. may resemble the European phenomenon in various ways, whatever cultural dynamics that may emerge within the religious life of the United States will still be uniquely culturally American. Just as it would have likely been difficult to predict the dramatic rise in global Christianity 100 years previous, it is difficult to give a definitive forecast of the future religious landscape in North America based purely on the decline of the American church.

There have been historic revivals on the heels of periods of decline before. Whatever the future holds, it is becoming clear that the Christian church in North America has been struggling to retain her prominence. Survey after survey reveal a dismal picture, so it does appear that at this moment in history a downward turn of some sort is occurring regardless of our abilities to predict the future with any real precision. The reality of decline in the present may have an effect on our theological vision for the church going forward and upon ministry practices in a changing context.

Reflecting on the Canadian context—where religious attitudes appear to sit on a cultural continuum somewhere between the religious adherence in the United States and the more extreme secularization of Europe—Joel Thiessen argues that "individual religious belief and practice are less likely to exist in plural and diverse societies, because no single sacred canopy dominates social life." Rather, a number of worldviews and ideologies of various sorts compete for the attention of potential adherents. In a multicultural and religiously plural setting it is virtually impossible to assume that allegiance to one religious community or another will result from a dominant social expectation. "Pluralism, therefore, reduces the social stigma once attached to being irreligious, and in the Canadian circumstance, one might argue that social stigma is reserved for those who are deeply religious" (Thiessen, 2013, pp. 134-135).

While the portrait of religious trends in North America seems dismal and certain downward trends appear to be quite real, the actual state of religious life in North America may be more dynamic and complex than at first glance. After all, affiliation doesn't necessarily equal active participation. Identifying with a particular denomination or historical church tradition in response to polls or religious surveys is likely an indication of Christendom's lingering influence in Western society, but is not necessarily an indicator of church participation or an ongoing devotion as a disciple of Jesus. Therefore, polls have seemingly always painted a prettier picture than what might in fact be reality.

While pollsters find that many Americans may identify themselves with a particular church or faith tradition, David Olsen, utilizing an alternative research methodology, has argued that actual participation in a Christian church during a given year dropped from 20% in 1990 to 17% in 2005 (Olson, 2008, pp. 26, 36). Participation in the life of a church is experiencing a downward trend, and when read in conjunction with studies of the rise of the religiously unaffiliated, an overall change in landscape of American Christianity is apparent. Comparing and contrasting various research reports on the status and decline of the American church, the exact figures do not always perfectly match, but overwhelmingly, the majority of studies agree that the American church is in sharp decline. However, it is possible that many ethnic churches, as well as grassroots efforts to start house churches, simply go unnoticed by many religious researchers. With many new church forms out of sight of mainstream perceptions, there is hope that perhaps the decline is not as steep as it might seem. In addition, a look at the statistics of church decline always raises the question of whether there is actually a decline in devoted faith, or is the church as an institution losing those adherents who were only nominal in their devotion to begin with? Perhaps it is some degree of both. These matters are worthy of further exploration, but these pages are not intended for working out this statistical debate.

While the established base of American Christianity appears to be shrinking, the church of Jesus Christ in North America is not nearly dead. Consistent with the growth of the church in the majority world, many of the immigrants populating American cities are Christians. There are few studies to actually help us pinpoint to what degree an influx of Christians from other nations might slow—or even reverse— the overall decline of church participation in North America. Until recently, much of the growth of ethnic churches in North American cities has seemingly been off the radar of many church-growth researchers. For instance, there are some indications that ethnic churches may be significantly undercounted in New York City

(Clayman, March 22, 2014). The United States' quintessential secular city may in fact be far more religious than most might perceive. Similarly, discussions around immigration in Canada may actually reflect less upon "the de-Christianization of Canadian society per se, but the de-Europeanization of Canadian Christianity." Through international immigration, an influx of Christian migrants to Western nations may be transforming the cultural tone of congregational life (Thiessen, 2013, p. 134).

Nevertheless, there is undoubtedly a loss in participation in the traditionally Western venues of Christian faith in the North American context, and it is unlikely that immigration alone would bring this downward trend to a halt. While traditional American expressions of church grapple with an emerging minority status, many ethnic churches are even more likely to be given a marginalized status, and it is not uncommon for ethnic evangelists to struggle to overcome cultural barriers for reaching unbelievers in the dominant culture. Nevertheless, immigration may be a key factor in reorienting our understanding of Western nations as "mission fields" (Thiessen, 2013, p. 134). Christian immigrants may in fact help sustain a declining Christian church in Western cities, and as a result due in part to declining faith participation among North Americans, another transition is actually taking place that very much reflects the global trend of a surging Christianity in the majority world. That is, the face of American Christianity may be increasingly non-White (Rah, 2009, p. 14). Similar to Western Europe, ethnic churches continue to bear witness to the Gospel of Christ in pluralistic and secular cities while the portrait of historic American Christianity struggles to find its identity. The American church faces a well-documented decline; however, there is a ray of hope with the influx of immigrants from the majority world representing the Gospel of Christ in American cities. A Christian witness will likely persist in North America, and Christian immigration represents the potential missionary force for the future church in the West. Again, Christian believers should benefit from neighboring with their brothers and sisters from around the world and renew their identity as citizens of the Kingdom of Heaven.

Unreached Peoples & Creative Access

Despite the dynamic growth of global Christianity, there remain a considerable number of people throughout the globe who lack an active engagement with the Gospel. The Joshua Project identifies more than 7,000 distinct people groups, totaling almost 3 billion people who are considered "unreached" or "least reached" by the Gospel of Jesus Christ. According to The Joshua Project, a people group may be defined as, "a significantly large sociological grouping of individuals who perceive themselves to have a common affinity with one another." Joshua Project defines "unreached" or "least reached" people groups as those people groups "where there is no indigenous community of believing Christians with adequate numbers and resources to evangelize this people group" (www.joshuaproject.net). Despite a growing global church, there remain numerous people groups with little to no church presence or even missionary engagement among them.

In many cases, unreached people groups are culturally or geographically based in nation-states that limit access to the Gospel to citizens and limit access to communicate the Gospel by expatriate missionaries or even local church leaders. With the deconstruction of Western colonialism, many new nation-states began closing access to their citizenry by Christian—and especially Western—missionaries. Often the political environment of these countries may be largely hostile to Christian evangelism and sometimes to the presence of a Christian church in general. Within many nations, sharing the Gospel with unbelievers is a criminal offense. For instance, in 2014 it was widely reported the young leader of North Korea executed some of his citizens simply for possession of a Bible. At the same time, in the last decades of the 20th century, a missiological impulse to engage the most unreached people groups once again emerged, and this is certainly in answer to the recognized need for evangelistic engagement where there is a vacuum of Christian witness. As a result, missions strategists began developing "creative access platforms." These creative access platforms are described as a "practical means for providing mission workers the opportunity and relational basis for effectively accomplishing their main goal" (Pocock, et al., 2005, pp. 209-213). No longer protected by the influence of a powerful Christendom, missionaries must find innovative ways to serve people and, sometimes covertly, communicate the Gospel in societies hostile to the Christian faith or at least what a resistant nation perceives to be Christianity. Creative access platforms provide access through business, education, development, or Christian service to demonstrate and to communicate the Gospel where open proclamation or church planting is forbidden.

It is not uncommon to meet missionaries traveling into the least-reached parts of the world as economic development workers, business people, teachers, or medical workers. The host nations are often aware of creative access platforms as well; therefore, there is always a risk for missionaries using an additional vocation to serve as a missionary in hostile areas. Nevertheless, many creative access platforms also meet real needs in the host nation, so doors continue to open for missionaries to serve people and seek opportunities to share the hope found in Jesus Christ. For example, the high demand for learning English as a second language has opened a doorway for Western Christians to serve in a number of cross-cultural settings from Latin America to the Middle East to Asia as well as a wide range of diaspora communities in the West.

Of course, creative access platforms may raise serious debates among missiologists and theologians as well. Are physical solutions to problems always a means to an end as a platform for evangelization, or should Christian service represent acts of Christian compassion with their own inherent value? Some advocates of creative access platforms argue that "the platform should be built to fit the objective or task and not the other way around" (Pocock, et al., 2005, p. 212). Evangelical tensions may arise if creative access feels like a "social gospel," and humanitarian criticism may arise when it seems missionaries are only interested in the salvation of souls without regards to the condition of the poor or needy. Western approaches to missions have often forced evangelism and church-planting ministries and compassion or development ministries into a dichotomous relationship. A Gospel-driven response to the human condition cares for the well-being of people, and that has both temporal and eternal implications. Of course the Gospel offers a mandate for compassion in our physical condition and a profound concern for our eternal condition. However, despite these inherent tensions, there are reasons to be hopeful. Perhaps evangelical fears and tensions over the "social gospel" may find some reconciliation in creative access platforms that serve physical and economic needs of unreached people while not only resisting marginalization of verbal proclamation of the Gospel but instead intentionally sharing the Good News as an objective of the work. There are now numerous efforts evolving to address the need to bring the Gospel of the Kingdom to people groups that may not otherwise have access to the message through traditional missionary service. Creative access platforms are a strategic response to societies closed or hostile to the message of salvation in Jesus Christ. As long as access ministries are not marginalized, much human suffering may be lifted while evangelistic pathways open opportunities for Gospel proclamation.

Yet while tremendous efforts are being made on behalf of unreached peoples to creatively penetrate cultural, religious, and political barriers, additional global shifts are taking place that provide new opportunities and challenges for the Gospel. Even as mission efforts began intentionally targeting the least reached regions on the planet, millions of people from these regions have been migrating out of their homelands into other parts of the world—especially to more developed nations—often next door to churches and agencies sending missionaries to their homeland (Pocock, et al., 2005, p. 25). We may say that where economic development has fallen short, international migration has taken over. Many unreached people are still far out of reach and require missionaries to be relocated into their local context; however, many unreached ethnic groups are now only "culturally distant." The geographic, political, or legal gaps have been narrowed. While unreached, they live within close proximity of potential Christian witness in the world's large cities (Bakke, 1999, p. 2).

Creative access platforms should continue to be utilized by missionary agencies around the world, but global migration provides new opportunities to evaluate evangelism strategies among people groups that are considered unreached. As communication technologies become increasingly accessible throughout the planet and ethnic diasporas remain connected to networks of friends and family in their homeland as well as similar diasporas, global migration raises not only new challenges but new opportunities for addressing the Gospel mandate to reach the nations.

Global Migration

There can be no doubt that we are currently experiencing the greatest global migration in the history of our planet. One in every 35 people in the world today is a migrant (Wan, 2011, p. 13). According to studies conducted by the Center for the Study of Global Christianity, in 2010 the total global diaspora was made up of 859 million people belonging to 327 distinct people groups (Johnson, June 2013, p. 82). The sheer volume of international immigration is of such a magnitude that its ripple effects are felt in nations throughout the world. Violent conflicts, famines and disasters, poverty, and economic opportunities are among some of the primary drivers of an unprecedented global migration (Claydon, 2004, p. 7). For a variety of reasons, both individuals and entire families are relocating. Refugees, international students, expatriate employees of multinational corporations, economically motivated migrants, and others are developing global networks and transforming local neighborhoods. Cities are being remade as new populations land in urban settings seeking new opportunities and confronting new challenges. "Migration movements affect urban environments by reshaping the landscape of city life" (Garcia-Johnson, 2012, p. 116).

Migration is not new. The Christian story is a narrative of migration. Abraham was a migrant. Joseph was sold into slavery as a forced migrant to a foreign land. Daniel was an exile. Jesus was a political refugee to Egypt. Paul was taken to Rome for trial. The church grew by being scattered by persecution. In the American story, our national myth is one of pioneers building a new country in a new land, and for Native Americans and African slaves it is one of forced relocation. Our history is filled with stories of migration. However, one of the key differences that is felt today lies in the increased technological advances in communication and transportation (Rynkiewich, 2011, p. 199). Modern communication and transportation technologies are opening bridges of mobility that didn't exist in a previous era. Around the world, people are on the move. International immigration is now a new global norm reaching statistical heights never seen before. For instance, at the end of 1999, an estimated 34 million Chinese were living overseas (Wan, 2003, p. 1). That's more Chinese living outside of China than the total population of many nations. Today, more than 8 million Filipinos reside in more than 197 countries, including more than 1 million official Overseas Filipino Workers with Saudi Arabia as the leading recipient of these migrant workers (Tira & Wan, p. 4-7). Could one strategy for reaching Saudis with the Gospel actually be to establish missionary efforts in the Philippines? Sending evangelists into Saudi Arabia, one of the most closed nations in the world, may actually mean intentional missionary initiatives increasing evangelism and equipping believers in the Philippines, especially training Overseas Filipino Workers for covert missionary work.

Estimates during the 1990s suggested the United States had become home to approximately 1 million Asian Indians, with the vast majority of that population being foreign born (Lessinger, 1995, p. 2). While church-planting efforts in the large Indian subcontinent should continue, there is a need to increase efforts to provide a Christian witness to the hundreds of thousands of Sikhs, Hindus, and Muslims living and working in North American cities. There is a great need for Christians in cities like Houston, Chicago, and New York's New Jersey suburbs to be trained to reach Hindus, and there is a pressing need for missionary engagement among Sikhs in Vancouver, New York City, and San Francisco. Around the globe, people are on the move, and believers in North America have an unprecedented opportunity to represent the Gospel of grace to immigrant communities.

Sixty percent of migrants settle in what we think of as developed countries with three-fourths of all migrants residing in only 28 nations. While nearly 10% of the British population in 2005 was foreign born, the majority of international migrants find their way to North America (Kalu, et al., 2010, pp. 71-72). In 2000, an estimated 11% of the United States population was foreign-born. Some predictions suggest that by 2050, Hispanics and Asians will make up 33% of the total American population in the United States, and by midway through the 21st century, the United States is expected to be one of the largest Hispanic nations in the world, having a smaller Hispanic population than only Mexico and Brazil (Claydon, 2004, p. 54). Global migration is affecting the demographic landscape of entire nations.

With a rise in international immigration from every corner of the globe, cities in North America are experiencing an ongoing demographic transformation. As newcomers arrive in metropolitan areas, they often develop or join networks of others from their homeland or ethnic group. Over the years, "scholars studying chain migration naturally noticed that newcomers moving from the same hometown not only became neighbors in the new world, but often worked alongside one another." Migration often moves along networks of relationships with family and friends sharing a common culture, history, and journey from one nation to another. Ethnic concentrations can be found in specific jobs throughout the city (Scott, 2001, p. 302). Not long ago, the brother of one of my Liberian friends in the Bronx called me to ask for help in typing up his resume. He needed to begin a job search because he was moving his family from New York City to Boise, Idaho. My first question was, "Why Boise?" It turns out his mother-in-law lives there, and one of his friends that first came as a refugee to the Bronx within weeks of his own arrival had also relocated to Boise and had bought a house there. He was following his natural network of relationships as he advanced along another link in the migration chain.

These networks naturally develop as new arrivals in a host country utilize these connections for finding housing, employment, cultural foods, and supportive relationships. At times, clustering leads to ethnic neighborhoods within a city or a nearby suburb generating a transitional space that helps close the gap between home and the new host culture while particular businesses or professions become populated by a new wave of workers and entrepreneurs. Living in New York City, at the risk of promoting stereotypes, it is actually common to see Chinese running laundromats, Koreans operating nail salons, Yemenis opening up *bodegas* (convenience stores), or Afghanis working at Kennedy Fried Chicken. Albanians often move into areas that were historically Italian, and neighborhoods once considered Puerto Rican *barrios* are steadily transitioning to Mexican. In Panama City, many of the Panamanians refer to the little grocery stores scattered across the city as "Chinos" because they are so often operated by Chinese living in Panama. It became so commonplace that locals simply began identifying the stores themselves by the ethnic entrepreneurs running these types of businesses.

Cities' gravitational pull usually results in large communities of migrants located in specific urban areas. Indeed, "one of the key defining features of most global cities is that they are the destinations of large numbers of highly diverse groups of immigrants" (Abrahamson, 2004, p. 48). Often, earlier migrants are the first link in a migration chain connecting an ethnic network between homeland and the host country. Once the first wave of migrants arrives and establishes a "beachhead," newer migrants from the same culture of origin follow behind finding comfort in familiar faces and utilizing cultural connections for finding employment and resolving other basic needs (Scott, 2001, p. 306). Could it be that a missionary strategy among diaspora networks may be to identify these outliers as the courageous first links in the migration chain and share the Gospel with them so that they might influence those coming to the city after them? Not unlike disaster relief ministries, what if missions agencies were prepared to send evangelism and church-planting teams into cities receiving a new wave of immigrants following international events that trigger new waves of migration?

The dynamics of migration and settlement vary. Vocational networks along ethnic lines develop, and new ethnic enclaves evolve in specific metropolitan areas. While some migrants seek opportunities for assimilation into the dominant culture, others form a new "home away from home," giving rise to new ethnic neighborhoods. Simultaneously, while some migrants make their host country their home, others settle in their new city only temporarily. "Some migrants settle in, but then move again to a secondary diaspora community. This can create a diaspora archipelago ... Multiple centers are linked—not by geography —but by sentiment, that is, real or imagined common origin, ethnicity, or religion that does not reduce one to being a subject of a host country" (Rynkiewich, 2013, p. 109). This phenomenon reflects the linkage of networks as international migrants move from one diaspora community to another. "Corey" told me how he had been living in New York City for three years while actively reaching out to migrants from a specific unreached people group from West Africa. After moving to the Dallas area, he connected to a suburban professional from Africa who is the brother of a New York City taxi driver. Through that connection, he discovered that a small concentration of the same African unreached people group lives in Arlington in the Dallas/Ft. Worth area and began making plans to connect with that community as a witness of the Gospel. Diaspora missiology often implies ministry along the relational channels of grassroots networks. Living in New York City, it is commonplace to meet individuals who have kinship connections in multiple countries including two or three continents and to have relationships established with individuals and families in at least two or three additional cities in the United States. One member of our house church has maintained family ties in Tanzania, Germany, England, Nigeria, and the United States. A Liberian friend in the Bronx has told me of visiting households in his kinship network in Rhode Island, and he traveled, as the oldest in his family, to Michigan to negotiate a marriage for a family member. Migration patterns often form a web of relationships across geographically distant locations and connect communities through networks of relationships.

It is difficult to overestimate the impact that global migration may have on the advancement of the Great Commission. New challenges confront church planters and missionaries as they wrestle with issues of contextualization in the midst of constantly shifting demographics, and new opportunities emerge as unreached peoples move in next door or majority-world Christians migrate with evangelistic zeal to Western cities. Simultaneously, migration and urbanization go hand-in-hand. As people from around the planet move and resettle in new countries, they gravitate to cities seeking new opportunities. Immigration today is "a quintessentially urban phenomenon" (Scott, 2001, p. 299).

Acceleration of Urbanization

At the start of the 20th century, the planet was 86% rural (Palen, 1992, p. 3), but something dramatic has taken place in the course of the last century. For the first time in the history of planet earth, more than half of the world's population is now living in urban areas. The world is more than 50% urban. The world has always been a place of cities, embodied in regional centers such as Ur, Tenochtitlan, or London. However, the rate of urbanization has radically accelerated, and we may be living in a world that can be considered "post-rural" (Rynkiewich, 2011, pp. 214-216). Even as urban families consider relocating outside of the city, one of the key considerations is deciding how far they are willing to commute because they are still connected to the city whether for economic, cultural, or educational motives. Suburbs, exurbs, and edge cities are part of the makeup of expanding metropolitan urban mosaics.

In the United States, even as urban dwellers sometimes make their pilgrimage to nearby suburbs, they are replaced by new residents to the city originating from around the world. "As people migrate throughout the globe in search of better lives, they most often head toward cities. They see cities as places that offer education, housing, jobs, entertainment, health care, and social services—and also anonymity and concentrations of fellow countrymen" (Kling, 2010, pp. 98-99). Through urbanization, the city acts as a magnet pulling new residents to the urban environment (Bakke, 1999, p. 2). As we consider ministry and evangelism among diaspora communities, urbanization is an inseparable reality impacting the church and missiological practice. While many of the world's poor and marginalized are drawn to cities as opportunities that they perceive to provide a better set of circumstances for their families, the church has often viewed the city negatively. However, "urbanization is one of the most profound expressions of migration in the world today" (Kling, 2010, p. 99).

The distribution of urban growth is more nuanced than is often recognized. Contemporary society is expressed in the megacity, but megacities are more than their sheer enormity of size. Large cities are nodes in the global network. They are urban centers where economic and cultural power is concentrated. While not every megacity plays a dominant role in the global economy, many cities in the majority world forge strong connections to the global network as they connect massive populations from the majority world to this network (Susser, 2002, p. 337). Furthermore, despite the obvious rise of megacities scattered across the globe, medium and small cities are also seeing substantial growth as recipients of the forces of urbanization (Conn & Ortiz, 2001, pp. 212-213). Although world-class cities persist as strategic locations for mission, the majority of urban dwellers today inhabit small to medium-sized cities. While cities like New York or Tokyo are international actors connecting through a global network, most of these smaller or intermediate urban areas act as regional nodes connecting the global network to their regions. Indeed, the links between regions are often manifested in the actual links between the urban "nuclei" of those regions (Borja & Castells, 1997, pp. 203-204). Regional cities play an important role in the surge of urbanization as they form the link between global megacities and their regions. Nevertheless, the patterns of urbanization are felt most profoundly in the growth and development of megacities since one-fifth of the population of the world lives in cities of more than 1 million residents (Clark, 2003, pp. 27-28), and it is these megacities that raise some of the greatest challenges for mission and some of the greatest opportunities as well. In addition, cities are continually changing and evolving as the urban ecosystem adapts and grows. Cities are experiencing greater decentralization even as resources are increasingly concentrated in urban space. Information technologies are allowing the functions of businesses to spread out across metropolitan regions. As a result, with an increasingly mobile work force and the ability of businesses and public services to network across vast territories, cities may evolve into increasingly multicentered urban places. Communication technologies allow cities to distribute their functions and processes across the urban landscape. Furthermore, there is not a single pattern followed by the evolution of urban space; the transformation of urban layouts will vary from city to city depending upon any number of historical or institutional factors (Susser, 2002, pp. 330-332).

For many Christian traditions that began during westward expansion in the United States, the rapid surge of urbanization presents a challenge that confronts a largely rural historical narrative. My own tradition of Stone-Campbell congregations or Churches of Christ and Independent Christian Churches is inherently rural in its history and culture. Many of the colleges and universities were intentionally founded in rural areas, and most of the congregations have historically been located in the South and Midwest where they generally remained functionally rural for most of the 20th century, even as urbanization was picking up steam. This tradition serves as an easy example, but the same anecdotes may be applied to varying degrees to any number of Christian denominations. Much of the religious narrative of American culture has been a rural tale maintaining a tense relationship with urban centers that consequently have been the drivers of the economic story of the same society.

If the "frontier" of mission is where people live and work, then the church's call to participate in God's mission will most often lead her into urban places (Rynkiewich, 2011, p. 214). In a world that is increasingly urban, the ministry of redemption will lead to cities where multitudes do not yet bow their knees to Jesus. For many Christians in the United States, the new reality of urban mission is in contrast to the spirit of a Jeffersonian past that sees cities as a detriment to society (Fischer, 1984, pp. 14-15). We may be more influenced by Thomas Jefferson than by Paul of Tarsus when it comes to addressing the needs and challenges of urbanization as the church in American society. However, an impulse to walk in the footsteps of the church described in the New Testament opens the door for a return to a missionary enterprise that is largely urban (Conn & Ortiz, 2001, pp. 120-150). Since the earliest Christian mission was largely an urban enterprise, it is hardly a biblical concept to resist urban mission. I am sometimes still puzzled when I attend missions conferences and find urban missiology remaining at the margins of the program. In a world that is now mostly urban, wouldn't urban mission represent the majority of missionary work as the primary context for most missionary efforts, while rural missions ought to be thought of as a necessary specialization? Our contemporary missions history seems to stand in contrast to the world that exists at present.

Even churches and ministries in largely rural areas in developed countries are unlikely to escape the impact of urbanism. With the impact of social networking and entertainment media, worldviews that have an inherently urban imagination exist in rural areas as well. People living far from cities are still affected by the values of the city, as rural residents are engaging through communication technologies in ideas and cultural images emerging from urban life. Through urbanism, the transmission and magnification of a culture that is inherently urban originates in the city and resonates into the wider society (Bakke, 1999, p. 2). I remember recognizing the expansive influence of urbanism while in the locker room at a YMCA in the largely rural region of west Texas. I was getting dressed in the men's locker room while the television was turned to the country music station. I watched as a music video played, and it struck me that the country music singer with his cowboy hat, blue jeans, and acoustic guitar was performing on the rooftop of a building amidst an urban skyline. It struck me that country music had been inducted into urban landscape. Similarly, several years ago, I was visiting my grandfather in Sabinal, Texas, a small rural town of about 1,500 people. As I was walking from the nearby convenience store to my grandfather's home, I strolled past an agricultural mill on one side of the street and a few houses on the other side. Parked on the lawn in front of one of the houses was a car playing music. Resounding from the car's speakers was contemporary rap music—a social resistance genre born in the South Bronx and unmistakably urban in worldview and in every other way imaginable. Culture, art, and worldview flow from urban centers and often spread globally, and these cultural expressions even reach areas that could hardly be described as "urban." "The world's rural areas are progressively being exposed to, and are being forced to come to terms with, urban influences both from within their own countries and from societies which may be both culturally, as well as geographically, distant" (Clark, 2003, pp. 134, 136). Urban ministry—in one way or another—is now on the doorsteps of most churches in North America.

Turning our attention toward cities realigns us with Pauline strategy in the New Testament. In Acts Chapter 16, the Apostle Paul and his team are laboring to proclaim the Good News of Jesus the Lord, but he repeatedly encounters closed doors. Then, he receives a vision of a man inviting him to come share the Gospel of Christ in Macedonia. Then, the story of Acts gives us a glimpse into Paul's sensitivity to the strategic importance of cities for global mission. Paul doesn't become a wandering preacher visiting the villages of Macedonia. Rather, upon hearing the call to proclaim the Gospel to Macedonians, he takes his team directly to the leading city of that district. For Paul, the strategic nature of urban centers as points of influence and leadership in a region is intuitive. We don't have a Pauline commentary on the need for urban missions because it is simply assumed. Pursuing urban missions is synonymous with accomplishing God's global mission. "Christianity was birthed in the city, spread from city to city, and grew to maturity in the city. That is where people are, and the people are in need of a Savior and friend" (Rynkiewich, 2011, p. 231).

Cities: Nodes in a Global Network

It is difficult to divorce the processes of globalization from the twin force of urbanization. These two social currents are not only taking place at the same time but have a symbiotic relationship as each affects the momentum of the other. As the planet shifts to a largely urban existence, the world's vast and diverse populations and cultures are more interconnected than ever before. There is an increasing global consciousness as individuals become aware of world events in real time as a result of rapid flows of information (Davey, 2002, p. 24). Increasingly, individuals are living in the midst of a global network as they walk the streets of their city, use their cell phones, or go to work. In metropolitan centers, urbanization and globalization dance to create a new global space in the city.

Through the processes of globalization, cities have become "the principle nodes of relationship, production, and interchange" in a global network (Borja & Castells, 1997, p. 203). With the increase of global connectivity and the emergence of postcolonial economies in countries such as Brazil, India, Panama, and China, some have popularly argued that the world is now indeed "flat" (Friedman, 2006). However, others have insisted the world is "spiky" with concentrations of power, talent, and, creativity in key urban centers with the rise of a "creative class" (Florida, 2004). Indeed cities have become more than regional headquarters or imperial capitals. Rather, they are nodes in a global network with city-to-city links connecting regions and nations. Connections between cities transcend national boundaries even as regional urban centers connect to global cities as a linkage to the larger global economy. Not every city is connected directly to the global network to the same degree or with the same economic or cultural influence, but regional centers link to the global economy through bridges to larger global cities that act as key players on the world stage. This web of larger and smaller nodes creates a cultural and economic network that transcends traditional boundaries. In reality, "thousands of residents in New York City are far more connected to the Philippines, Haiti, Colombia, China, and Nigeria than they are to New Jersey or Connecticut" (Kling, 2010, p. 103). I've known countless people in Manhattan and the Bronx who have seldom, if ever, traveled elsewhere in the United States beyond the five boroughs of New York City but have routinely traveled to another continent to visit family or conduct business. Cities are the places where "population, activities, and power concentrate" (Borja & Castells, 1997, p. 203).

"Cities provide the setting where global forces operate, because they provide the infrastructure, labor, stability, and services to support the spread of neoliberal capitalism, representative democracy, and modern culture; the hallmarks of globalization" (Rynkiewich, 2011, p. 214). If, as some might suggest, globalization is merely an expression of the expansion of the free market, then global cities have become the town square. As urbanization gives rise to the importance of urban space, cities act as nodal players in a global network. People, capital, and information move with significant fluidity between key urban centers

(Davey, 2002, pp. 33-37). "Traditional urban systems" were rooted in the political support of the nation-states organized along territorial and political hierarchies. That world is now being transcended by global networking through the free market. Now, we may envision nodal points in an urban network that interacts with the nation-state but also transcends it (Borja & Castells, 1997). Cities are "no longer simply subordinate to the state, but rather engage in competition and cooperation with a global network of cities and corporations" (Rynkiewich, 2011, p. 232). It is not that the nation-state has passed out of existence, but the role of the city has emerged in recent decades with vigor and taken on new significance.

In recent history, missionaries have often traveled to rural areas seeking to avoid going where the Gospel has already been proclaimed, and perhaps, it may be suggested, there has been some intentionality to avoid the challenges of cities as well (Rynkiewich, 2011, pp. 217-218). Many Christian missionaries prefer the village hut to the high-rise. However, when considering the strategic importance of cities in a networked world, the intensity of contemporary migration movements, and the accessibility of unreached people groups within cities, missionaries once again are beckoned to walk in the footprints of the first apostles and engage the world's urban centers. Today, any global missions strategy must consider the importance of cities if it is to take contemporary culture seriously at all.

Many Christians who desire to contribute to God's global mission may only need to walk across the street or jump on a subway. When seeking to evangelize unreached people groups, some of the key leaders of that society may actually be residents of Los Angeles, Miami, or Paris while maintaining significant influence among a cluster of family and friends. Globalization, international migration, communications technology, and urbanization forcefully challenge us to reimagine global missions for a world in transition.

Conclusion

The missionary task is standing at another crossroads of change. The world has been undergoing tremendous transformation, and missionaries face the daunting challenge of adapting to a new world. This new global context presents both opportunities and challenges. Local ministry may potentially have a global impact even reaching around the world, and practically no local context is left untouched by forces of globalization. The missionary endeavor has always been to enter a new culture and represent the Gospel in that culture in word and deed. That missionary mandate is persistently true for the global church as cultures and worldviews intersect with one another on a daily basis.

The church of the majority world is on the rise. Evangelism and church planting have been accelerating, but the church in Europe and North America has been grappling with decline in overall membership and involvement. There remain multitudes of unreached and least-reached people groups that have little to no Gospel presence among them; however, global migration is closing the geographic gap between Christian witness and representatives of unreached ethnic groups from around the world. Urbanization is rapidly transforming the context for world missions, but the impact of globalization is transforming cities from simply the places where the most people are into strategic mission fields for both global and local evangelism. Missionaries are confronted with the transformation of physical space while pushed beyond spatial limitations to engage relational networks. The current global context is forcing us to reconsider the strategic implications of a mobile world where the context for global mission is a web of cities that are increasingly international.

Reflection Questions

1. How do you see the current global trends impacting your local church?
2. How do you think these global trends might affect the practice and study of Christian missions?
3. What opportunities do these global shifts present to the church? What challenges does the church face?
4. How do you imagine the role of the American or European church in the missionary task in light of these global shifts?

Chapter 3
Loving Our Neighbor:
Foundations for Witness in a Pluralistic Society

Beginning With Our Own Hearts

Recently, I was riding in a taxi in Manhattan and spent most of the ride speaking to the driver. He was from the Dominican Republic. He had entered the United States legally and had lived in New York City for 17 years. He discussed life in his country and how sincerely he desires to return home. He literally aches for his homeland and the culture that he knows and loves. He explained, however, that returning home would be an economic impossibility. He discussed how he believed that corruption in the government keeps money out of the hands of ordinary people, and while he would rather return home, working in New York has provided a life for his family. His heart is in another land, but economic realities keep him grounded where he is.

A few months ago, I was in a conversation with another leader of a ministry organization based in a city in the southwest United States. We were discussing the challenges and opportunities found in ministry among migrant or diaspora communities, and he explained how he guarded his language when speaking with members of churches in his area. He steered clear of using the term "immigrant" because he didn't want to evoke negative emotions. He instead used the term "migrant" because it wasn't as politicized in his cultural context. I've used these terms interchangeably in this book; however, the very term immigrant often drums up negative reactions within the dominant culture. There has often been suspicion or even hostility toward the "others" entering "our" country.

I want to argue, and passionately so, that attitudes of resentment or hostility toward immigrants is antithetical to the Gospel of Jesus Christ, but I also want to assume that Christian readers of a text discussing diaspora missiology already embrace a compassionate attitude toward immigrant communities and hopefully recognize common cultural blind spots. I have no intention of wading into the nuanced and complex debates of public policy here; however, as I focus on urban evangelism and missions among migrant communities, it is impossible to dismiss the notion that there are negative feelings toward immigrants even among Christian churches—despite biblical commands to the contrary. Can even the people of God fall prey to resentment and anger toward the foreigner and alien? I can't help but recount the negative comments or scapegoating I've overheard while listening to discussions playing out in the media, and I've certainly encountered negative assumptions about new arrivals to the United States among Christians who are active in church and ministry. I'm deeply concerned that the church of Jesus Christ might completely miss what God is up to in our world as doors open for evangelism among even some of the most resistant ethnic groups in the world. It would be heartbreaking if one of the greatest opportunities for evangelism and church planting in our time is unfolding in our cities and the priorities of nationalism trump our commission to see the nations become disciples of Christ. It really seems to be part of our human nature—that is, our fallen nature—to harbor resentment for newcomers to a country we call our own. We too easily consider others to be invaders even when they come seeking the peace of our city. Whether it's European hostility toward immigrants arriving in droves from nations that were once Europe's colonies, Americans' suspicion or underlying envy of their new neighbors arriving literally from around the world, or even the tension one small nation has with another such as Costa Ricans' feelings toward immigrants from Nicaragua, the human tendency to marginalize and view the "other" as an invader of sorts persists in our imaginations. This book is about evangelism and strategies related to reaching the nations flocking to our cities. I've intentionally focused on strategic implications and the practice of mission rather than a complete theological treatment of the subject as this is a text dealing with the practice of ministry. However, I hope the next few pages may encourage readers to check in with their own hearts and perception of Scripture as we encounter the "other" in our neighborhoods and cities. Our missionary efforts should grow out of our Christlike love for those unlike us.

Despite assumptions to the contrary, the Bible takes a very different attitude toward foreigners and aliens in our midst. I'm hoping that anyone reading this book addressing diaspora missiology in urban contexts will not be a victim of extraordinary resentments toward foreign immigrants. We really cannot be too empathetic toward our brothers and sisters who have migrated across borders. Anyone who has never immigrated to a foreign context will never quite understand just how traumatic the experience really is in the life of the migrant. Newcomers to a foreign culture must figure out where to find housing, food and other basic needs, transportation, and schools for their children in a system they don't yet understand. They also must learn how to communicate while still learning the language, master social acts such as how to greet new people, and the culture's perception of time (Rogers, 2006, pp. 28-36). The challenges for any immigrant are many, and the first response of a follower of Jesus Christ ought to be deep and sincere empathy for the plight of the foreigner. Whatever the reason, something motivated them enough to risk everything to enter a new land, culture, and way of life. This is no small leap. When we read tales of Europeans taking this journey across the Atlantic to escape hardship and build a new life, we often listen with nostalgic admiration.

When we take a step toward evangelism among diaspora communities living in cities, the crucial beginning point is our own heart. Members of diaspora communities are more than our missions strategy; the Gospel propels us toward love (Baxter, 2013, p. 122). In many countries and certainly in the United States, there may be negative attitudes or unhelpful stereotypes toward immigrants in their new community. In *The Meeting of the Waters*, Fritz Kling quotes Nick Park, an Irish pastor of a multicultural church in Dublin, "Migration is the key moral issue of our day. It used to be slavery, then integration, then abortion. Now it is immigration" (Kling, 2010, p. 91). Of course, the previous issues mentioned certainly have not gone away, nor have they ceased being moral issues each in their own right. Slavery is certainly alive today, and great work is being done in the name of Jesus Christ to combat the global slave trade by such organizations as International Justice Mission, Rapha House, and others. Integration made great headway in the 1960s Civil Rights Movement in the United States, followed years later by the fall of apartheid in South Africa; however, much ground still needs to be gained in undoing systemic injustices and facilitating racial reconciliation. That fight is not nearly finished until all racial prejudice is extinguished. Abortion is certainly far from rare, and many ministries are working to replace that alternative with adoption. Many are working tirelessly and peaceably for the opportunity for others to live. However, immigration is the key moral issue of our time if for no other reason than the evangelical church in developed nations has in large measure failed at recognizing it as a moral issue. From cover to cover, the Bible is explicit in the mandate to God's people concerning the treatment of the foreigner. If our hearts are more ruled by our concern over one's legal status in our nation or participation in our tax system, perhaps we are more ruled by nationalism than by our own obedience to the Christian Scriptures? I do not pose this question as a political commentary, but rather as an opportunity for theological and personal reflection. If we are to become effective in ministry among the nations living in our cities, we should begin by addressing our own hearts toward immigrants in our land. My hope for this chapter is to simply remind us, through the Scriptures, how greatly concerned our God is for the plight of the immigrant.

Often believers who have never migrated from their homeland need to hear the stories of others who have taken this journey. The following excerpt is from a letter by a Christian migrant leader quoted in a document from a Lausanne Committee meeting on World Evangelization:

> Poverty, inequality, civil conflicts, persecution, and desire to survive forced us to leave our country and people. Regrettably, we do not feel a 'warm Christian welcome.' Instead, we are blamed for the crisis of your profit-driven society. We are seen as a wave of plague that must be turned back and controlled. There is now fear and trembling in our midst, not knowing what the future holds for us. What keeps us going is the satisfaction that our euro remittances help our families to survive, that soon we will return home—a dream which is getting to be a myth and illusion. In order to survive and have hope and meaning in life, we organize 'migrant churches,' which seem to fascinate some of you, for reasons we sometimes cannot understand. (Claydon, 2004, p. 14)

In reality, the Gospel narrative itself has far more in common with the journey of international immigrants than our own attempts at middle-class preservation. Indeed, the genealogy of Matthew's Gospel begins with Abraham being called out from his homeland, and it ends with Joseph and Mary as political refugees (Zapata-Thomack, March 22, 2014). The story of Jesus entering the world is "about an Asian-born baby, born in a borrowed barn, who became an African refugee. In that simple story, Jesus is in touch with the greatest migration in human history, because over half of the world's babies are born in Asia and over half of the world's 30 million refugees are Africans" (Bakke, 1999, p. 4). The earliest expansion of the church beyond Jerusalem took place through the scattering of religious refugees fleeing violent persecution.

Migrants—such as Priscilla and Aquila—followed economic opportunities from city to city and pressed the advance of the Gospel from Corinth to Rome, and as a bicultural evangelist, Timothy lived in the dual worlds of the Jewish diaspora and the Greek dominant culture. Our faith story is wrapped up in the journey of immigrants. The Christian narrative speaks to immigrants in a way that may be difficult for some to understand. For many of us, our ability to listen to their stories brings us closer to the story of our Christian faith.

The following sections are in no way meant to be an exhaustive account of the Bible's treatment of immigrants or of diaspora communities as a whole, nor is it designed to be an in-depth exegetical analysis. Indeed, an exegetical work along these lines would make an important contribution for discussing this theme within the Body of Christ. Nevertheless, this chapter is taking the reader on a brief excursion from the impact of globalization upon missions strategy and urban evangelism to the biblical values regarding the church's stance toward the foreigner and alien. My aim is to take a brief survey of the worldview of Christian Scripture toward immigrants across the pages of our Bible, and my purpose is to rekindle a love for the "other" as we seek to have the mind of Christ in our ministries and in our daily walk with him. The foundation for urban missions among diaspora communities is reteaching our own hearts to love our neighbors as ourselves. That must be the foundation of any strategy to engage diaspora communities in any part of the world.

Welcoming the Foreigner

"When immigrants live in your land with you, you must not cheat them. Any immigrant who lives with you must be treated as if they were one of your citizens. You must love them as yourself, because you were immigrants in the land of Egypt; I am the Lord your God" (Leviticus 19:33-34, CEB). In the Torah, God repeatedly reminds Israel that they too were once foreigners, and they retell this history because it should stimulate compassion within them toward others. The

Law emphasized repeatedly that God's people were to show kindness and hospitality to foreigners in their land. Leviticus 19 even directs them to treat foreigners as if they were equal to citizens, to love the foreigner even as they love themselves. Again, in the Deuteronomic law, the people are commanded: "... you must also love immigrants because you were immigrants in Egypt" (Deuteronomy 10:19, CEB). Later in Deuteronomy 24, God includes the foreigner with the plight of orphans and widows, instructing farmers to leave food for widows, orphans, and immigrants to gather from among the leftovers. Israel's de facto welfare system was aimed at the fatherless, the widow, and the immigrant. In the Western church, we often take up the challenge to care for widows and orphans, but the Old Testament doesn't stop there. It includes the foreigner among those who deserve compassion from members of the host nation. Loving the immigrant as we love ourselves is as unconditional in the biblical text as is caring for orphans and widows. At the heart of loving your neighbor as yourself is the mandate to love our new neighbors who have come from a seemingly strange and distant land.

This emphasis upon compassion and hospitality to migrants isn't limited to a few verses nor does it stop at the Law of Moses. For instance, in Malachi 3:5, God's judgment is pronounced against: sorcerers, those committing adultery, those swearing falsely, those oppressing orphans and widows, those cheating day laborers from their wages, and those "who brush aside the foreigner and do not revere me" (CEB). Perhaps we are sometimes quick to cheer on God's judgment against witchcraft or a cheating husband or someone committing evil against widows or orphans. However, if we take the Bible seriously, God is just as frustrated when we lack hospitality to the struggling immigrant. The prophet's voice carries down through the ages and confronts, with no less forcefulness, the landowner who cheats the Mexican worker picked up from the corner as a day laborer or any believer who would lack hospitality for the El Salvadorian striving against all odds to provide a better future for his children. God's people are clearly commanded to respond to foreigners in their land with hospitality and mercy.

Throughout the Old Testament Law and the Prophets, the theme of concern for the poor, the abandoned, and the foreigner repeats itself sufficiently enough to warrant our attention. Even as we wade through those difficult, frightening, and sometimes exciting Old Testament narratives, hospitality toward the migrant is a biblical standard, and the declaration for compassion sounds loud and clear. The starting place for diaspora missiology is God's deep concern for immigrants and the struggles they face. The challenge that confronts God's people today is to see the immigrant not through our American or British or Canadian eyes, but with the eyes of the Lord himself—to see the immigrant, the undocumented worker, and the refugee, as our brother, our sister, our mother, our children.

The Blessings of Exiles

Much of the story of Israel is a story of sojourning. Abraham is called to leave his father's house. Joseph is sold into slavery only to rise to the height of the ranks of Egyptian government. Moses leads the twelve tribes out of slavery through the wilderness wanderings. Despite the warnings of the prophets, the people are taken into exile and displaced in Babylon. In Jeremiah Chapter 29, we find the letter Jeremiah sends to the leaders of the exiles in Babylon. He instructs them:

> This is what the Lord Almighty, the God of Israel, says to all those I carried into exile from Jerusalem to Babylon: "Build houses and settle down; plant gardens and eat what they produce. Marry and have sons and daughters; find wives for your sons and give your daughters in marriage, so that they too may have sons and daughters. Increase in number there; do not decrease. Also, seek the peace and prosperity of the city to which I have carried you into

exile. Pray to the Lord for it, because if it prospers, you too will prosper."(Jeremiah 29:4-7, CEB)

Throughout the Bible, God's people are often migrants rather than in the role of the receiving country. When they arrive in Babylon, they arrive as exiles. They have been conquered and made subject to a foreign crown. However, they are told to seek the peace or welfare—the shalom —of the city. They are to build lives there, integrate into the life of the city, and work for its well-being. Their lives are wrapped up in the welfare of the city. They share in the blessings of the city and are called to contribute to its health and prosperity. Many of us reading this book share life circumstances closer to that of the Babylonians than of exiled Israelites. As we host new immigrants arriving in our cities, many come and contribute to the welfare of the city. Christian entrepreneurs from around the world come and build new businesses in North American cities, and many come adding to the *shalom*, the welfare, of our city. By welcoming new families to our churches, our neighborhoods, and our businesses, we are inviting the blessing of exiles as they seek prosperity in our communities and desire revival in our churches. Several months ago, I heard a story of German churches being revitalized by Iranian Christians resettling in the European nation despite these Iranian Christians being shocked by what they perceived as lethargy of many German Christians. Often immigrants bring economic, religious, and cultural revitalization to communities struggling for creativity and renewal. Many churches are in need of the fervor and courage characteristic of many migrant Christians arriving in their communities. Rather than suspicion, a new and more hopeful way to view new immigrants in "our" land is to see them as the bringers of blessings as they arrive as exiles seeking the welfare of the city.

Jesus the Refugee

Right in the first pages of our New Testament is the story of a refugee escaping to a foreign land seeking political asylum. Amidst our yearly Christmas carols it might simply be too easy to forget that Jesus's early days were spent as an illegal immigrant in a foreign country. In Matthew's account, Herod is set on assassinating any potential rival for his puppet throne. When the visitors from the East follow the directions given in a vision to avoid reporting the child's whereabouts to Herod, he kills any child that might be his young rival. The contrast between the foreign visitors (who we often assume might have been travelers from Persia) and the puppet king of the Jews is obvious. The righteousness of pagan foreigners who traveled to recognize the true king of Israel far surpassed that of Herod who occupies Israel's throne. When Joseph is warned in a dream to escape, Jesus's family members become refugees and escape to Egypt. As we sing Christmas songs in worship to Jesus as our King and Savior, we are singing praises to a child refugee seeking political asylum in a foreign land where his own people were once held as slaves.

Indeed, Jesus's own refugee journey to Egypt resonates in the heart of many undocumented immigrants making long secretive journeys today. This is a point that might appear so strange to those native to the host nation that it may even be offensive for me to suggest it. In order to seek refuge from Herod, Jesus's family traveled to Egypt "secretly." Perhaps we should let that description sit with us for a moment. What does "secretly" imply? It is indeed unlikely that they knocked on the door of the embassy seeking permission to enter the country or sought a visa in order to settle in Egypt. No, their journey was one of secrecy. Our Christmas story involves Jesus's parents literally sneaking into the neighboring country. For many struggling immigrants fleeing hardship for a hopeful future for their children, they affirm: "We too have made that journey" (Zapata-Thomack, March 22, 2014). Joseph's responsibility was to protect Jesus and his mother. His responsibility was not to the political integrity of Egypt or to Herod's rule in Israel. As our faith story begins, Jesus's first years were spent as an illegal alien. When we love the alien and foreigner, the immigrant and the refugee, we are extending our hand to the Lord himself.

Embracing Samaritans

I grew up aware that racial or ethnic prejudice was not a modern invention, and I knew this was true because I went to Sunday School. As young as I can remember, Bible class teachers would explain how Samaritans were regarded with racial disdain during Jesus's time in order to help us grasp the dramatic and countercultural moves unfolding in the New Testament narrative. As we explored stories of Jesus's interaction with Samaritans, it was exciting to see Jesus break the rules, but the more I learned through the years of our own racial injustices and deep-seated prejudices, the more I sincerely appreciated the power behind Jesus's reconciling moves and counter-moves in a tense and segregated society. What to our modern ears may appear subtle was deeply subversive in Jesus's first-century world, so it is likely to have been no mistake that ministry among Samaritans plays a significant role in the early ministry of Jesus and the church.

The Good Samaritan: Imitating the "Other"

In Luke 10:25-37, a story begins with a Jewish leader questioning Jesus. He asks Jesus, "What must I do to be saved?" Jesus asks him how he interprets the Law of Moses. What answer does this expert in the Torah offer him? He answers plainly, "To love the Lord . . . and to love your neighbor ..." Jesus congratulates him. Perhaps the discussion could have ended there, but he further questions Jesus, seemingly seeking some greater justification or loophole for who he is actually required to love. He asks, "Who is my neighbor?" Then begins the story we know as the Good Samaritan. A man is robbed, beaten, and left for dead. A priest passes on the other side of the road. A Levite passes him by as well. Then, it is the Samaritan who stops and helps the victim on the roadside. I suppose it would have been easy to tell the story with the victim as a Samaritan and a good Jew stopping to help. A more traditional protagonist and a Samaritan victim would have still answered the question, "Who is my neighbor?" For a Jewish keeper of the Law, going out of one's way to help a Samaritan would have been quite challenging enough. It may have even still revealed the teacher's apparent desire for self-justification. If someone isn't technically my "neighbor," am I still compelled to love him? Telling the story of a Jew helping a Samaritan or even a Roman colonist would have accomplished the same lesson in many respects. However, Jesus chooses a protagonist that is far more provocative. His use of cultural dissonance raises the stakes for everyone listening.

The protagonist in the story is wholly "other." The divide between Jews and Samaritans was both theological and racial as well as political, and the division between these peoples was dug deep over a period of hundreds of years (Bruce, 1983, p. 103). The Samaritan wasn't just racially "other" though he was that too, but he was theologically wrong as well. Yet we are called upon to imitate this Samaritan. The Samaritan demonstrates tangible love of neighbor even as we are called to love him, the Samaritan, as well. Can we not only love a man beaten and left on the side of the road but also truly love the antagonist of our faith, ethnic pride, or nationhood as well? The contrast with the expert in the Law is unmistakable. Right practice by one outside of right orthodoxy must challenge Jesus's listeners—and indeed us—with how far we actually may be regarding a true understanding of faithful and obedient practice of God's Law. The Samaritan, who likely lacked a right understanding of God's Law, was the player in the story who demonstrated one of its primary tenets in action. Despite the intellectual and the orthodox understanding of the Law by the teacher of that Law, he was lacking the tangible demonstration displayed by the Samaritan. It is perhaps no different for us. I have often taught on the importance of hospitality but realize that I have much to learn about actual practice from my Muslim neighbors. Political battles wage in American society over whether we may post the Ten Commandments in public space while African immigrants express their confusion by our society's apparent fascination with dishonoring father and mother. We have much to learn from the Samaritan indeed.

The parable does not argue for religious relativism or imply a modern display of anti-Western sentiment. It never makes the leap to say that right theology is meaningless. Rather, it does insist that our love for others be without condition, and it does appear to argue that we possess the humility to learn from our neighbors who do not yet share in the truth that we proclaim when aspects of their life demonstrate that same truth beyond our own testimony. As we encounter the "other," we may be certain that Jesus is King of kings and salvation is in him alone, and as a result, we can rest in confidence in him. That confidence allows us to listen and learn from our neighbors' example when they unknowingly imitate aspects of our Lord's example. This parable boldly demonstrates that our cognitive understanding of loving neighbor is insufficient when not accompanied by radical practice. When we see others who do not know the grace found only in Jesus Christ living out one of the principles of the Gospel, a living parable emerges calling us back to obedience to love the "other" as we love ourselves. Certainly, it is unlikely that Jesus's use of such cultural and theological dissonance was accidental.

In our imitation of the Samaritan, a key task of mission is to love others without condition. The racial and theological divide between Jew and Samaritan was no less bitter and broken than many of the racial tensions in our cities today. Yet Jesus tells a radical story of loving others without condition. We demonstrate unconditional love to migrants who may or may not have entered our land through legal documentation. Our relationships with Muslims may be characterized by compassion instead of fear. Our encounters with followers of world religions in our cities and suburbs may be characterized by a deep longing for their discovery of grace and a new allegiance to Christ rather than religious arrogance or ethnocentrism on our part. When we share the mind of Christ, our treatment of foreigners will embody the command: "Love your neighbor as you love yourself" (Matthew 22:39, CEB).

Meeting at the Well: Pathways for the Gospel

The story of the Samaritan woman is well-known among both missiologists and in countless Sunday School classes. Jesus's use of evangelistic discourse in the face of potential opposition is striking. They are passing through the land of Samaria, moving between Judea and Galilee, and while his disciples are looking for food, Jesus sits by a well and asks a Samaritan woman for a drink of water. The woman is surprised by his request since sharing a cup with a Samaritan woman would have made Jesus ritually impure (Bruce, 1983, pp. 102-103). She may be shocked at his request for a drink from her cup, but she may also have taken this as an opportunity to object to the typical treatment of Samaritan women by Jewish men as well (Brown, 1997, pp. 342-343). Jesus goes on to offer her "living water," but she doesn't grasp the concept. Jesus then takes another step, asking her to bring her husband, knowing quite well she doesn't have a husband but has had a bad and shameful history with men and is now living sinfully with a man. Finally, at this point she brings up political and religious controversy between Jews and Samaritans, raising a point of debate on the correct place of worship—the temple in Jerusalem or at this mountain. When someone gets personal, what's the best way to change the subject? Bring up religion or politics, of course. Jesus brushes it aside and explains that worship is not bound to a holy place but embodied in a holy people. Not quite satisfied with his response, she suggests that the coming Messiah will settle the controversy. However, Jesus forces her to make a decision about him. His declaration is clear. "I am he."

The story of the Samaritan woman speaks volumes to Christians seeking to be a witness in a pluralistic world. From the very beginning of the exchange, Jesus is breaking cultural barriers. He is completely unconcerned by the religious defilement that taking a drink from the cup of a Samaritan woman would bring upon him. Jesus's offer of living water to the woman transcends the political, religious, gender, and ethnic barriers that would normally inhibit a conversation even taking place between the two of them. Rather, when the woman raises the controversy over the correct place of worship, he presents a different way that negates the battle lines that have traditionally been drawn. To be certain, he is not issuing a call to an archaic form of religious universalism, but his invitation is certainly universal in nature. Worship is not restricted to a certain place or among a certain type of people. Obedience to the God of creation is not simply built along the lines of tribal loyalty. Instead, all peoples may have access to God through a true relationship with him.

In this story, Jesus calls a woman to faith, teaches his disciples a lesson, and brings the message of salvation to an entire community by crossing real cultural barriers. One of the most striking aspects of this story is that Jesus reaches this woman and her community not from a position of power or privilege, but from vulnerability. His physical thirst and his disregard for maintaining his ritual purity is the launching pad for reaching an entire community through a sinful and shamed woman.

For missiologists, crossing cultures is not a new challenge. However, in an urbanized and globalized society, the challenge is not simply for missiologists to enter another culture in another land. Rather, missiologists now are faced with the task to train a Western and sometimes insulated church how to interact and engage with a pluralistic and international society that is both near and far. Western believers accustomed to reaching others much like themselves while sending missionaries to foreign lands are now living in an urban global community where their nearby neighbor is thoroughly "other." The Christian mandate to take the Gospel to every nation, love the foreigner as we love ourselves, and to forge new paths forward in racial reconciliation as ambassadors of Christ is now an opportunity that nearly every Christian has the potential to embrace. It simply requires crossing the street or driving across town.

A Truly Great Commission

The passage commonly referred to as The Great Commission in Matthew 28:16-20 is well known. It's repeatedly been the topic of conversation in forming sermons, workshops, mission statements, and countless articles unpacking the importance of our participation in the mission of God. Following his resurrection, Jesus instructs his disciples that their job is now to make disciples. He tells them to teach new disciples to obey all things that Jesus has commanded them, and their baptism is to be into the faith in the triune God. Much ink has been put on paper to offer commentary on one of the most striking aspects of this passage. Jesus charges his disciples to make disciples not only among the lost sheep of Israel, but what would have been an extraordinarily new vision was the call to make disciples among all ethnicities, all peoples. Panta ta ethne literally means all ethnicities. Jesus's instructions were no longer to simply go to the lost sheep of Israel. The command by Jesus is to teach every kind of person from every tribe under heaven to follow Jesus as their teacher, obey his commands, and be baptized, so the boundaries of race, ethnicity, language, tribe, or nation no longer apply. In Christ Jesus, there is one new humanity that draws from every tribe and people. When this command was first given to a group of Jewish men seeking to follow their resurrected rabbi, it was extraordinary. Were they to make disciples of their Roman conquerors? Were they to teach the Celts or the Turks to obey all Jesus commanded? Were they really to baptize Persians or Africans? The commission that Jesus gives leads us to a definitive "Yes!"

International Encounters: Ethiopian Eunuch

In Acts Chapter 8, Philip is directed by God to go to the road between Jerusalem and Gaza, and it's there that he sees a eunuch, likely originating from modern Sudan (Marshall, 1992, p. 162), from the court of the Ethiopian queen. As the eunuch was riding along the road on his way home from Jerusalem, he is reading Isaiah. Philip asks the eunuch if he understands what he is reading and accepts an invitation to join him in his chariot to explain. He explains the meaning of the text to the Ethiopian official, and when they reach water somewhere along the way, the eunuch asks to be baptized. Immediately after the baptism, Philip is whisked away by the Holy Spirit, leaving the eunuch to go on his way praising God for his newly discovered salvation. It's a seemingly simple story, but the missiological implications in a globalized world ought not to go unnoticed.

The mission of God extends beyond the reach of the original Twelve Apostles, and at this point in the story the Holy Spirit is moving through the church's newest bicultural leaders who have one foot in the Greek world and the other in Judaism. Philip would have already been familiar with moving between cultures and is apparently the first one to continue Jesus's work among the Samaritans. We don't know much about Philip, but we can see that he was used by God as a pioneer of the Gospel—a bicultural evangelist to Samaritans and Ethiopians when the church was virtually entirely Jewish.

As an Ethiopian official, the eunuch traveled quite a distance to worship in Jerusalem, and as a eunuch, he would have been unable to enter the temple. Eunuchs were often utilized for various duties in royal courts during ancient times, but even as a worshiper of God, he would have been denied access to full religious participation among the Jewish people (Bruce, 1966, pp. 186-187). We can't help but wonder if he was reading Isaiah due to Isaiah's vision recorded in Chapter 56 when foreigners and eunuchs will no longer be excluded from full participation with God's people. He then comes to the part of Isaiah when the suffering servant takes the injustices of sin and shame upon himself and wonders to whom this passage is referring. We cannot know for certain, but it is not difficult to imagine.

Philip is sent; that fact in the story is significant. Like so much of the story we find in Acts, the Spirit is directing the mission to the nations. Philip didn't dream up a plan for reaching the Ethiopian empire, but the Spirit of God was constantly advancing his redemptive mission to the nations. Philip is an obedient missionary who follows as the Spirit leads. It is the Lord that sends Philip to the road for an encounter with one completely outside his typical religious boundaries, just as it is the Lord who directs Peter to Cornelius's household, and it is the Lord who sends out Barnabas and Saul. As the story of Philip's adventures wraps up, the Spirit leads him to the city of Azotus, historically a Philistine city of Ashdod north of the area of Gaza (Bruce, 1966, p. 191). It is fascinating and thrilling that the story of Philip leaves off with him landing in a city that represents the pagan enemies of Israel. I wish we knew the next chapter in Philip's story, but we're left to imagine how a cross-cultural mission to the Gentiles and former adversaries of Israel may have potentially continued through Philip.

Fellowship with Pagans: Finding Cornelius

Just before his ascension, Jesus tells the disciples that when the Holy Spirit comes, they will be his witnesses to the ends of the earth. Following the episode, for the rest of the narrative throughout the book of Acts, the Holy Spirit is intent on driving God's people to be a missionary presence in the world. As the story builds momentum, Peter is led to proclaim Christ beyond his religious and ethnic boundaries and help launch the Gentile mission. He receives a vision of unclean foods and is told, "kill and eat" (Acts 10:13, CEB). Peter insists that he cannot break kosher laws, but the Lord insists that these foods have been made clean. The vision is repeated until Peter is called away to the home of Cornelius. Cornelius has simultaneously been receiving a vision to hear the word of the Lord from Peter. Peter breaks the rules by entering Cornelius's house, and as he is explaining the good news of Jesus Christ, the Spirit comes upon the household and repeats the Pentecost experience before Peter's eyes. By this time, Peter gets the point. Even members of this foreign army occupying his country may come to know the Lord and his grace. Peter realizes that the previous religious and ethnic and even political barriers can no longer inhibit them from entering God's Kingdom, so they are immediately baptized. Of course, now Peter has to explain himself to the remaining Jewish leadership of the church, and following a counsel in Jerusalem, Gentile conversion without becoming kosher was made the church's official position—although still debated for decades to come.

The cultural barrier of consuming unclean foods according to Peter's adherence to kosher laws was more than just religious ritual. It was a boundary that prohibited true fellowship. "Breaking bread" or sharing a meal would have been one of the main components of Christian worship at that time (Gehring, 2004, pp. 83-85). The church gathered mostly in homes and ate together. However, at this point Peter would only have experienced this table fellowship in Jewish households. For modern Westerners, we can easily imagine going into someone's home, spending an hour in Bible study, and going on our way without even opening a bag of chips, but for Mediterranean people at this time, hospitality was a cherished value. By Peter staying with Cornelius for a few more days, he is sitting at his table and eating foods that would represent breaking Jewish law and customs. Not unlike Jesus's request for a cup of water, Peter is making himself ritually unclean. Yet, it was the Holy Spirit that directed him to move beyond his cultural boundaries and religious customs and sit at the table of a Roman military officer. Much is at stake when dealing with kosher traditions in the New Testament. When Paul is arguing for a united fellowship of Jew and Gentile in Galatians, the issue is not simply whether they will sit together during the potluck "after" church or whether they could go out to dinner to the same restaurant, though these issues would still have importance today if some division were creeping into a Christian community. Rather, what is at stake is whether they can share fellowship as church because the meal is a central component of their worship as a body of believers.

When the Spirit drives Peter to respond to the invitation by Cornelius, the vision is more than a symbolic gesture of equality (though it is certainly that, too), but it is a call to join in fellowship with one who is completely foreign—in fact, even a foreign invader. It is a mandate to cross ethnic and religious barriers, and it might risk scandal as well since a Roman officer represented the imperial regime that was occupying Israel as a foreign power. However, the Kingdom of God transcends nationalistic interest, religious piety, or ethnic divisions.

Universal Access and a New Humanity

Throughout the letters of Paul, he is fighting for the mission to the Gentiles and a unified body of Christ. In Galatians, he recognizes that a broken table fellowship equals a broken church. Ironically, he must confront Peter who pioneered the Gentile mission at the table of Cornelius in the first place. In Ephesians Chapter 4, Paul argues passionately that there is "one Lord, one faith, one baptism," and two chapters earlier declares that Christ has removed the "dividing wall of hostility" (Ephesians 4:5; Ephesians 2:14, CEB). For Paul, the image of the temple would have made this tangible. If any one of his Greek converts had tried to enter the temple, he or she would have been restricted to the outer court of the Gentiles. However, now the significance of that dividing wall is no more. All peoples have access to the one God through the one Lord Jesus Christ, and therefore, there is no longer a theological separation between nations either. The dividing wall that separated God from people also separated classes of people from one another, but that wall is no longer valid in Jesus Christ.

As our cities are impacted by the forces of globalization, interaction with individuals and families from any number of nations is not only possible but likely. Many churches will serve multiethnic neighborhoods, and many disciples of Christ will live beside neighbors who practice Buddhism, Islam, Sikhism, Hinduism, or other non-Christian faith. A number of Western cities will become home to religious refugees seeking rest from violent persecution for their faithfulness in the Lord Jesus. For instance, just one of the missionary families currently working in New York City with Global City Mission Initiative has developed relationships with individuals from China,

Albania, Kosovo, Iran, Serbia, Yemen, Morocco, and Italy. Most of these relationships are within a few city blocks of one another while others are a subway ride away. As we encounter a wide range of diversity in our cities, each soul may be offered access to God's grace, and each person is of equal value in God's eyes. In Christ Jesus, we are one new humanity because the wall that separates Gentiles to the outer court is no longer relevant. It has been abolished by the cross and replaced by an empty tomb.

Renewing Our Minds For Mission

If we take these themes of Scripture seriously as part of the theological vision for the church, what are the implications for our missionary practice as the community of faith? Reflecting on the biblical vision for our witness among the nations, there are key character traits that we as missionaries, church leaders, and disciples of the Lord Jesus may put to practice as we encounter our neighbors from around the world. The starting point for developing a missiological response to the nations living in our cities is to turn our hearts toward loving the immigrant, the refugee, the day laborer, the undocumented worker. A diaspora missiology that reflects the Gospel of grace flows out of a love for all people from all nations regardless of class, legal status, country of origin, education, or gender.

Hospitality

From the earliest pages of the Bible, hospitality is a cherished value; however, welcoming others is not limited to our dearest friends and family. The Christian practice of hospitality is deeply rooted in our witness as followers of Christ. The church of the New Testament and of the earliest centuries that followed was known for her care of the weak and marginalized. "Hospitality—especially to strangers—is not just a Middle Eastern cultural value but a vital spiritual principle" (Claydon, 2004, p. 12). Yet it is commonly known and repeated among workers with international students that the majority of foreign students studying in American universities have never been in an American home.

I remember when I first invited a man from the West Bronx to my home for a Bible study. I was a new church planter, and we were hitting the streets trying to find someone (i.e., anyone) who was receptive to the message of the Gospel. My friend, "José," came and joined us. José was a heroin addict who, in his late forties, was fighting hard to kick an addiction that had plagued him for more than 30 years. While we sat and talked in my living room, he looked at me and shared with me that the thing that got his attention was that I had invited him to my home. It had, quite frankly, shocked him into receptivity to the Gospel. My own practice of hospitality is often dwarfed in comparison to what I've received from friends I've made that have come to New York City from around the world. Many times I sat in the apartment of a single mom from the South Bronx, and before any discussion of the Bible could begin, she would serve me coffee and some bread or crackers. It was sometimes nearly all she had in the kitchen to offer me. It hasn't gone unnoticed when my international friends offer me the best in their refrigerator knowing it was something they could have saved for themselves. Sometimes when I show up to visit a home, they run immediately to the store to provide something to drink despite conditions outside that may be rainy or cold. I don't feel that I deserve such honor, but they understand hospitality so much better than I do despite my vague intellectual awareness of its importance in Scripture and to Christian mission. I confess I have much to learn about true hospitality, and one of the benefits I've received from living in such an international metropolis is the lessons I've been taught by my neighbors from various parts of the world.

Hospitality is a Christian virtue that may soften the hearts of the unreceptive in urban settings. Although urban life sometimes promotes impersonal interactions, the Christian practice of hospitality breaks through and opens the door for authentic and loving relationships, and when we neglect our commitment to hospitality, we may risk weakening our potential witness of the Gospel among those who understand the importance of sharing our home and our table.

Vulnerability

Jesus modeled a highly powerful—but highly counterintuitive— missionary methodology when he sat by the well in Samaria and asked for a drink. His starting position was vulnerability. The Incarnate Word was thirsty, and he placed himself in the fellowship and care of a woman who was wholly "other." By the cultural standards of his time, her theology was wrong, her gender suspect, and her ethnicity offensive. Yet Jesus began the conversation that led to salvation by offering his vulnerability. Ultimately, Jesus emptied himself and became a servant, demonstrating submission through his acceptance of the cross. In imitation of Christ, the church must be a self-emptying community. When each member practically lives out the incarnation of Christ in this way, unity and reconciliation across cultural barriers becomes possible. The church of Jesus Christ representing a new humanity becomes possible (Oh, 1988, p. 69). Many immigrants come to us vulnerable, but their vulnerability was a product of moving into a new city and a new culture. Imitating Christ, those of us from the dominant culture may choose to enter into reconciling relationships by choosing vulnerability for ourselves.

While there are certainly diaspora congregations who find ways to participate in God's mission as sending agents and do so dynamically, many are confronted with their own lack of influence and resources as minorities among the dominant culture. Unfortunately, many established churches rooted in mainstream American religious life are in jeopardy of missing the opportunity to act as partners (Adeney, 2011, p. 16). Their own power and privilege may act as an obstacle to engaging in dynamic mission. The immigrant experience may be characterized by vulnerability, and in imitation of Christ's own self-emptying, there is much to learn from these faith communities on the margins. For Christians in the dominant culture, the Gospel compels us to embody the example of Christ with our neighbors. As we share fellowship with migrants in our cities, we embrace vulnerability. Diaspora communities represent opportunities for Christians from the dominant culture to step out of their own carefully managed space and to make themselves vulnerable in shared space with others. One of the greatest challenges for North American Christians may be to live outside of the privilege that our position affords us and to embody the Gospel from a stance of vulnerability. Practically speaking, this may imply that white Christians listen to the voices of non-white and non-Western leaders. It may mean that evangelists in American cities begin by listening well to outsiders and adding ethnographic research to their valued ministry tool belt, and it may imply that churches now surrounded by a changing neighborhood demographic learn to serve beyond their own interests, meeting the needs of others so much unlike themselves.

Boldness

The Gospel is for all of creation. Westerners confronting the emergence of a post-Christendom society are often reluctant to share the good news of Jesus the Savior, and in our individualistic society it is unfashionable to call others to change their faith allegiance. Nevertheless, the good news of God's Kingdom calls citizens of that Kingdom to be courageous. In each of the biblical examples we touched upon previously, there is no lack of boldness concerning the Gospel of Jesus Christ, nor shyness about making the Gospel's exclusive claim on eternal salvation. In some respects, it is not difficult to understand why many American Christians may have become reluctant to share such amazing news. We are often repelled by bad examples from within the Christian community and are desperate to find ways to overcome negative stereotypes. If evangelistic proclamation is carried out in arrogance or without love of neighbor, our proclamation may be viewed as nothing more than religious switching. I will argue in a later chapter that evangelism as a ministry vocation in and of itself must represent much more than religious proselytizing as its endgame. Gospel proclamation is embodying the integrated practice of verbal explanation and vulnerable service. Accompanying the practice of vulnerable service is the expression of bold proclamation.

Conclusion

For the church, global migration represents opportunities to join God's mission to reach the nations with the Good News of the Kingdom. While the challenges are very real, the evangelistic opportunities are unprecedented. The starting point for any church, missionary, or Christian leader will be the condition of our own hearts. Those of us who are well established in our homelands are challenged to listen to the voices of those who have migrated across boundaries and navigated the experience of living in cultural dissonance in a strange land. For followers of Christ, rereading the Bible through the eyes of immigrants opens a door for our own transformation so that we may love the immigrant as we love ourselves. For the missionary serving among diaspora communities, it is a vital step to view people in the full scope of their humanity. We want each one to know Jesus fully and deeply, and simultaneously these neighbors are more than targets of our religious marketing. Even as we intentionally seek to evangelize the nations in our midst, our international neighbors are bringers of blessing. Their journeys, in some cases, may even have more in common with the story of Christ and of God's people through the ages than our own. May our hearts be softened and prepared to receive the alien and foreigner as our brother, sister, mother, son, and daughter.

Reflection Questions

1. What images come to mind when you hear the word "immigrant?" What emotions does the word conjure?
2. How easy or difficult do you find relating to the themes of exiles, refugees, and migration in the Bible?
3. The Law often spoke of receiving orphans, widows, and foreigners in the same breath. How does this affect your outlook on immigrants arriving in your community?
4. What does it mean for Christians to be aliens and foreigners even when residing in the land of one's birth?

Chapter 4
Diaspora, Globalization, and Migration

Globalization

The impact of globalization can be felt in nearly every corner of the planet. Whether we are walking into a McDonald's serving up *gallo pinto* in Costa Rica, a Korean rapper becoming an American YouTube sensation, or a Congolese immigrant handling household affairs back in his hometown through a cell phone while standing on a street corner in Montreal, the effects of a globalizing world are felt everywhere. Yet despite the fact that globalization touches nearly everyone in almost every part of the world, it is still somewhat elusive as a concept.

Globalization may simply be the global expansion of the free market mixed with the rise and spread of technology (Pocock, et al., 2005, p. 37), and while the cause of globalization may indeed be the evolution of a globally connected free market, the outcomes are increasingly complex and interconnected. Globalization may be viewed as a multifaceted movement rooted in the free market but still affecting so much more than merely open market exchanges. More precisely, we may understand the phenomenon of globalization as "the widespread engagement of people with an expanding worldwide system of communication, commerce, and culture that is producing broad uniformities across selected sectors of many societies as well as generating multiple hybrid cultures in various stages of reception, rejection, and reinvention of innovations" (Rynkiewich, 2011, p. 234). Globalization, in many respects, represents a brand new world. However, the old industrial systems and established metropolitan regions are not vanishing. Rather they are simply being rearranged by new information technologies interacting with the global network (Susser, 2002, pp. 328-329). Globalization is certainly affecting virtually everything, and it is rearranging what we already knew.

The rise of the processes of globalization is leading us to see "the world as a single place" with greater and greater connectedness between once distant locations, and borders between nation-states are less and less of a barrier to religious, cultural, and commercial exchanges. Time and space are being compressed through information, communication, and travel technologies, as international trade blurs the distinction of local and global (Hanciles, 2008, p. 15). While one danger of globalization to missiological concerns could be a persistent American ethnocentrism wielding its cultural influence around the world (Pocock, et al., 2005, p. 38), the United States is as much a recipient of the effects of globalization as it is a player in the process (Hanciles, 2008, pp. 32-37). Western cultures, markets, and technological advances are helping shape other cultures and places around the planet; yet Western nations, including the United States, are also on the receiving end of the impact of cultural influences, a global economy, and scientific advancement riding on the wave of globalization. Certainly globalization involves the expansion of Western ideas and cultural expressions throughout the world, but the West is just as much a recipient as the global South or East. While globalization may often be thought of as synonymous with Westernization, such an assumption not only discounts the phenomenon of hybrid cultural expressions emerging in world-class cities and proliferated in pop culture but also overlooks significant non-American and non-Western agents making their impact on the global stage as well. To assume that globalization is strictly the advancement of Westernization overlooks the consistent impact of migrants from both East and South upon American and European cities, the integration of artistic expressions, symbols, and holidays from around the world into Western consciousness, or the highly integral nature of what is now a global economic system. Even if the influence of Westernization is operating as a global force, it is not the only cultural force at work in a global world. The reality of globalization is far more complex than our underlying assumptions. The rise of China's economic impact alone displaces the concept of a singular global dominance of only one Western nation. For instance, China now services the greatest number of imports and exports in the world and has surpassed the U.S. in manufacturing (Wan, 2011, p. 182). Will China's growth continue? Will the United States' persistence endure? Political and economic commentators regularly volley these questions back and forth in discussion and debate. Yet I'm sure the future is far less known than many political commentators suggest. While China continues to have its own internal struggles and the United States remains a prominent power in the world, a plurality of centers of global power including this non-Western juggernaut signals a shift from recent decades. However, in reality globalization is far more than these two competing powers, and the fact that discussions on globalization so often gravitate to these national influences may actually illustrate how much we lack a real grasp on the true complexity and fluidity of globalization. Nation-states are certainly key players in the movement toward greater globalization, but they are not the only players. Different individuals, as well as ethnic networks, private institutions, and government entities, interact with the processes of globalization to varying degrees. Multiple players interact across global networks impacting local realities in big and small ways. Some benefit from the advantages of a global marketplace with a widening group of options while others are impacted negatively and truly suffer under injustices that now play out on a global scale. Still there are others who remain unaware of globalization's powerful force upon the world—even if it is indeed having a real impact on their everyday lives (Rynkiewich,

2011, p. 236). The dramatic unfolding of globalization points to an interaction of a multitude of individuals and groups, private and public entities, and any assortment of cultural players. Indeed, "even at its most oppressive, globalization has never been unidirectional. Rather, it has always been about intercultural encounter and exchange" (McKenzie, 2011, p. 1). A missiology that engages with an interconnected globalized world will confront a fluid set of challenges rooted in geographic displacement, cultural interchanges, corresponding polarization, and cultural hybridization. Consistent and constant change is the new norm confronting evangelism and missiological efforts at Gospel contextualization.

Globalization affects us all to varying degrees. In essence, "globalization is a relational concept explaining how technological, economic, and cultural forces have fostered cultural contacts, which have reduced vast distances in space and time and, at the same time, brought civilizations and communities into closer degrees of interaction" (Kalu, et al., 2010, p. 25). Globalization is not an isolated phenomenon. It is powered by increased technology, and it fuels ongoing urbanization—and vice versa. It spurs international migration and connects once distant places with the push of button. As globalization accelerates the processes of urbanization and stimulates widespread international migration, the church does indeed face significant challenges and sits on the edge of incredible opportunities. A reorientation toward global mission playing out in global-urban contexts opens a pathway for the church as well. As the missionary enterprise addresses the needs of a world that is rapidly and consistently changing at a rate at which it's difficult to keep pace, targeting missiological initiatives in key urban centers places the ministry of the church at the leading edge of global and societal transformation. Indeed, "the city in an age of globalization creates a forward space that enables us to see the present and future of the church and world" (Gornik, 2011, p. 8). If we want to see the church of tomorrow, we may need to look no farther than immigrant-led churches, urban house churches, and multiethnic congregations in cities like Los Angeles, London, Hong Kong, or Vancouver.

The nature of globalization is profound. We once thought that the domain of the missionary was in a far-off land, but globalization brings the missionary experience close to home and is now a nearby reality for nearly every follower of Christ. Cross-cultural ministry and global missions are now within close proximity of virtually every local church or Christian household (McKenzie, 2011, p. 1). In some cases, church leaders may hope to resist the changes brought by globalization. The changes implied by such a cultural phenomenon may feel too threatening, but as one futuristic race in the *Star Trek* universe once stated: "Resistance is futile." Without question, the church should challenge injustices inherent in the processes of globalization, and additionally the church is also challenged to be an adaptive community in a changing environment as she proclaims the message of the Kingdom of God. Globalization is not likely to be reversed. Rather the new stage on which our drama now unfolds is certainly one that is definitively global. We now live in a connected world, and our cities are increasingly places defined by diversity and pluralism. Confronting global injustices may need to take into account not only local institutions or cultural systems but forces at work on the other side of the planet. It may no longer be sufficient to organize community development projects in a neighborhood without taking into account global factors playing out many miles away. Bringing the Gospel to unreached people groups may require evangelistic engagement between multiple nations as ethnic groups find themselves scattered across multiple cities sometimes worlds apart from where they originated. Developing leaders should include a preparedness to adapt in a world where change is normative, making it essential for theological formation to be rooted in dynamic hands-on learning situations. Urban mission must not be a marginalized area of missiology or ministry studies, but a central theme as we participate in God's mission in the urban world that is now emerging. We live on a planet that is interconnected and urban. "In missiology, we need to engage the world as it is, full of cities that are all products of urbanization and globalization" (Rynkiewich, 2011, p. 216).

People on the Move

In the United States, despite having a long history of repeating periods of immigration, since 1965 there has seen a seismic increase in the sheer number of immigrants, along with their global diversity, pouring into North American cities. While the development of the United States has always been affected by immigration, the story of immigration to North America was largely—though not exclusively—a European tale. Despite the forced slave labor of Africans or the role played by Chinese laborers, our stories were predominantly those of English pilgrims, German immigrants, or Irish refugees, among other European sojourners. However, the immigration waves impacting U.S. society today flow from Asia, Africa, Latin America, and the Middle East and are inevitably transforming the cultural landscape (Borja & Castells, 1997, p. 72). In reality, the story of the United States was never a fully European story, but today the fact that American society is not just a European narrative is obvious to far more than just the historian. In the United States, cultural diversity is on the rise in virtually every region of the country.

Through modern transportation and international access, migrants enter host countries through a number of different means and for a variety of reasons. Many stay permanently and may even obtain citizenship, even if they did not originally intend to make their host country their new home. Others are temporary residents, such as international students, business people, diplomats, or contract workers. Still others have been displaced by tragedy and trauma and are refugees or are seeking asylum and safety from traumatic events or persecution in their homelands (Claydon, 2004, p. 9). In the past, migration was thought of in fairly simplistic terms. People migrate to a new country and finds a way to survive in the new society. They attempt to assimilate, and they or their children eventually merge into mainstream society. Now, with the accompanying forces of globalization and advances in technology, migration processes are far more nuanced. Sometimes migrants move to the city and stay and build a life there. Sometimes migrants move to a city but then eventually return home to their country of origin. Still other migrants relocate to the city for a period of time, decide they desire to relocate to a better location, and then do so. Migration is not unidirectional; rather it now flows in a multidirectional manner (Rynkiewich, 2011, p. 201).

My wife's family illustrates the multidirectional movements within an immigration experience. Until she married me (a missionary presently in New York City), her intention was to return to London, where she was born and the culture with which she most identifies. Her mother still lives in the Bronx—the area where she first settled upon her arrival in the United States. My wife's father has relocated back to his native Jamaica. Her sisters have resettled in other cities in both the northeastern and southwestern regions of the United States. A single family has followed nearly every pathway a migrant family might typically follow as they have settled and resettled over the years. Understanding the immigration experience is not a single story but a dynamic and nuanced multidirectional movement of people and cultures. The example of my in-laws alone illustrates the point.

As a result, missiology is challenged to adapt to a new global mobility. Urban communities were never completely monolithic or static to begin with, but today the degree of fluidity that characterizes urban lifestyles would be dizzying to many in previous generations. Populations are in motion, and global society is a mobile culture. This will certainly challenge the church to develop new strategic perspectives and will likely confront some of our more intuitive assumptions that have been with us as a reversal of these trends seems unlikely. How does living in a globally connected and highly mobile society affect such areas of ministry as evangelism strategies, ideas about church planting, or theological education? While few would argue against the idea that such a demographic shift is presenting a challenge to the church, it also provides significant opportunities for the church to engage in God's mission for his world and to participate in that mission both locally and globally. Even as some mission fields have become more difficult places to work, representatives from those same nations have become urban neighbors with followers of Christ.

The church of Jesus Christ is a body that unites race, socioeconomic standing, gender, age, and education. It is a movement that transcends our social distinctions and supersedes national borders. In a time when people from around the planet are moving, shifting, and resettling, Christian leadership is needed in order to courageously and creatively engage mission in this new world. Missiologists are faced with questions of how to contextualize for a more globalized and urban world. Churches face a more mobile and transitional society than the one in which many churches were first planted or sending agencies first organized. Individuals are called to step out in vulnerability to reach out to their neighbors around the block. Some demographics may provide natural leadership for the church serving the nations through grassroots global networks. Often the second- or third-generation children of immigrants as well as immigrants who have learned to be bicultural in a diverse city, may possess the most potential for carrying out the Great Commission in such a dynamic society. It may be those who historically were on the margins of our society that are emerging as the new torchbearers for Christ's church in pluralistic and multicultural cities. "The natural bridge-builders should be liminal, hyphenated, polycentric, multilingual Christians" (Adeney, 2011, p. 7). Second-generation immigrants, immigrants who have adapted well to living in more than one culture, third-culture kids growing up in missionary or diplomat homes or other sojourning households, younger leaders who are not only technologically savvy but grew up in a more multiethnic society, and emerging leaders from uniquely marginal backgrounds may provide insight as leaders and key members of ministry teams as we envision ministry in the global network.

Global Cities

In our Bibles, we read of at least a few encounters at a well. It's where Moses first encountered Jethro's daughters and where Jesus opened a dialogue with a Samaritan woman. When Eliezer was sent to find a wife for Isaac, he waited at the central well of the community because he knew that the settlement's well was a place where he wouldn't remain alone for long. As the source of water for the community, it's where women would fill their buckets or shepherds would water their sheep. Ages before coworkers gathered by the water cooler in high-rise offices, a nation's towns, villages, and cities were built around sources of water. Natural resources and early urbanization were inherently linked as early settlements developed and grew. Sources of water were perhaps the early expressions of nodal centers, as human settlements formed around them.

Today, metropolitan centers are providing a global network with the resources of economic capital, clusters of human talent, technology infrastructures, and relational centers for interpersonal interactions between institutional leaders. Replacing the village well, cities themselves have emerged as "node points in vast interconnecting networks and systems that are oblivious to national boundaries" (Davey, 2002, p. 25). While nation-states continue to play a significant role in humanity's affairs, global cities often transcend borders and form a global network connecting across nations and continents. Metropolitan areas become nodes in a global network of individual, community, and institutional exchanges. Urban centers are undeniably the focal points of human civilization. They are the points of connection for modern human civilization, and human interaction most often takes place between cities on a regional, national, and international scale. As cultural centers, they reinforce cultural connections between once distant locations as mobile populations create lines of relational and cultural connections between international cities, and simultaneously the free market on a global scale utilizes urban space as command-and-control centers on the stage of world economic exchange. Large global cities connect to one another and connect to regional urban centers as their influence expands into surrounding regions. Cities are nodes in a global web of relationships and institutions, exchanges, and processes.

The church has found herself in a world of cities, and to participate in God's mission is to engage worldviews and cultures in an overwhelmingly urban society. In my experience, I've felt a degree of dissonance whenever listening to a discussion while visiting a Bible college or seminary campus and hear a student brush off the need to learn about urban life or culture, claiming that it is simply not his or her context for ministry. Maybe this way of thinking will soon be a relic of the past and fade from the halls of seminaries and colleges, since the new realities of globalization are quickly becoming the only world anyone will know. If not, we will be dangerously out of touch with our contemporary context for the ministry of the church.

Regardless of how well we are paying attention, the societal shifts I've been discussing here have been accelerating for decades. If we do not reshape our missiological vision for the church now, then when? A disclaimer for abstaining from cross-cultural ministry and the woes of urban life couldn't be further from the reality of an impending ministry context in today's world. Cities are centers of cultural influence, and with contemporary technologies the expansive influence and power of cities as regional, national, or global command centers touches life that formerly was beyond the reach of their city limits. "The urban experience is increasingly common, presenting previously unanticipated challenges and opportunities. Although regions and cities are at various stages of their development or decline, the culture of the city is increasingly global, and this has far-reaching consequences even for the most rural societies" (Davey, 2002, p. 6). Urbanism is a cultural phenomenon with a long reach well beyond the cityscape.

Ministry contexts are less and less isolated from one another, removing our ability to ignore urbanism. "The world's rural areas are progressively being exposed to, and are being forced to come to terms with, urban influences both from within their own countries and from societies which may be both culturally, as well as geographically, distant" (Clark, 2003, p. 136). Not only has the gap between cities been shrinking as urban centers are more and more connected as a global-urban network, but the space between urban and rural seems to be closing as well since technology brings urban perspectives and images to rural locations. In today's world, even when engaging a rural ministry context, it is unlikely for the church to avoid the influence of urbanism. The world is an increasingly connected place with cities at the intersections of that connectivity. The church's missionary task will overwhelmingly be an urban endeavor. In a world that's population is already more than half urban with a fierce expansion of urbanization continuing to advance, to engage in mission is to interact with urban society. Whether from a distance or up close, urbanization is a reality for everyone. Furthermore, the impact and role of cities in human civilization is continuing to evolve and have an increasingly important role. It may be necessary for us to reconsider whether urban mission is truly a subdiscipline of missiology or to think of urban missiology as simply contemporary missions. It seems that thinking of urban missiology as "mainstream" is way overdue. Rural missions must continue as we are called to go to all the world, but it requires special consideration in a world now run by cities. This is not to say that we should abandon the study of urban missiology. The complexity of urban systems requires a specialized understanding to contribute to strategic conversations and inform missionary practice, but it also seems that most church leaders and missiologists should gain a basic understanding of urban culture in a world that is undeniably populated by cities. An urban society is simply the context that more missionaries will confront when sharing the Gospel, and the underlying issues associated with urbanization and globalization will, without a doubt, be a contributing factor for both opportunities and challenges facing evangelism efforts by the church.

While processes of globalization and urbanization intersect and overlap in countless towns and cities, global cities—the primary global command centers in the global network—have been particularly challenging for Christian evangelism as well as gateways for vast opportunity. Saskia Sassen, an urban scholar, has argued that New York City, London, and Tokyo are the archetypes of this powerful urban force in the global village (Sassen, 2001). While it is unlikely that this status will remain static, global cities such as New York City, London, Tokyo as well as Paris, Toronto, Sao Paulo, Houston, and many other key urban centers are of strategic importance for the present and future church. Such cities are centers of global influence and points of connection between nations and cultures. As the Gospel moved along the Roman roads through the cities of the Mediterranean world and people gathered at wells in ancient villages, global cities are now nodes in a global network and are of strategic importance for the mission of the church. These are the centers of human activity that connect people and institutions through city-to-city and city-to-region interactions.

The global city is a hub of cultural influence. "The analysis of the 'global city' as the production site of the informational, global economy has shown the critical role of these global centers in our societies, and the dependence of local societies and economies upon the directional functions located in such cities. But beyond the main global cities, other continental, national, and regional economies have their own nodes that connect to the global network" (Susser, 2002, pp. 345-346). Global cities are key nodes in the network, but they also function to connect to regional centers, political capitals, marketplaces, religious headquarters, and similar points of influence as conduits for the global marketplace. International, national, and regional leaders are drawn to global cities where they may carry out interpersonal exchanges among their peers and with other leaders of industry, art, government, academia, or economics. For instance, not only can New York City boast the largest diplomatic community in the world, but it is also home to almost 2,000 foreign companies ("NYC Mayor"s Office for International Affairs," 2014). Cities are emerging as institutional centers on a global scale. Simultaneously, struggling immigrants are pulled to global cities as gateway destinations from all over the planet, and the working poor and middle-class professionals populate the machinery of the city and its institutions. The influencers and changers of culture often congregate in global cities where they may share direct human interaction and take advantage of direct accessibility to their peers who have come to the city for similar reasons. With an increase in urban gentrification and a kind of gravitational pull of the global city among the cultural elite, high-income residents and commercial enterprises find their home in global cities. As a result, there is an increased need to supply low-wage service-sector jobs, therefore attracting low-wage earners, to meet the service demands of this high-end population (Sassen, 2001, pp. 8-10). To illustrate the contrast within global cities, once I was walking along Central Park West in Manhattan, and outside of the Museum of Natural History, I spotted a stretch limousine and 10 feet down the block from the limo was one of the city's rickshaw-type tricycles that have become popular in Manhattan in recent years. Somehow the juxtaposition between these two vehicles-for-hire seemed to fit well in the global city. Urban economies in the global city represent extremes of elites and those laboring in the service sector. Workers from around the world are attracted to new opportunities and are motivated to seek open doors through hard work in the city. Global cities may be characterized as places of significant economic polarization with elite citizens of the metropolis at one end of the continuum and struggling immigrants and poor urban dwellers at the other. Indeed, this symbiotic process of urban growth presents a challenge to church planting as high economic demands may make an impact on the availability and energy level of the average citizen due to an intensive environment of productivity in a highly competitive economic system. Individuals often commute long distances, work long hours, experience an inevitable strain on family relationships, and are constantly laboring to get to the next step of social advancement. This tension challenges disciple making and leadership development since the essence of evangelistic ministry is a life-on-life activity. Making disciples and training leaders takes time, involves relationship, and requires at least some degree of availability. It's difficult to form disciples when new missionaries have limited accessibility to potential candidates for discipleship and training. Missiological strategies must take into account unconventional working hours, long commutes, and a general physical exhaustion. The church should encourage and partner with missiologists to find imaginative solutions to address these challenges. These realities may also challenge the traditional binary debate of either/or when it comes to drawing a rigid ideological line between either "tent-making" ministry or full-time missionary service. On the one hand, "tent-making" may provide points of relational access to those who seem to be "always working." However, "tent-making" leaders then face the same issues of long commutes, work hours, and additional strain on their family life. Conversely, full-time missionaries have the bandwidth to develop and adapt new strategies and contextualize ministry approaches and training opportunities as well as creatively coach emerging leaders while building their ministry activity around their contacts' ever-changing work schedules. While the traditional binary between these vocational choices is sometimes a challenging debate drawn out along ideological lines, the realities of life in the global city likely require both kinds of leaders learning how to partner in order to develop and nurture new disciples, leaders, and churches in the demanding—sometimes oppressive—context of the global city. Old ways of dichotomous ideologies concerning one's missionary vocation are less useful in the midst of urban complexity. A mosaic of different types of evangelists will be needed to address a mosaic of urban diversity.

Furthermore, global cities are often major cultural, economic, and even religious centers for international diaspora communities. "One of the defining features of most global cities is that they are destinations for large numbers of highly diverse groups of immigrants" (Abrahamson, 2004, p. 48). While economic pressures characteristic of world-class cities present a formidable challenge to the church, these strategic cities also provide an opportunity for engaging a variety of diaspora communities arriving from around the globe. Many churches or mission agencies are sending missionaries to engage unreached people groups on the other side of the planet while tens of thousands or even hundreds of thousands of that same people group may reside in a nearby metropolitan area. This is not to say that missionaries should not be sent overseas to foreign cities. There is immense value for sending missionaries into the homeland of unreached people groups. In fact, it will be strategic for missionaries in a majority-world city to coordinate with ministries among diaspora communities in cities outside their homeland. What if mission strategies took into account that, due to remittances sent home and the perceived success of immigrants in the United States by family and friends remaining in the homeland, some of the key cultural leaders of this people group reside in an urban diaspora community in a North American city? What if the church were mobilized to creatively develop strategies for reaching internationals arriving in American cities from some of the most closed nations in the world? What if mission teams formed around a coordinated effort between two distant but dynamically connected destinations with half the team going to a diaspora community and the other half relocating to the corresponding city in the majority world? What if sending agencies began seeing people groups as global networks moving through key urban centers linking specific communities in their homeland with influential diaspora communities? Addressing such questions potentially transforms contemporary missions strategies.

In Mark Gornik's study of African churches in New York, he highlights the significance of New York City as a major global city in the life and flow of African Christianity. He points out three characteristics that emphasize the important interplay of the city as a global node with the worldwide expansion of African Christianity. First, he says, "The global city is a switching station for the development of African Christianity across borders." In other words, migrants in the city establish churches that embody their African roots as a way of coping with and adapting to the global environment. They view the world around them through the filter of African Christianity. As new arrivals from African nations relocate to the city, these urban churches become an outpost for their home culture. "Second, global New York City serves as a hub for the worldwide operations of African church movements." New York City is not simply where lots of immigrants from the African continent settle. While it may seem to the casual observer that the immigrant presence is nothing more than a handful of storefront churches, it is in fact far more than that. Rather, the city is a key point in the global network for church movements worldwide and a base of operations for expansion into North America. New York City, as a global hub, has become a foreign headquarters for many African church movements that are now church planting throughout the United States. For African Christianity, New York City is both a major link between Africa and North America and is a launch pad for ongoing missionary expansion into the United States. "Third, African Christianity in New York City illuminates a new cross border urban geography, one that features African cities." While the major market forces of global economics connect New York City to affluent centers such as London or Singapore, African migration and African church planting in the city forges new and dynamic connections between New York City and major African cities such as Lagos, Accra, or Monrovia. Cities that may appear to be merely regional or national centers now play a greater international role in the global network due, at least in part, to these grassroots connections between homeland and a major global city such as New York. African churches in New York are not simply cultural islands for struggling immigrants. They are helping to shape African Christianity on the global stage as well as a jump-off point into a new land. Indeed, they are essential players in the global flow of African churches worldwide (Gornik, 2011, pp. 46-47). The global network may actually function through multiple layers involving both high-powered institutions as well as grassroots interpersonal and religious connections.

The global city is so much more than a new place to live and work. As diaspora communities emerge, cities like New York, Toronto, or Los Angeles become headquarters for cultural change, the flow of ideas, economic exchange, and more. Links are created both by major economic exchanges and by grassroots links connecting cultural groups across geographic distances. They are cultural centers, not only receiving newcomers into diaspora communities but sending finances, cultural concepts, and media back into their culture of origin. These cities are being shaped by the presence of diaspora communities but also play a role in shaping the societies of sending countries through the transnational relationships initiated by international migrants. Global cities are strategic centers of world missions not simply because they are where a lot of people live; although, that alone is reason enough to focus significant resources on engaging world class cities with the Gospel. Our missionary task is indeed to transmit the Good News to people everywhere, and cities are certainly where most people live and work. Nevertheless, cities are so much more than the millions of people that reside in and around them. Global cities are centers of international connection and cultural influence. They are the nodal points of exchange in global networks. As the world continues to evolve as a network connecting once distant urban areas, the impact on missiology is potentially game-changing. Learning to engage global networks with the Gospel through ministry in global cities, represents a new and vastly important wave of missionary pioneering.

Diaspora Churches: Transplanted Witness

One of the clear transformations taking place in the religious landscape of Western cities is the transplanting of immigrant churches. In New York City, some of the largest churches in Queens are Korean, and across the city assemblies are springing up meeting in a variety of languages and dialects. In virtually every major city in the United States, it is not at all difficult to locate a Spanish-speaking assembly where first-generation immigrants gather to worship sometimes from a single nation, such as Honduras or Dominican Republic, but at other times coming together from across Latin America, sharing the same language among a myriad of nuanced intercultural differences. Chinese churches have been reported across Asia, nations of the former Soviet Union, the Middle East, South America, Africa, Australia, and the United States (Wan, 2011, p. 191). It is common to walk the streets of the South Bronx and observe the names of pastors or bishops written on church signs hanging above storefronts to be of either African or Latino origin. Whether Haitian congregations in Brooklyn, Korean churches in Los Angeles, Spanish-speaking assemblies in Chicago, or Indian churches in the New Jersey suburbs of New York City, the religious fabric of North America is being transformed once again by transplanted expressions of Christian faith from around the world. In the past, Quakers, Dutch Reformed, Irish Catholics, or German Lutherans landed on an unknown continent and changed the landscape of religious life in North America. Today, African Methodists, Latino Pentecostals, Jamaican Baptists, or Korean Presbyterians are rearranging the look and feel of religious experience in Western cities.

Churches that exist as a result of international migration are neither monolithic examples of religious life in their homeland nor do they reflect strictly American expressions of religion. They most often reflect a cultural hybrid that may serve as a bridge between the cultures of here and there. The religious life of immigrants represents the tension between preserving their cultural frameworks for interpreting reality and adapting to the practices and worldview of their new cultural environment. The very nature of immigration forces believers to adapt to new circumstances, and religious life is no exception. One noteworthy change occurring through diaspora church planting may be the rise in congregationalism among immigrant churches. While some communities of faith are officially tied to denominational structures in their nation of origin, they become functionally much more congregational as they address the immediate needs and adaptations of their own faith community in a new pluralistic society.

Congregationalism is certainly not new to religious experience in the United States. However, it is a new innovation among some migrant churches even when some of them may share ties with highly structured denominations. While congregationalism is a strong force in the story and culture of American religious life, the shift of many immigrant churches toward greater congregationalism has less to do with adopting American structures than it does their practical need to behave more congregationally in order to address their unique cross-cultural context (Warner & Wittner, 1998, pp. 20-22). They are simply facing a different set of circumstances than the churches of their homeland. Perhaps through a mix of conscious attempts to adapt or subconscious changes forced by external circumstance, diaspora churches are working out different ways of expressing their faith within their cultural experience. Congregationalism is essentially a contextualized response to their new situation.

As social scientists observe diaspora communities, it seems that processes are at work that might, at least to some, seem inherently contradictory. That is, globalization leads to a greater degree of cultural integration and interaction while simultaneously there is a noted rise in religious and traditional cultures reflecting local flavors in the midst of global processes (Rynkiewich, 2011, p. 209). Local and global considerations fight and dance at the same time. It seems that the more global our society becomes, the more tribalism and localism rise as cross-currents. With this apparent tension, congregationalism becomes an expression of theological ritual and cultural customs rooted in local memories while maintaining an interaction with their global network through the ongoing forces of rapidly spreading globalization and accelerating urbanization. Missiologists and missionary practitioners, as cross-cultural agents, live in the dissonance between cultural adaptation and resistance, and developing relationships with diaspora churches may provide another pathway for shared ministry in a global network. Diaspora congregations may provide opportunities for forging partnerships between potential ministry partners that were once geographically distant. However, many diaspora congregations will be viewed as marginal by American churches, and cross-cultural agents may need to invest significant energy in cultivating a relationship of mutuality between Western churches and diaspora congregations. For many American congregations, diaspora churches provide partnership opportunities for connection points for mission among a people group in their city and beyond, but creating a foundation of mutuality will be an important step in the development of partnerships. Migrant churches must be given more than second-tier status for potential partnerships to thrive on a global scale.

From a missiological perspective, one of the primary interests for this book is the role of diaspora churches as a missionary presence. What role will immigrant congregations play in the evangelism of a city? Currently, it is difficult to determine to what extent diaspora churches are evangelistically impacting their host societies. Many Christian migrants struggle to connect effectively with the dominant culture and lack training in cross-cultural evangelism for secular societies, and many immigrant churches may actually represent migrant Christians preserving their culture rather than a missionary presence in a new land. However, the potential for migrant ethnic churches to forge new pathways for mission is easily imaginable. It is reasonable to believe that the potential of diaspora churches, as an "uncoordinated movement," in Western cities represents a significant opportunity for reenergizing mission in North America (Adeney, 2011, p. 7). There are hints throughout the urban landscape of this potential becoming reality. There are overwhelmingly large diaspora movements around the world that, if unleashed as a missionary force, would inevitably make a deep impact on international diasporas, communities in their homeland, and within highly secularized host cultures. While it may take time to determine the actual impact upon households in the dominant culture in secularized societies, it is clear that a missionary zeal follows many diaspora churches. A new wave of evangelism could indeed rise from the margins of North American cities. For instance, I met an African woman living in a U.S. city who not only continues to be a witness for the Gospel among her own people in the diaspora community, but she feels called to reach out to addicts and those on the margins in her urban community as well. She is bringing individuals to faith in Christ from American backgrounds while she also has been a partner for American Christians reaching out to Muslim African women. Indeed, "it appears that the poor of the world are the great missionary force of the present stage of mission history" (Escobar, 2003, p. 66).

There are numerous diaspora communities on the move ranging from the Middle East, Africa, Asia, and Latin America, while fewer and often smaller—but still persistent—movements take place from parts of Europe. Observing only a few examples of diaspora movements along with diaspora church planting reveals both tremendous missionary potential and significant challenges.

For Latinos, diaspora may be a complex and nuanced subject. Many Mexican families in California, New Mexico, and Arizona became residents of the United States in a single day at the conclusion of the war between Mexico and the United States without ever migrating anywhere. Yet, one Latino church leader describes, as a teenager, Anglo-Americans telling him to go back where he came from. He said he had felt genuine confusion since his family had come from right there in California for generations before him, long before the ancestors of his White antagonists had arrived.

Nevertheless, migrants from Latin America have often traveled to destinations in the United States for more than a century, and growth in Spanish-speaking communities in U.S. cities has accelerated in recent decades with a growth rate of more than 500% in just two decades. Today, Latinos are approaching 20% of the U.S. population, with two-thirds of that vast and diverse community originating from Mexico. While recent decades have experienced a rapid rise in Spanish-speaking communities, many churches in North America lack experience ministering to their Hispanic neighbors moving into their cities (Martin, 2014).

North American cities are becoming home to Latin Americans setting in metropolitan areas in the United States from coast to coast. While even cities like Nashville or Sacramento host scores of Latinos, places like Los Angeles, Houston, and Miami continue to represent large urban nodes in the global network connecting diasporas and homelands. For instance, the shores of New York City are nowhere near the borders of any Latin American nation, and yet it rivals cities across Latin America as a thriving Hispanic metropolis. Latinos arriving in New York City first appeared on a national census in 1845, and political exiles from Latin America continued to establish themselves through the end of the 19th century. The first half of the 20th century saw the influx of Spaniards, Cubans, Dominicans, and especially Puerto Ricans, and following World War II, working class Puerto Ricans continued to settle in New York City as well as additional Cubans, Dominicans, and Central Americans. With U.S. military and political intervention, overall population growth, industrialization, and widespread instability across Latin America, numerous Latino immigrants flowed into the city from the 1970s onward, and a steady influx of Latino migrants into U.S. cities continues. Latino communities dot the urban landscape of cities like New York, from Dominicans in Washington Heights to South Americans in sections of Queens (Haslip-Viera, 1996, pp. 3-21). New York City is more than 2,000 miles from the Rio Grande River and much more than a quick commute to the shores of the Caribbean, but it is a Latino city nonetheless with 2.4 million Latinos officially residing in the city's five boroughs ("NYC Department of City Planning," 2014). Due to more than a century of migration and increased momentum in international immigration in recent decades, New York City is a key urban center for the Latin American world, and during the early years of the 21st century, "the fastest-growing institution in Hispanic neighborhoods is the church" (Carnes, 2001, p. 3). The Latino diaspora, particularly in the United States, represents a vast array of rural settlements and major urban communities. Cities such as Los Angeles, Houston, San Antonio, Miami, and Las Vegas boast large Latin American communities that reflect a growing cultural force impacting nearly every aspect of North American society. Even in Suzuka, Japan, a Spanish-speaking church assembles as a congregation spanning the South American diaspora—Peruvian, Ecuadorian, Bolivian, Argentinian, and Brazilian—and the church has even reached a number of Japanese youth through the evangelistic efforts of the second-generation Latinos growing up bicultural in their Japanese context (Garcia-Johnson, 2012, p. 114). Indeed, while teaching a class in New York City, I recently met a Peruvian believer who became a Christian while visiting his sister and her church in Tokyo. Some Christian denominations in Latin America have been sending missionaries from Latin America to mission fields in Europe and Africa for nearly a hundred years, and today "Latin America is now a base for a growing Christian missionary movement to other parts of the world" (Escobar, 2002, p. 153). As hundreds of thousands of Latin Americans migrate to Europe, Asia, other parts of Latin America, and the United States, aligning the growing missionary zeal in Latin America with this ever increasing global diaspora holds the potential for a virtually unprecedented missionary force.

In his seminal text, *Diaspora Missiology*, Enoch Wan reports on Hispanics for Christ, a ministry based in Portland, Oregon, intentionally focused on working in Latin American communities. Hispanics for Christ was started in 2004 with the intention to plant Spanish-speaking congregations and train new Latin American leaders. They began by training nine church planters, which they referred to as "field coordinators." Most of these initial field coordinators were serving in their home countries; however, at the time of Wan's reporting, three of these leaders were operating in the United States with others working in Paraguay, Mexico, and Argentina. Each of the field coordinators are primarily supported by the churches they lead, and the three leaders in the United States are bilingual and know well how to operate within North American culture. In addition to churches started in Latin American cities, they have seen new churches spring up in and around U.S. cities as well. For instance, new church-planting efforts in Sacramento have resulted in six new groups around the Sacramento metro area in the smaller cities linked to the regional hub of Sacramento. While Hispanics for Christ began with the intent on evangelizing Latin Americans both in their home country and in the Latino diaspora, Hispanics for Christ has begun planting churches through transnational pathways as well. For example, one family moved from Portland to Mexico and immediately began to gather a new church. Wan describes the mission strategy of Hispanics for Christ:

> The model HFC employs is fairly simple. Field coordinators are constantly on the lookout for the person of peace in a village or neighborhood. This person may surface through existing social networks or through an evangelistic campaign. Once the individual is identified, the field coordinator begins working to equip and coach this person to lead a new group in his home, shop, or anywhere people can gather. The key elements of success of this model are: a biblical philosophy of church multiplication, materials for discipling new believers, and an apostolic leader to provide oversight and training to the new "shepherds" of the formed groups. (Wan, 2011, pp. 259-261)

The Chinese diaspora around the world is estimated at 65 million people, and less than 3% of that population is considered to be Christians. Nevertheless, despite the overall population of Christians being such a small percentage of the overall Chinese diaspora, the growth of the Chinese church among migrant populations has been significant (Claydon, 2004, p. 40). As Chinese churches emerge among Chinese diaspora in various parts of the world, they provide an opportunity for Chinese migrants to seek both spiritual care and social and cultural support. Church planting among migrants from mainland China often focuses primarily on providing support and reaching out to Chinese immigrants, so it remains difficult to determine what impact there actually may be upon the host culture or even among neighboring

Asian diasporas. Most churches are started as a result of Chinese merchants relocating as entrepreneurs; therefore, many churches owe their beginnings not to mission agencies but to global economic forces as Chinese relocate to seek business opportunities around the world. As Chinese migrants encounter Christian faith and stay in communication with their kinship network or return to their homeland, churches in China often benefit as the impact of the Gospel flows from believers in the Chinese diaspora back to China. This transnational influence of the Gospel flowing naturally from diaspora to homeland is an exciting development in world missions. It illustrates the opportunity to evangelize otherwise geographically distant peoples by making new disciples from among Chinese immigrants who then communicate the Gospel back through their kinship network. This raises the strategic importance of cross-cultural ministry in global city contexts where large Asian populations form strong ethnic communities (Wan, 2011, pp. 181-197). Some of our greatest missions opportunities for reaching out to China may in fact be evangelism to communities in cities like Toronto, San Francisco, San Diego, or Houston. New York City, for example, is home to the largest Chinese population outside of Asia ("NYC Department of City Planning," 2014). Reaching Chinese communities in these and other metro regions in North America may have a far-reaching impact upon our efforts for advancing the Gospel in Asia.

However, while churches in China benefit significantly from evangelistic work among diaspora churches, the diaspora churches themselves often struggle with a lack of stability and high turnover. As economic forces make their mark on the lives of Chinese immigrants, churches in the diaspora feel the impact as new converts and leaders are tossed about by various external forces and caused to change their life situations. Ironically, the same winds that bring Chinese churches in diaspora communities into existence are the forces that generate an ongoing instability for those churches in their new context (Wan, 2011, pp. 181-197). If the Gospel is moving freely through relational networks but diaspora congregations struggle with institutional stability, our first response is generally to find ways to bring greater institutional stability, and that may be quite helpful. Certainly, generating more stability and adding to longer-term sustainability by diaspora churches is a positive action. Unfortunately, from a church-planting perspective, we sometimes overlook these communities as mission opportunities because we recognize the challenges to institutional development. As we view the development of Christian institutions as our end-game, we may be missing the actual viability of these seemingly unstable populations for real advancement of the Gospel through the natural networks of relationships and high levels of mobility among migrants. Despite the challenges to building sustainable institutions, another perspective may be to prioritize movement of the Gospel through the natural relational flows within migrant communities above the need to maintain institutional stability. We should maintain strong Christian institutions when it is feasible to do so; however, if the organizational life of a new church is temporary, but her short existence resulted in clusters of new disciples now passing on their faith to both diaspora communities and to family and associates still remaining in China, such a church plant should be seen as a success. If the shape of our world is increasingly made up of global networks, perhaps one of the more effective visions for the church is to understand herself as operating within networks of relationships rather than static structures? Could a more fluid approach to Christian community and ministry be a new face of contextualization in a more mobile and interconnected global world? I am not arguing against the establishment of located congregations, but I am suggesting that we refocus with a wider lens in light of our global context for mission in and through diaspora networks. Applying evangelism and church multiplication principles in diaspora communities may require a fluid approach to contextualization. Individual community nodes in the network—that is, diaspora congregations of various shapes and sizes—may exist as an actual assembly for shorter periods of time as a congregational entity. Or, the congregational entity may persevere quite a long time, even through several turnovers of membership, but the relational network of disciples and communities continues to grow and flourish even as it too remains quite fluid. If we approach church planting and evangelism through this perspective of relational networks, we recognize that individual ethnic congregations, house churches, or cells may function as a communal node for a period of time, but the larger drama playing out is an expanding network of disciples where faith communities emerge, fade, and reemerge on a routine basis. Such an approach to contextualizing in global networks forces us to reimagine our metrics of church as an organic process driven by the proactive evangelism of highly mobile disciples. However, shifting our perspective to viewing the wider Kingdom impact while keeping in mind the context of globalization, diaspora, and flows of migration, may encourage us to work more effectively in our emerging global society. This bigger picture, in light of the processes and forces of globalization, may provide a changing point of view that informs our mission strategies as well as our organizational priorities. Such a shift in perspective may be counterintuitive for many, and it would likely cause us to necessarily reenvision our conceptual view of success and failure as well as our emotional responses as missionary workers to this sort of fluidity and apparent instability as it may at times play a key role in our strategic decisions within missiological disciplines such as church planting.

Despite the challenges that face diaspora churches among Chinese communities, the way that many Chinese congregations engage their community can be quite dynamic. I had the opportunity to listen to the story of a well-established Chinese church that has been adapting her ministry practices to the realities of a diaspora network that is constantly in flux and moving through their local community. I sat down with the senior pastor of Grace Church to the Fujianese in Lower Manhattan. I expected him to be open to conversation about their ministry efforts, and he was indeed gracious with his time and sincerity. I was even more impressed with his humility, his desire to keep learning, and this church's willingness to experiment with new strategies among a people group so impacted by globalization.

In Manhattan's historic Chinatown, many of the Cantonese are relocating and being replaced by Fujianese immigrants. As this transition occurs, Church of Grace to the Fujianese has taken a prominent role in serving the influx of migrants and serving as a witness to what is a highly mobile community. Many Fujianese arrive as undocumented immigrants, and as a result, immigration lawyers often refer them to Church of Grace in order to establish a case for residency in the United States on the basis of religious freedom. It is important to note that Church of Grace did not seek these referrals. However, as a result, they regularly receive immigrants in need of a religious identity. At the same time, it is an opportunity to serve people with tangible needs and teach the Gospel of Christ to those who have not yet heard. It is impossible for the leadership of Church of Grace to determine the sincerity of each individual, nor do they advertise themselves to law offices as desiring to fill this role for undocumented immigrants. However, they see the opportunity resulting from the hand they have been dealt. They recognize that the unsolicited referrals are an opportunity for compassionately sharing the Gospel with people in need of a friendly face. They recognize that they cannot judge individuals' hearts or intentions, so they put a process in place in order to attempt to strengthen the potential for true conversions among Fujianese immigrants coming to them for help. Eliya Shira, the senior pastor, explains that they wait for a new visitor to participate four times before other opportunities for participation in the church becomes available to him or her. They then provide four weeks of membership classes, which must be completed before they can move to the next stage of church involvement. Before moving to the next step, each individual must speak with one of the church's leaders, and only then may they participate in an eight-week baptism class. Church of Grace to the Fujianese begins by serving the need for new arrivals from Fujian to identify an institution willing to help them transition to life in the city and the specific advantages for them to identify with a religious or Christian institution. Meeting migrants at their point of need, church leaders are sifting through a steady stream of newcomers to discover the truly receptive. Normally, from a strategic standpoint, I would typically argue that there ought to be as few barriers to conversion and full participation in the church as quickly as possible. My missiological thirst for rapid reproduction of disciples tugs at my heart. As a principle of church multiplication, we want new disciples to easily reproduce ministry and evangelism among their peers and remove the barriers keeping this from becoming reality. However, listening to the conversion process and specific circumstances surrounding Church of Grace, it became obvious that this congregation is creatively adapting to a set of political, international, religious, economic, and legal factors that does not challenge the average congregation to the same extent. They have thoughtfully contextualized their approach to address the opportunities and challenges they have inherited through this new wave of immigration. They are carefully contextualizing effective evangelism in their community. I left the interview feeling deeply encouraged by the ministry of Church of Grace to the Fujianese. This humble congregation on Manhattan's Lower East Side may be making one of the most dynamic evangelistic advances in the city as they respond to a set of external circumstances completely outside of their influence.

Nevertheless, this ministry is not without its challenges. Migrants in the global city often work around the clock and oftentimes at unconventional hours, so Church of Grace organizes five church services throughout the week utilizing both Fujianese and Mandarin languages in various worship services. Three worship services meet on Sunday, one service is conducted on Monday afternoon, and one assembly takes place on Wednesday afternoon. This sort of organization is congruent with the realities of the global city operating in an around-the-clock global marketplace. They intentionally offer a number of contact points through the week to accommodate the scheduling demands pressing upon new arrivals in the global city. In addition, one of their services specifically targets the unbaptized. Many of the new arrivals come as Buddhists, so virtually all the classes for them are taught by Christians who are also former Buddhists and can naturally relate to their worldview and directly address their concerns and questions.

As I sat with the pastor of Church of Grace, he explained that a person could walk into Chinese restaurants practically anywhere in the United States, and if the people working in the restaurant are Fujianese, they likely have been to Church of Grace early upon their arrival into North America through harbors in New York City. Since Fujianese scatter from New York to locations across the continent, the church offers Bible studies through teleconferencing several nights of the week. Nearly every night of the week, there is a group Bible study with several in "attendance" over the phone through teleconferencing. They utilize phone-based radio stations and conference calling to provide ongoing biblical instruction to new converts living in cities throughout the United States. Former participants in Church of Grace call in from all over the country to these conference calls. It's entirely possible that the workers in the back of a Chinese restaurant in Dallas or Nashville, may be receiving biblical instruction over a telephone-based radio channel from a church leader in New York City. As the pastor and I talked, he shared his vision for planting churches in Chinese restaurants in various locations across the nation. He openly confessed that they did not yet actually have a plan for how this might work, and I appreciated his humble admission since international migration on this scale is new territory for the majority of ministries and churches throughout the United States. However, he sees the opportunity and recognizes the great need for the Gospel to advance along the continuing migration patterns of Fujianese immigrants as they pursue entrepreneurship or seek employment in the United States beyond the harbors of New York City. This network stretches across the nation and opens opportunities to reimagine church multiplication. His passion for spreading the

Gospel among the Fujianese was contagious. As I walked from his office out onto the streets of Manhattan's Lower East Side surrounded by an expanding and diversifying Chinatown, I felt rejuvenated by the zeal and determination of a church that acts as both the "Grand Central Station" for Fujianese entering the United States and the support group for these struggling migrants even as they go out from New York City to other destinations across the country to find work or start businesses. I'm confident they are poised to make a significant impact among this people group, especially if they become increasingly unhindered by conventional structures and are able to contextualize church forms to intersect with the realities of global migration and relocation. I was encouraged to hear the leader of Church of Grace exploring ways they can see the Gospel advance along the lines of natural immigration patterns, and they are continuing to experiment with potential contextualization among a people group on the move.

In his ethnographic study of African churches in New York City, *Word Made Global*, Mark Gornik points out, "In New York City, you don't have to travel to another country to experience African Christianity, all you need to do is get on the subway" (Gornik, 2011, p. 3). Indeed one only needs to walk the streets of Harlem, the Bronx, and sections of Brooklyn to encounter African congregations from tiny storefront churches to large mainline denominations gathering migrant communities ranging from Ghana, Liberia, Nigeria, and other parts of the African continent, as well as an ever growing number of West African mosques dotting the urban landscape. Reading the average sign on the front of a church building in New York, it is normal to recognize an African name listed as the pastor, elder, or bishop. African churches are becoming a common presence in New York and other cities throughout North America.

Global conditions have set the "perfect storm" for a massive African migration that has been unfolding over the last 40 years. With high population growth rates and overwhelmingly high rates of economic hardship on the African continent, Africans often migrate seeking better conditions than the harsh standard of living in their homeland. Around the world, they are a people on the move. As a result, despite the numerous economic hardships confronting various nations from this continent, African peoples represent "perhaps the most mobile population in the world" (Hanciles, 2008, pp. 220-221). It is interesting to imagine that perhaps the previous generation of missionaries forging new evangelism and church planting in Africa were unknowingly doing more than reaching African communities but were developing a movement of global church planting. Naturally, as African Christians relocate to host nations seeking relief from difficult economic conditions or escaping violent circumstances and go in search of new opportunities to improve their family's standard of living, they become carriers of the Gospel. While, for some, the words Africa and missions put together brings to mind American or European missionaries crossing an ocean and teaching Africans in a village hut, African Christianity has often had a missionary impulse, and it should be no surprise that the majority of Africans have been taught the Gospel by other Africans (Hanciles, 2008, p. 218). The step toward a more global presence is a logical one in the current climate of global movement and relocation. Sending may actually be the more common picture of "African" and "missions" than that of receiving a Western missionary. With increasing globalization, diaspora churches are transforming the fabric of global Christianity. Africans are highly mobile and highly connected, and as they migrate to destinations circling the globe, churches often spring up reflecting their unique cultural and theological perspective. A picture of globalization through African migration provides a snapshot of the grassroots impact and important role migrants may play in the global church.

Gornik points out that observing African Christianity in New York City is not simply the experience of "an isolated inner city, but part of an interconnected world" (Gornik, 2011, p. 19). Over the years living in New York City, I cannot recall a single incident of speaking at length with an African believer and not hearing of some more globalized connections with kinship, or vocational or religious contacts beyond their local New York neighborhood. To encounter Africans in New York City is to speak with global citizens navigating an international society, and in some cases doing so with very limited material resources. Many struggling African families relocating to some of the poorest neighborhoods in American cities are often far more globally connected than the average U.S. citizen. They are connecting their families, churches, cities, and nations to Western resources through grassroots networking on a global scale. While many Americans still do not own a passport, many of their African neighbors are becoming players on a global stage.

Gornik points out that these migrant African congregations represent a missionary worldview. However, he explains that this missionary impulse is not so much a preconceived "re-evangelization of the West" but rather a natural relationship between mission and migration. A missionary ethos and the journey of migration are inherently joined in the worldview of many African believers. Much of the African missionary movement will likely go unnoticed by typical Western measurements because they are less connected to Western missionary agencies but more driven by individual church initiatives (Gornik, 2011, pp. 182-183). As grassroots ministries emerge and diaspora churches adopt more congregational structures to contextualize in their new host city, they represent a growing presence in Western contexts but may remain "off the radar" for many ministries just a short drive away into the suburbs.

Observing case studies from different streams of Christianity—from indigenous African movements, mainline Protestant denominations, and Pentecostal traditions—Gornik observes distinct characteristics of the missionary strategy of African churches in the city. First, African churches are a source of care for their members. Providing counseling and pastoral care, they help their members navigate the adjustments to life in a new culture and offer cultural continuity in the midst of inevitable culture shock. For these churches, pastoral care is an aspect of their mission as they serve an immigrant community in a pluralistic city. Even staying connected to a community of faith may be a challenge for many immigrants as they struggle through long commutes, sometimes unreasonable work hours, and undeniable culture shock. These churches provide a source of care and help through transition for many who would otherwise become displaced and perhaps disillusioned in their faith. Second, these churches see prayer and intercession as a characteristic of their missionary engagement with the city. Their Christian identity and the nature of their mission is rooted in being a praying community. Prayer for many African churches is a practice of evangelism. Third, they are actively starting churches, and church planting is a key characteristic of their missionary life. Fourth, African churches often see healing as a part of their mission. Their concept of salvation includes their physical life, and they believe the power of the Holy Spirit is at work to counter harmful spiritual and physical forces. Also, mission is seen as a way of life. It is not a program of the church, but every believer shares the message of Jesus Christ. As they seek to share the Gospel with the broader population of an international city, they don't determine their evangelistic success by the number of non-Africans that attend worship assemblies. Rather, they see the workplace and the streets as their context for evangelism. African Christians are sharing the Gospel in their day-to-day encounters. Finally, African churches in the city are not confined solely to local engagement, but their witness is multidirectional. African churches in New York City are actively supporting ministries in Africa as well as their local activity in the city. These congregations exist at the intersection of local and global (Gornik, 2011, pp. 191-213).

Of course, many African church leaders in the United States express the desire to mobilize their congregations for mission resulting in disciple making and by extension church planting or church growth in the wider culture. Naturally, leaders from any culture desire to recognize outcomes from their labor and ride a wave of progress and growth. Some African leaders have expressed frustration at the slow pace of mission mobilization to reach their host culture in North America. Making a deeper impact on the wider multiethnic society seems presently to be "a remote potentiality" (Wan, 2011, pp. 226-229). While many African churches are effectively serving their own diaspora community in the city and members are actively sharing the Gospel at work and on the streets, these congregations still face the challenge of closing a gap between their church and the broader culture.

Of course, it's understandable that African churches might struggle to effectively communicate the Gospel across cultural lines to Americans or among other ethnic diasporas. "Many African immigrant Christians find themselves ill equipped to initiate, build, and nurture churches and ministries in the West. On arrival to the United States, they grapple with survival issues and cultural values they must relate with but which they find difficult to connect with" (Gwamzhi, 2013, p. 5). Among the key contributions that missiologists may offer these diaspora churches is training in cross-cultural missions. Africans should in no way abandon the cultural and worldview strengths that they bring to a secular city. Many of these traits will be gifts to the Western church. However, they also will need to be further equipped for reaching out within a secular or pluralistic city in Western contexts. Of course, many are in need of pastoral care as leaders wade through the issues of culture shock both within themselves and in their congregants. This experience is one to which many missionaries can relate and offer helpful guidance.

In addition, many migrant Christians face enormous challenges outside of ministry as they seek to adapt to the new culture. Many are experiencing racism for the first time. For example, an African who migrates to the United States is now classified as Black and inherits a foreign history of racial tension and derision. In other cases, migrant believers are already considered a minority by the dominant culture in their host country, and as a Christian, they may in some cases already be a minority among their own people. Now, already considered a minority by their own people and adapting to a new dominant culture, they may struggle with their own fears of rejection, which becomes a hindrance to sharing the Gospel with their new neighbors. Diaspora churches are also in danger of becoming insular, seeking only to preserve their own culture rather than establish a beacon of light and shalom in their new surroundings (Claydon, 2004, p. 20). North American missionaries who have served overseas and wrestled with their own family's experiences of reentry culture shock have the opportunity to forge a new phase of ministry among their brothers and sisters from overseas who are resettling in an American city. Returning missionaries walking beside a diaspora community with whom they share a language as well as other commonalities can become a precious ministry for both the diapora community toward the missionary and for the missionary to the diaspora church since both are walking though the liminal space of culture shock and transition together. Migrant Christians arriving in North America often come with the desire to evangelize within their new culture; however, they need support and mentoring as they adapt to their host culture. They are working through the trauma of migration, culture shock, and adjusting to a new way of life. Former overseas missionaries will share a unique insight into the worldview of migrants while simultaneously having a unique way of seeing American culture as they reenter their own country of origin with the ability to see it with a different set of eyes. They bring a unique insight and set of experiences to serve diaspora communities. Many former overseas missionaries may serve to equip, train, and support new migrants who desire to serve as evangelists in their host culture. The potential bond they may share as they both live between worlds has potential for powerful ministry partnerships and healing pastoral encounters.

One of the key steps for an African ministry leader serving in North American culture is to dismiss the misconception that the United States is a Christian nation (Gwamzhi, 2013, p. 10). Equally, as former missionaries to Africa return to their country of origin, it is essential that they recognize they have not returned to a Christian homeland but rather are simply shifting their field of mission as an ambassador of the Gospel. This recognition will not only help them stay engaged in God's mission in a spiritually struggling North American continent but will certainly increase their effectiveness as mentors and trainers of African Christian migrants. For example, when Dave and Jana Jenkins and their children returned from Rwanda to the United States, they settled in Chicago, recognizing that they were returning not to a Christian homeland but to a new phase in their life as missionaries. In the last couple of years since settling in Chicago, the Jenkins have been developing relationships with African believers living in Chicago and seeking ways to help advance ministry efforts among their African brothers and sisters.

Migrant church leaders are confronted with the need to adapt and change constantly. They must be consistent learners. The nature of contemporary culture in an urban world is constant change, and the ministry leader from the diaspora community must be prepared to never stop learning and adapting to an ever-changing global and technological society (Gwamzhi, 2013, p. 14). For Christian leaders coming from the majority world, there is much to learn in order to impact a post-Christendom North American culture. Indeed, American Christians are struggling to make a genuine impact themselves. However, many African believers bring a key ingredient to mission that is often lacking in Western church settings where ministry is produced through an abundance of resources. They have a relentless perspective that ministry is spearheaded by the Holy Spirit. The advancement of many of the ministries of poorer nations is forged through prayer and a radical dependence on God's intervention through his Spirit. There is a recognition that it is the Holy Spirit that goes with migrants departing the African continent into cross-cultural contexts (Gwamzhi, 2013, p. 20). One of the greatest gifts from diaspora churches to North American Christianity may be to offer a rejuvenation of Christian spirituality. Western Christians often lack the sort of radical dependence present in many Gospel movements. "The key issue for

Christianity in the Global South is the prevailing worldview that subscribes to a belief in direct divine intervention in the daily lives of people" (Kalu, et al., 2010, p. 63).

Even as numerous ethnic congregations spring up from diaspora communities throughout Western cities, there remain significant challenges. In one Hispanic church association, there are more than 26,000 congregations involved; however, very few of these have an official missions program. This may largely be due to the temporal nature of the immigrant experience along with the regular hardships faced by Latin American migrants (Adeney, 2011, p. 18). However, it would seem that the temporal and highly mobile nature of Hispanic diaspora communities should lead to a strong emphasis on missionary initiative. This may again be a moment in which leaders should reevaluate current structures and priorities in favor of recognizing a network of discipleship in which congregations, cells, or house churches are nodes in that relational network. In this way, it may be possible that such instability becomes an opportunity for missionary activity rather than a liability for building static structures. As we read about the church in the book of Acts in the Bible, mobility and migration in the Roman Empire seems to have helped stimulate the practice of Christian mission. If church was experienced as a more organic and fluid structure, it would make sense that mobility, migration, and relative instability in the labor force would have led to an increase in church planting and cross-cultural evangelism through the experience of regular dislocation and mobility. In light of the effects of globalization, critically evaluating self-imposed constraints on Christian mission is an essential discipline. Certainly, if Hispanic immigrants facing all sorts of cultural and logistical challenges, are expected to reproduce the structures of typical American churches, or if they have in mind competing with the stature of the cathedrals or megachurches of Latin America, it is unlikely that mission through the diaspora will go far. In fact, it is even possible for some success stories to establish a standard for ministry that most cannot hope to reach unless they are among the most skilled and resourced entrepreneurs. Nevertheless, in our reading of Acts and stories of the early church, the Gospel spread through the proclamation and service of believers who often relocated across the Mediterranean region whether due to persecution, economic hardship, or financial opportunity, and as they did so, the church expanded throughout the Roman Empire and beyond. With the steady flow of Latino migrants into the United States and the emerging mainstream presence of Hispanic culture in the dominant culture of American society, evangelism, church-planting initiatives, and leadership development among Latino immigrants is crucial not as a marginal evangelistic enterprise but as an attempt to impact an emerging mainstream culture.

One of the most significant barriers to a unified church-growth movement in the United States may be the resentment and suspicion felt by many church members from within the dominant culture. However, missiologists may seek to develop grassroots leadership for raising Latino believers as a missionary force. Another function of mission leaders among diaspora communities should be to help them to contextualize evangelism in accordance with the realities of immigrant experiences and to envision church as a community that exists much more organically so that it may reproduce and flow in congruence with the fluidity and mobility of life in the global network. Our cities are international mosaics, and many diaspora communities represent a significant Christian population before even encountering an American or Canadian church. One of the great opportunities confronting the global church is to effectively mobilize Christian citizens of the diaspora for mission in their new cultural context. While I have briefly mentioned examples of African, Chinese, and Latin American diaspora, churches are being started across the full spectrum of international diaspora communities and networks. Indian, Filipino, Ukrainian, Persian, and numerous other ethnic communities are establishing Christian congregations in cities and suburbs throughout North America, Europe, and beyond.

In the last few years, Jessica Udall has conducted research on the Ethiopian community. Her research focused on preparing Ethiopian Christians for cross-cultural ministry. As should be expected, there are traits unique to Ethiopians, but her analysis is helpful for anyone hoping to mobilize believers in diaspora communities for cross-cultural evangelism in international cities. While working among Ethiopian diaspora will lead one to seek effective strategies for equipping believers in cities such as Washington, Los Angeles, or New York, where sizable Ethiopian communities can be found, Udall's study will likely provide useful insights for equipping other diaspora churches for cross-cultural missions in their cities. Many Christian migrants live and work alongside migrants belonging to least-reached ethnic groups and historically closed countries. In addition, these ethnic migrants are less likely to attract criticism for political or economic policies of the host nation because they too are facing many of the same barriers and struggles. Mobilizing believers among diaspora communities represents a viable strategy for evangelism among the unreached in our cities.

Udall points out that, although it is nearly impossible to pinpoint a specific number, there are potentially thousands of evangelical believers in Ethiopian diaspora communities in North American cities. With evangelical believers making up 18% of Ethiopia's population, it is not difficult to suggest that many evangelical believers are living and working in cities in the West. Washington, D.C., is the second largest Ethiopian city in the world with only Ethiopia's capital boasting a higher Ethiopian population. Although Udall's initial research was focused on discovering how to best prepare Ethiopians (in Ethiopia) for cross-cultural missions, her research led her to believe that a ministry investment in mobilizing Christians in the Ethiopian diaspora would be an important missions strategy. They "are likely already ensconced in a diverse community—often living in a large apartment complex with immigrants and refugees from various other cultures and working in a similar environment." Many Ethiopians living in North American cities are likely to settle in neighborhoods with cultural proximity where they are surrounded by neighbors originating from countries traditionally "closed" to Christian missions (Udall, March 29, 2014). With the very real potential for Ethiopian believers to be mobilized as cross-cultural missionaries in diverse North American cities, considering how to best equip these believers for not only reaching their own people but reaching out cross-culturally to the diverse communities around them is an important task. By considering Udall's research, we may gain additional insights for equipping other Christian migrant communities as well.

Udall interviewed several Ethiopian Christian leaders and asked what they saw as the barriers keeping the Ethiopian church from becoming a major missionary sending body. Some identifiable challenges surfaced during her interviews, and interestingly she noted that there was not a difference in the responses between interviews with leaders in Ethiopia and those leading diaspora churches outside of Africa. The responses were consistent across both groups. First, Ethiopians need training in cross-cultural ministry. Even those leaders already living in diverse communities in the United States felt this need in their churches. Ethiopia was a nation never colonized by European powers, and they possess a strong national pride. While there is much to admire about this strong Ethiopian heritage, it can negatively contribute to looking down at other cultural groups, and for evangelical Christians, it may lead to isolating themselves from the host culture or other diaspora communities in order to keep themselves pure from sinful influences. Of course, if Ethiopians isolate themselves from other cultures, it perpetuates the cycle of less ability to communicate the Gospel cross-culturally into differing worldviews. In addition to these nuanced cultural tendencies, like so many other immigrants, Ethiopian migrants are facing numerous life challenges. Often their reason for migrating was economic, and these financial concerns continue to apply pressure on their families while they adapt to the new culture and seek to build a more prosperous future. Finally, for some, a stereotype—however false—that only Westerners do cross-cultural ministry might undermine the potential for mobilizing Ethiopians to their neighbors from other diaspora groups living in close proximity in the same urban neighborhood (Udall, March 29, 2014).

Desiring to respond to the challenges to mobilize Ethiopian diaspora for cross-cultural evangelism, Udall asked Ethiopian leaders to offer real steps for preparing Ethiopians for cross-cultural mission. Her interviews resulted in 10 practical suggestions that might help equip and mobilize Ethiopians to evangelistically engage nearby diaspora from non-Ethiopian cultures living in proximity to them in diverse metropolitan areas.

First, Ethiopian migrants need to grasp the bigger picture. Most have resettled in a foreign land for economic purposes, and while they will indeed seek to achieve financial advancement for their families, they must see that God's purposes go beyond individual economic freedom. Ethiopian believers must begin to see that their role as migrants is parallel with their role as missionaries.

Second, leaders must catch the vision for empowering and mobilizing their churches for cross-cultural mission in a diverse urban society. Practical steps are needed to educate and inform leaders in churches. One suggestion is the use of the Perspectives course. The Perspectives course has been well received in Ethiopia, so utilizing this course in Ethiopian churches in Western cities may have the potential to educate leaders and congregations for missionary engagement (www.perspectives.org).

Ethiopians in diaspora churches should be taught to pray for the nations. Prayer is already an important dynamic in Ethiopian churches, so this aspect of Christian worship is not a new concept for Ethiopian believers. However, praying for the nations living and working among them may be a new concept for Ethiopian diaspora churches.

Fourth, it is not enough for leaders to receive training, and diaspora churches should not stop at prayer. Members of diaspora churches must be equipped for sharing the Gospel cross-culturally and catching the vision for ministry to the nations. Practical training should be made available to congregations in order to mobilize church members for mission in an international context.

In addition, diaspora churches should learn to foster collaborative relationships with other ministries. Often there are other churches— whether from the host culture or another diaspora community— reaching out to some of the same ethnic communities, and they may have much insight to offer. Sharing information and finding common ground for collaboration will do much to advance the Gospel in diverse international cities.

In order to make an impact for the Gospel among nearby ethnic communities, believers from one ethnic group must be open to the culture and customs of another group. Opening up to other cultures creates the opportunity to build bridges of relationships that can lead to Gospel witness. Of course, this may be challenging at times for new migrants because they are struggling to hold onto their own cultural identity in the face of adapting to a new society. However, if they are able to open their hearts to the cultural characteristics of neighboring diaspora communities, migrant believers will have the opportunity to be ambassadors for Christ beyond their own ethnic enclave. For believers in one diaspora community reaching out to a neighboring diaspora community, learning the dominant language of the host culture will be important in order to communicate in what may be emerging as the common tongue for all of the city's diaspora communities together.

Seventh, Ethiopians are great at being witnesses during special events. Special occasions such as weddings or funerals are wonderful tools for sharing the Gospel. However, Ethiopian believers must practice evangelism as an everyday lifestyle. By not limiting their Gospel witness to special occasions, much more Gospel sowing can be unleashed in the city. This may require additional equipping to serve as everyday witnesses for the Gospel.

Eighth, migrants should use technology. There are some ministry initiatives emerging that are actively utilizing technology, but there is plenty of room for more. There was agreement that Ethiopians love technology. International migrants are global citizens increasingly using technology to communicate across vast networks that transcend national borders. Being intentional about using technology to facilitate Gospel proclamation may increase the church's impact in a mobile and connected world.

Ninth, churches in diaspora communities must equip the younger generation. A great deal of concern has gone into second-generation immigrants and rightly so. One pastor interviewed by Udall commented that the church must "work to equip [the] young generation spiritually but free them to integrate culturally." The children of immigrants are growing up between cultures, and as bicultural citizens living between the dominant culture and the diaspora community, the church should be equipping the younger generation in diaspora churches and unleashing them for cross-cultural mission.

Finally, diaspora churches should strive for Christian unity. Often —especially in smaller urban areas with a less sizable diaspora population—believers are forced together in the same congregation if they desire to worship in their heart language. The need for unity is forced upon them. Simultaneously, diaspora churches should strive for unity with other ethnic churches and with churches in the dominant culture. Migrants face many stresses both outside and inside their church life as they live and work and raise families in a new cultural situation. Christian unity must flow from intentional efforts to maintain the brotherhood of believers and work toward cross-cultural collaboration (Udall, March 29, 2014).

Conclusion

Globalization is challenging the historical categories of missions, and globalization is working symbiotically with urbanization to simultaneously transform the global context of Christian missions. While a new frontier of Christian missions will be to engage the context of the global city, a new missionary presence is seen in diaspora churches. A new opportunity for North American churches to develop cross-cultural partnerships with these new communities of faith may provide a gateway for evangelistic ministry that was otherwise out of reach. With the emergence of globalization, missiologists need to evaluate existing categories and strategic frameworks with the new urban and global landscape in mind. The church of God is facing unprecedented challenges and an amazing array of opportunities in the new global context for world missions.

Reflection Questions

1. How have you seen globalization impact the daily life of your community or city?
2. What role do you see your city playing in the global network? Is it a commercial or cultural center for a region? A leading global city?
3. How would evangelism in your city impact people living beyond your city through natural relationship networks?
4. How are churches in your city partnering with diaspora churches?
5. What are some ways that returning missionaries or local church leaders in your church or ministry organization may serve migrant leaders in your area?
6. How might you imagine evangelism and church-planting strategies adapting to the new context of a global network?

Chapter 5
Evangelism Among the Nations

A few years ago a missionary who has worked a great deal in South Asia told me a story. He recalled when he was studying the Bible with a group of men who were encountering the Christian Scriptures for the first time. He was leading them in an inductive Bible study process, and at one point one of them asked a question, "If we follow Jesus, must we stop beating our wives?" As shocking as it may sound to most readers, it was a sincere and honest question from a seeker of truth. The missionary, showing extraordinary restraint, asked the group of men to continue exploring the Bible story and determine how they think God's Word might be answering that question. After further reflection, the whole group of men concluded, "Yes, if we follow Jesus, we will have to stop beating our wives." They then informed the missionary that they must think about this new revelation and consider the implications for a few days; they would then return with a decision. After a few days had passed, the group of men returned to the missionary and shared with him that they were committing to follow Jesus and, therefore, would no longer beat their wives. They then explained to him how this was a challenging step for them to take because literally every man in their community beats his wife. They believed that they would appear weak to their neighbors, but they would take this step of obedience in following Christ nonetheless. This story is not unique. Such tales often emerge from missionary encounters of sharing the Gospel in pre-Christian contexts around the world. However, it illustrates the power of the Gospel to begin transforming the fabric of a society through the transformation of individuals and families resulting from evangelistic encounter.

A few years ago, I was speaking to a seminary class, and I was asked by one of the students what our ministry did in the area of social justice. I kept thinking about the question. Works of social justice are dear to my heart and of great importance to God's Kingdom, and caring for the poor and the marginalized should be a natural characteristic of the Christian community. I understood the nature of the question though as my ministry team in the city is focused on the work of evangelism and church planting. However, I felt as though I was being asked to define our ministry along the lines of a common dichotomy. The vocation of our ministry in the city is evangelism; however, we certainly desire to see peace overcome injustices and for compassion to be offered to the suffering. While we've helped people with their life circumstances in the city with things such as teaching English, tutoring immigrants for their U.S. citizenship test, welcoming refugees and helping them transition to the city, offering educational seminars, or intervening to put marriages back together, the driving focus of our ministry in New York City has always been evangelism. We are making disciples through sharing the message of the Gospel. Through the evangelistic work of presenting the Gospel in the Bronx, I've seen families once marked by violence and infidelity brought to wholeness and unity as they encountered the risen Christ. We've seen youth once discarded by their families and society find family and begin to understand the meaning of being loved. The Good News of the Kingdom of God is life-giving and transformational. Therefore, I kept thinking about the question because I wasn't satisfied with the corner I was being backed into if I were to answer his question using the philosophical categories that, I believe, were being applied through his inquiry. To begin a chapter on evangelism, I must wade into the tensions inherent in our current cultural and religious climate. In order to adequately address urban evangelism and diaspora missiology, I must address issues impacting evangelism in the Western context as well as the specific impact of globalization and the concerns of diaspora missiology. In urban environments in North America and elsewhere, these diverse factors intersect quite dynamically. I want to offer a perspective on evangelism that will both transcend the historical tensions rooted in Western dualism and challenge current feelings of uncertainty toward the practice of evangelism in our contemporary Western church settings. As a result, I hope that evangelism among diaspora communities comes into focus as we work through the particular dynamics, the amazing opportunities, and the unique challenges.

Evangelism in Tension

One of my key goals in writing this text is to equip and enhance the evangelism of the church among diaspora communities as the body of Christ navigates its way through an age of globalization. I also hope to encourage urban evangelism in general; although, in many urban settings it is getting more difficult to separate the two. This task is certainly not as simplistic as it might seem. The church in the Western context has often wrestled with a dichotomy between addressing primarily physical needs or exclusively addressing spiritual needs. In response to this polarizing categorization of the human condition, some missiologists have responded with a call to ministry that is "holistic." That is, caring for the whole person both body and soul. Caring for the whole person resonates with me and appears to have much alignment with the vision of the New Testament for Christian behavior and ethics. However, our uses of language often present additional challenges. Terms can mean different things in different places spoken by different people. In my own observation, holistic ministry sometimes actually means holistic ministry. It indeed integrates the full implications of the Gospel as the Gospel is presented verbally and embodied in works of service by active ambassadors of Christ. Yet sometimes the terminology of holistic ministry is used to describe the swinging of the pendulum from an evangelical emphasis on spiritual salvation to an exclusive focus solely on physical needs. That is, a flip from one dualistic side to the other. Such a response is more aligned with a post-conservative stance than with a truly integrated approach. Therefore, the issue of semantics strikes yet again. Looking from another angle, the ministry in Houston where I served as a youth evangelist for a few years following my college graduation was every bit as holistic as one might imagine proclaiming the message of salvation and actively serving the poorest in Houston's toughest neighborhoods, but I never once heard the language of holism used to self-describe our ministry despite its apparent accuracy. Finally, another problem arises. We often have difficulty seeing holism on the relational level—one life holistically impacting another life in all its dimensions—but we typically frame our definitions and understandings in programmatic ways. This limits the scope of our vision. I want to challenge my readers to view evangelism through a more multilayered spectrum than such a singular and monolithic approach.

I do not expect to solve the historical dualism so apparent in the context of the Western church, but I do hope to contribute to the discussion with some degree of nuance and offer a view of evangelism that may transcend the apparent tension. I assume that I will have readers from both ends of the philosophical spectrum and several points between, so I hope I might offer some reconciling ideas within the discussion in this chapter. The church in the United States in particular is, in my view, in a tense relationship with both the concept and the actual practice of evangelism. Divorce may not be imminent, but harmony is difficult to imagine. While evangelical churches in the United States in the past may have been accused of ignoring physical needs while preaching in the streets, today the practice of evangelism seems to risk marginalization in at least a few Christian circles. In other settings, evangelism is discussed often but may actually be better equated with church membership or a number of "decisions" at an event. Such a utilitarian approach to evangelism illustrates well a need for criticism toward some forms of evangelistic practice. In order to address evangelism in and through diaspora networks, it is important to work through some of the ideals of evangelism as a Christian expression. Allow me to propose some key points that are foundational to the thoughts shaping this book. These are key factors that may help us hold the tension while living in the middle of it. From there, I'll continue to further discuss both concept and practice in terms of evangelism in Western cities, where radically different worldviews—representing both the host culture and diaspora communities—often share the same space in urban settings.

Transcending the Dichotomy

Historically, the church in Western society has—knowingly or unknowingly—split ministry into caring for the body or caring for the soul. As long as the Western church continues ideologically bouncing back and forth between seemingly opposing poles representing a kind of sanctified dualism, evangelism will suffer as a Christian practice. Rather, I contend that our mission is to care for people . . . period. When the church abandons care for the poor, the widow, the orphan, and the foreigner, we are at risk of losing our grasp on the deep ethics of the Kingdom Gospel. Equally, when the church swings to the opposite end and ignores the profound need for eternal salvation, we are at risk of losing ourselves as ambassadors proclaiming the Gospel of grace.

I don't dare to claim any universal expertise or understanding of all cultures and Christian worldviews around the globe, but it does seem that this dualism is primarily a problem for the Western church and wherever our influence has expanded to embed our ways of reasoning into local faith communities. Perhaps that is overstating the case, but it would be worth conducting further research of the practices of ministries outside of a heavy Western, or at least American, influence. It would seem that an undefined holism is present in a large portion of indigenous faith communities outside of Western contexts. Often issues throwing the American church into crisis are not as paramount in other regions of the world. Regardless of ideological divides, it is essential that the church's missionary practice is driven by a deep love for God and an unyielding concern for people.

Disciple Making as a Holistic Practice

When evangelism leads to making disciples, it is also a holistic practice. Much of our categorization of social justice and compassion ministries takes place at the institutional level. This is, to some degree, quite reasonable, but it is also problematic as far as gaining a more full-bodied view of ministry through relational channels and in different contexts. Many of our efforts in the church in Europe and North America are rooted in institutional initiatives and involvement, so we might overlook grassroots expressions of justice and mercy accompanied by verbal proclamation of the Christian faith. However, when a single woman takes in a troubled teenage girl and acts as a surrogate mom, she is attempting to intervene and address the underlying inequalities affecting the girl's life choices, but she is doing so on a much more personal level. When this act took place in our house church community in New York City, it made an impact on more than one life in the community. When the Gospel enters a household or neighborhood and brings an end to domestic violence, it is creating a much more just environment where families may thrive. The presentation of the Gospel is expanding the shalom of the Kingdom. When a new believer sells possessions to address the needs of his neighbors, it is a signpost of the transformation sparked by the Gospel of Jesus Christ. It begins a shift in allegiance from solely love-of-self to love-of-neighbor.

When we make disciples, we are developing agents of transformation in the city. It is a holistic ministry; it is simply taking place on the personal rather than institutional level. To follow our

Master is to care for our neighbor. Works of justice, compassion, and love take place and potentially flourish at the level of personal daily interactions as new believers learn to live out the "one another" statements of the New Testament and love their neighbors as themselves. This may fly below the radar of institutional initiatives—as important as such works truly are—but the emergence of a new imitator of Christ has a ripple effect, beginning purely at the relational level, throughout her social world. Disciple making represents life-on-life transformation and calls new believers to imitate the Lord Jesus. As such, at the relational level, disciple making is a practice that ultimately cares for people and brings deep change to the fabric of the city beginning as a grassroots movement. It does so by replicating agents of mercy and peace from within the formerly lost households of the city. When the work of evangelism is aimed at making disciples of the Lord Jesus, it leads to deep transformation and presents an alternative vision for human interaction. This explanation, of course, roots discussions of evangelism in the act of making disciples rather than counting "decisions" or adding to our membership rolls.

Evangelism as a Ministry Vocation

Throughout this book, when I am writing about evangelism, I am generally referring to the work of attempting to make disciples of the Lord Jesus. Evangelism points to the work of shaping unbelievers into disciples through the leadership of the Holy Spirit. As such, many organizations or missionaries engage in evangelism as their primary vocation. An argument for evangelism as a ministry vocation should not mean that the real needs of hurting people should be swept aside. Not at all. However, I do wish to argue that some missionaries will focus the majority of their time and energy in the work of Gospel proclamation and disciple making, and these evangelists may partner with others whose primary vocation is meeting the needs of hunger, housing, or medical care. This is not meant as further polarization but rather as a vocational function. One whose primary vocation is evangelism should still care for those who are poor and marginalized, just as one whose primary vocation is community development or mercy ministries continues to be an ambassador of the Kingdom who verbally affirms hope in Christ. I want to argue for a framework of ministry vocation rather than a philosophical dualism between evangelism and service. Evangelism—as the communication that leads to making disciples—can be the primary vocation of some missionaries or missions organizations as they participate in the larger mission of God. Such a concentration on evangelism aims to bring genuine change throughout the relational threads of society by creating agents of transformation through grassroots relationships.

Evangelism in Contemporary Society

The very idea of evangelism elicits a variety of responses. For almost 20 years I have supervised college students coming into the city for short-term missions internships. Some are excited to gain experience in evangelism while others are terrified by the thought of it. Still others—despite their obvious attraction to the activity of Christian missions—represent a philosophical tension with the concept of evangelism itself. The idea and practice of evangelism rarely goes without eliciting a reaction of one sort or another. Nevertheless, at times the idea of evangelism seems to simply be fading from the conversation altogether. I was once overseeing a supervised practicum for a graduate student studying missions in a Christian seminary, and after sharing some insights on evangelism, he paused and told me, "In our school, we don't ever talk about evangelism." I wouldn't have been quite so surprised if he had been pursuing a degree in finance or culinary arts and happened to be studying in a Christian college. However, he was a graduate student studying missiology, and evangelism was apparently left out of the conversation altogether. Evangelism in our Western culture and within contemporary Christian thought seems to find itself in an awkward position even in some sections of the church.

For some, the very word "evangelism" might carry the impression more as a four-letter word of sorts than as a theological mandate or joyful witness. Who could be so presumptuous that they would claim their religion is true and try to convince others of such a claim? Shouldn't we just keep our opinions about religion to ourselves? For many Christians, the concept of evangelism leads to emotional dissonance. We know that we are told to share the story of Jesus Christ with others, but how can we do so without looking like the negative examples that we've seen on television or on the street corner who appear to do it so combatively? Members of my team in New York City have witnessed subway preachers intentionally and aggressively confronting passengers on the train and purposefully starting arguments as if such conflicts will inevitably draw others to the joy of the Gospel. Is that what we're supposed to be doing? I quite doubt it.

At times, the way evangelism is conducted appears to be nothing more than recruiting members to a religious institution or simply proselytizing individuals to an intellectual acceptance of a sectarian ideology or political persuasion. As a result, it does appear that for those who (rightfully) oppose these tactics, evangelism gets too easily brushed aside due to its perceived failure to address social concerns and compassionately respond to physical pain in our world. As credible as this criticism may be in any number of specific contexts, rather than proclaim Christ and simultaneously help the suffering as we may recognize in early church history and in contemporary ministries around the globe, evangelism is cast aside altogether as a reactionary response to poor examples. Of course, this is often in response to others who fail to serve the physical needs of the poor while preaching in their streets. Certainly, if expressing faith in Jesus Christ is nothing more than a cognitive belief in a deity lacking any real transformation or deep shifts in allegiance, it may do little good to change our world or provide hope that has any real meaning behind it. Indeed, faith without works is dead (James 2:17, CEB). In an attempt to escape the accusation of overemphasizing religion at the expense of other tangible concerns, evangelism then fades from regular ministry practice. Indeed, I have increasingly heard the stories of evangelistic ministries that have begun to face shortfalls in mobilization and recruiting in recent years. This likely points to a deeper theological dissonance.

Our society is seemingly trapped by dueling options. In some cases, the argument that evangelism may be more concerned with religious piety or institutional growth certainly has merit. At least some reactions to evangelism are due to bad examples of evangelism. Evangelism, at least in many Western contexts, has at times been converted into membership recruitment to a particular church or denomination rather than the work of developing obedient disciples to Jesus Christ among individuals, families, and communities who were formerly unbelievers. Where this is the case, our understanding of evangelism has been seriously misguided. However, rather than reforming evangelistic practices or perspectives, the response has too often been a swinging of the proverbial pendulum, giving aid to historical dichotomies that forced a binary choice between one or the other. Rather than responding to a one-sided form of evangelism with a more integrated approach, many just switch sides of their dualism, emphasizing social justice instead while leaving evangelism in the void. Or on the other side of the coin, ignoring physical needs altogether while preaching about being saved.

However, the dualistic split between two options doesn't seem to reflect the concerns or the comprehensive nature of the Gospel. Certainly Matthew chapters 25 and 28 are uttered in the same Gospel. Obeying Matthew Chapter 28 should lead to a great deal more activity that reflects the spirit of Matthew Chapter 25 if our evangelism leads to making disciples who obey what Jesus commanded. When I began my involvement in urban ministry during my college years, I didn't have a grasp of the historical separation between liberal and conservative or the religious split between caring for the body versus caring for the soul. Such an ideological split seemed unimaginable at the time. My gateway into formal ministry took place in urban churches that were both very evangelistic—regularly teaching the Word of God and baptizing new believers in the cities' poorest communities—and extremely compassionate—helping the homeless, prostitutes, impoverished children, and struggling immigrants. As I digested missiological studies from a wide range of authors, I came to realize that there existed a tension between those who stress social justice at the expense of evangelism and those who stress evangelism at the expense of addressing systemic injustices. While I believe one's primary ministry vocation may share an intentional emphasis in one direction or another, the ideological divide puzzles me to this day.

In our current cultural climate in the Western church, reigniting our imaginations for evangelism is, I believe, sorely needed. However, it's important that I express my deep dissatisfaction with the ideological split that does a disservice both to ministries of justice and to ministries of evangelism in the Western church. My task in this text is to address the vocation of evangelism in light of urbanization, globalization, and international migration. Evangelism is, of course, an essential missionary vocation. At the core of evangelism is the prayer we were given, "Your Kingdom come on earth as it is in heaven." While all of our works of grace represent signposts pointing to that Kingdom breaking into our world, calling human beings to shift their allegiance to the God of the universe is a central missionary task of the church. Improving that vocation of evangelism among the nations gathered in our cities is my primary task in this book.

Evangelism that is focused on Jesus as Lord should result in citizens that are seeking the peace of their city and that are more just, merciful, and compassionate toward their neighbors. When evangelism is not merely a membership drive but calling people to come under the reign of God, it should increase works of justice flowing from the lives of Jesus's individual disciples and churches. Cities start down the road to transformation when each individual convert is loving God and their neighbors in a way that reflects God's work of transformation in their lives. Worldviews are turned upside down as a new reality in Jesus opens before their eyes. One new believer in the Bronx once told me about his teenage neighbor. He built a relationship with him and kept pushing him to go to school when he was on the edge of dropping out during his senior year. Finally, the young man graduated high school and invited his Christian neighbor to come see him graduate. It was because of the persistent and attentive push by a brand-new believer that a teenager persevered to finish school. When these stories repeat and multiply across the city at the relational level through the agency of individual believers and Christian families serving others in their communities, the shalom of Christ expands throughout the city. It is the yeast of the Gospel of the Kingdom working and expanding in the city through human relationships.

Nevertheless, in an age of pluralism, others who have yet to discern the difference between the Gospel and other claims on reality, may ask, "Why evangelize?" One young Ghanaian man once told me, "Anyone who does not tell others about the Gospel does not really understand what he is a part of." It's difficult to disagree, and yet such disillusion with the concept of evangelism is fairly common in various corners of Western Christianity. In light of the apparent tension, some also are wrestling with the question, "What is evangelism anyway?" Walter Brueggemann offers a clarifying response:

> As discipleship is not simply church membership, so evangelism is not simply church recruitment of new members. Evangelism is the invitation and summons to resituate our talk and our walk according to the reality of this God, a reality not easily self-evident in our society. The call of the gospel includes the negative assertion that the technological-therapeutic-militaristic consumer world is false, not to be trusted or obeyed, and the positive claim that an alternative way in the world is legitimated by and appropriate to the new governance of God who is back in town. (Brueggemann, 2008, p. 233)

In Jesus's often-quoted parable of the farmer, he tells the story of a man who scatters a large number of seeds on a variety of soils. Some of the seeds are quickly eaten by birds. Some of the terrain is rocky, and while the seeds hint at growth in the beginning, they have no root and quickly wilt and die. The farmer throws some seed onto ground that is filled with thorns, so when the seeds begin to grow the thorns choke them out. Finally, some seeds land on soil that produces a crop that is harvested and multiplies to feed countless hundreds as a result (Matthew 13:3-9, CEB). I'm often struck by how generously the farmer cast out the seeds. Maybe there is some contextual nuance to the story I have missed, but it seems wasteful to throw seeds on the ground where the birds may steal it or where thorns are a danger to the life of a new crop. Of course, like all of Jesus's parables, there is greater truth underlying the simple story. The Good News of the Kingdom is offered to all, and certainly the receptivity of the soil is completely out of the farmer's control. The farmer is to scatter the seed generously. The starting point of evangelism is sharing the hope of Christ with those who may or may not turn out to be fertile soil for the Good News. Evangelism that leads to the emergence of new disciples is at its core a relational act, communicating a profound truth to another person or group of people. It is an act of proclamation and explanation accompanied by genuine compassion and empathy.

The wider implications of evangelism include the impact that the lives affected by the Gospel will in turn have within that society. When we make new disciples, we are calling people to be ambassadors of the Gospel. We are asking them to become agents of transformation within their social circles or communities. While evangelism will certainly have systemic implications as the ripple effects of the Gospel wash over a community, the engagement of evangelism is undeniably extremely personal as well. Through evangelism, the Gospel may transform an entire community, but it is equally profound as it takes root in a single human heart. At the core of our experience with the Gospel of grace is the call to share the hope found through faith in Christ with others. "Anyone who proclaims a gospel which omits or deemphasizes the justification and regeneration of individuals is, as Paul said, preaching his own message, not God's good news of salvation in Jesus" (Snider, 2008, p. 191). Nearly 20 years ago, I was attending Houston Graduate School of Theology while serving as a youth minister with Impact Ministries in Houston's center city, and my evangelism professor at the seminary used to tell us, "Evangelism is simply gossiping the Good News." I'm not sure whether he was quoting someone else or came up with that explanation himself, but it stuck with me ever since. At its most basic level, the starting point of evangelism is passing on the news of God's glorious and redemptive reign through Jesus the Lord to others. As we pass through others' lives, we share the hope of the empty tomb. Among our ministry partnerships in New York City, we often speak about mouth-to-ear evangelism. To see the Gospel sown in the hearts of those who do not yet believe, we want to see the Gospel expressed through human interactions and communicated in our relationships. While evangelism is our communication of Good News of the Kingdom of God to others, it also must be understood through the impact of its deeper implications. Evangelism is to result in disciples of Jesus, who in turn are ambassadors of reconciliation in our world. David Bosch writes:

> Evangelism may be defined as that dimension and activity of the church's mission which seeks to offer every person, everywhere, a valid opportunity to be directly challenged by the gospel of explicit faith in Jesus Christ, with the view to embracing him as Savior, becoming a living member of his community, and being enlisted in his service of reconciliation, peace, and justice on earth. (Bosch, 2008, p. 17)

When we address the subject of evangelism, we are primarily focusing upon our communication of the Gospel of the Kingdom to those who have not yet yielded their life to Jesus the Lord. Furthermore, as evangelism calls people to serve Jesus, it will develop individuals into agents of justice and kindness representing "with ever increasing glory" the character of God's Kingdom. We are saved by grace *and* for grace. In this text, the vision for evangelism is to form disciples of the Lord Jesus; therefore, we are calling individuals and families to begin imitating Christ. When new disciples are formed, our evangelism has not only resulted in new belief. It certainly has generated new belief and should, quite frankly, turn pre-existing worldviews upside down, but furthermore, our evangelistic efforts have generated new agents of justice, compassion, and salvation in a community and cultural group. Certainly not all of our evangelistic activity will actually result in conversions to Christ, but making disciples of Jesus is the goal of all of our evangelistic communication.

Evangelism is often traditionally viewed as a verbal act with religious implications and, as a result, is sometimes accused of being irrelevant to people's real needs right now. Certainly, if our practice of evangelism just equals membership in a local church or repeating a prayer and not much more, then such an accusation is quite justified. However, evangelism equals much more than religious switching. Each one should contribute what he or she can to causes that are battling injustice for the poor and cheer the efforts of ministries that rescue sex slaves from brothels or jumpstart the economy of an impoverished community or help a child who has no opportunity to transcend extreme poverty without intervention and assistance. And many ministries adopt their primary ministry vocation as focusing on systemic injustices and intervening through those sorts of acts while sharing the hope of Christ with those they encounter. In addition, the ministry vocation of evangelism with a view toward making disciples of Jesus is both personal and holistic. Some ministry vocations may involve launching an extensive initiative to relieve suffering or organize for long-range community development. Evangelism as a ministry vocation should lead to forming new disciples of Jesus Christ, and disciples of the Lord will be agents of love, peace, and mercy in their communities and families. In one parable, Jesus shares an image of the yeast multiplying so that the texture of the whole society is transformed (Matthew 13:33, CEB). Applying his meaning, I argue that evangelism is transformational in nature, occurring at the relational level of individuals, families, and communities. Evangelism leads to an alternative worldview, loving community, and intentional change in ethics and behavior. As individuals and households shift their allegiance to Christ, they become agents of transformation, justice, and compassionate love in their cities. The multiplication of disciples is a city's most profound social movement, with the inherent potential to bring systemic change from the grassroots while prophetically challenging the city's power structures. As churches emerge through evangelism in a neighborhood, they become communities of transformation bringing shalom to their communities and kinship networks. At its heart, evangelism brings change from life-to-life, household-to-household, community-to-community. We see this change begin and gain momentum, flowing from a relational response to the Good News.

On one occasion, a man with whom I had been studying the Bible came to me and told me a story. He explained that he had never felt compassion for anyone before and had only looked out for himself, but something had recently changed within his heart. He explained that some friends of his were about to be evicted from their apartment, so he took all of his gold jewelry to the pawnshop and gave them the money to pay their rent. He wasn't yet a Christian, but he had been participating in a Bible study and engaging the Gospel of grace for the first time in his life. The power of the Gospel was just beginning to do its work in his heart. He didn't fully understand what was happening to him at the time. It was a radical reworking of his worldview and personal motivations at the most basic and instinctual level, but something was changing in his heart as he interacted with others who were struggling. For the first time, he cared about the well-being of others. Prior to this, he had never embraced feelings of compassion for others around him and was willing to hurt anyone who stood in the way of his pleasure and personal power, but now something was different. The Gospel, through the influence of the Holy Spirit, was beginning to do a work of transformation in his heart. A new compassion toward others was emerging, and it was evangelism that was the activity giving birth to this act of mercy.

Repeating this story is not to say that the church shouldn't engage in initiating programs that attempt to bring about systemic change in a neighborhood or propose large-scale initiatives led by organizations that battle injustices taking place in megacities or nations. However, I do want to reframe evangelism as a holistic act if aimed at making disciples of Jesus who in turn become agents of light and salt in the city through relational encounters. As a missionary vocation, we are in fact multiplying agents of God's mission to his broken world. Evangelism should transcend ideologies that separate ministry into binary options. Rather, evangelism is in itself a holistic practice—which may or may not be accompanied by other large-scale works of service sponsored by Christian institutions on any given occasion—when its central aim is making disciples and teaching those new disciples to imitate Christ, thereby becoming agents of the Kingdom of Heaven.

The Gospel transforms worldviews, and ultimately sharing the Gospel is the work of developing lost persons into agents of grace and salvation within a community of people. That's not to negate organizational initiatives or the corporate efforts of the church. We should applaud them and participate in them as much as possible. Rather, it is to say that evangelism is as holistic as it is personal. As we live into the story of God, we are also changed by it. If the aim of evangelistic communication is making disciples of Jesus, then the implications of evangelism are transformational—although obviously tangled up in the realm of interpersonal relationships and ordinary human interactions. Serving the city through evangelism, we are sharing a story that resets how we live in the city. The proclamation of the Gospel becomes the hope of the city.

As an aspect of our humanity, we live within the stories we tell. We don't simply articulate narratives absent of meaning, but we see ourselves within our stories. Our ethical and moral understanding and our perceptions of reality are rooted in the stories in which we live (Esposito, Fasching, & Lewis, 2008, p. 15). When we tell the story of the Gospel of Jesus Christ, we are making a claim on reality, and we are staking our claim for what is real for the rest of humanity as well. It is indeed through our story that we understand the world. As Christians, we believe and proclaim that the Gospel of Jesus Christ is good news for all people everywhere. If there is one God who put creation into motion and sustains its existence and if that single Creator stepped into human history to offer salvation by paying the ultimate price within human experience and then rose from the dead therefore validating that vision for humanity, we are saying that this story really is for all people everywhere. While the claims of the Gospel are exclusive, the Gospel's invitation is universal. Our story is about the one God who made all things and is working to redeem humanity's brokenness, and the invitation to join this God is offered to all people from every place in creation. Jesus is the fullest expression of God. God alone is worthy of worship, and the mission of God is to redeem all ethnicities, all nations, all tribes. Our story, the Gospel narrative, is not simply for one people at one time. As we serve the city through evangelism, we have the opportunity to share the story with the nations gathering in our cities.

Nevertheless, evangelism in contemporary urban contexts faces a renewed set of challenges. Globalization and urbanization working as tandem social currents force narratives to coexist with a myriad of worldviews, which in turn make their own claims on reality. In our contemporary world, cities are centers of cultural pluralism. In many urban contexts, especially in the West, personal narratives are often pushed into private space where individuals stick with their own story while each narrative remains marginal to the society as a whole. The grand storyline has become the idea that everyone has his or her own independent story that should remain private, and the only story that prevails is the one that says there are many equally true stories. Of course, that narrative is itself making its own claim on reality. Ministry in world-class cities brings us to stand at the crossroads of deeply contrasting worldviews. Globalization has transformed "society into a pluralistic, multicentered reality subject to global influences" (Esposito, et al., 2008, pp. 5-6). Practicing evangelism, missionaries are forced to adjust to this new context without compromising the universal and exclusive claim of Jesus Christ as Lord while issuing a far-reaching invitation to all people everywhere. Evangelism in the pluralistic context of globalization is faced with the challenge of sounding a clear call to the life-giving Gospel of the Kingdom in the midst of numerous messages clamoring for attention. In addition, as a multitude of stories compete for attention and influence, they are often overshadowed by the grand storyline advanced by postmodernity that no stories should stake a claim on ultimate truth. Cities are mission fields where the Gospel is not simply engaging a single cultural history, but in the context of urbanism conflicting messages compete for our attention and for our loyalty from every direction. If we are to communicate the truth of the Gospel, we are faced with the challenge of navigating an urban world of dizzying diversity.

At times, those who desire to succeed religiously in Western culture are challenged to accommodate the pluralism of many stories as essentially equally true, but the urban evangelist is challenged to cut through the noise of ideological competition with the truth of the Gospel of peace. When a missionary serving in a city in the United States was told by a short-term mission team that a local imam had received copies of the Jesus film and was distributing DVD copies to the members of his mosque, the missionary decided he should pay the imam a visit. He made an appointment and met the Muslim leader in his office at the small storefront mosque. They sat down and began to talk, and the imam explained that he was glad to distribute the film because learning about all religions is good. The leader of the mosque was expressing how his own faith fit neatly into a pluralistic society. He understood and had embraced the message of the secular city, and as long as the Gospel is seen as one story among many and kept distant from any degree of conviction, it may remain disempowered without the ability to transform lives or shape worldviews. As one religious tradition among many, it is safe. It won't intrude on our allegiances or challenge our assumptions. However, after listening intently, the missionary paused and said, "I don't think you understand. Let me explain." He then took several minutes to use oral storytelling to explain the narrative of the God of the Bible and his plan of redemption through Jesus the Lord. At the end of the conversation, the Muslim leader was intrigued by the clear communication of the Gospel narrative—a message he had just heard for the very first time—and since that time, he and this urban missionary have had several meetings dedicated to studying the Bible. Evangelism in a pluralistic society implies that disciples of Christ will communicate the Gospel's claim on ultimate reality and simultaneously must do so in a manner that respects the ability of others to reject our explanation while continuing to cooperate with them as neighbors. The Gospel demands nonconformity to the religious standards of pluralism, but simultaneously champions respectful engagement that reflects the love of God for all creation. At least to some degree, it appears that the lack of experience of the American church with this sort of pluralistic environment has contributed, in part, to the church's perceived identity crisis as a missionary witness in the pluralism of contemporary cities.

While globalization brings with it a new range of diverse worldviews, allegiances, and religious practices colliding in urban space, our evangelistic engagement with historical populations of Western cities is also taking place on a changing playing field. Even as the church in North American cities begins to recognize the arrival of immigrants from around the world, the conditions for evangelism within the historic populations of Western cities has been shifting as well. Stuart Murray describes one aspect of the transition facing the church today as a cultural post-Christendom. In Christendom in Europe, the power of the church was historically embodied in her relationship to the state. Even as the Protestant Reformation took shape, theological lines of fellowship broke along national or regional boundaries and according to allegiances to noble benefactors. However, in the case of North America, Christendom is more of a cultural manifestation. With a persistent mantra of separation of church and state, Christendom was never fully manifest through a state religion but rather through cultural position. A cultural Christendom in the West assumed that the Christian narrative—or at least its institutional forms and structures—had a privileged position. Where ethnic and religious diversity existed, Christian institutions still held the dominant presence and maintained the loudest and most influential voice. Even as the United States dismissed notions of a state church, the cultural manifestations of Christendom persisted. However, today post-Christendom represents the increasing marginalization of Christianity as the prevailing narrative for Western society. Murray defines the shift to post-Christendom as "the culture that emerges as the Christian faith loses coherence within a society that has been definitively shaped by the Christian story and as the institutions that have been developed to express Christian convictions decline in influence" (Murray, 2004, pp. 1-18). I tend to lack confidence in the idea of an American history that was ever fully Christian in practice, but the favored position of Christianity even among those with little to no involvement in its institutions is undeniable. As the cultural landscape shifts, post-Christendom does not simply mean rapid secularization. Rather, in light of increased religious pluralism, it instead represents a diminished voice for institutional Christianity in Western society. "This marginalization of Christianity is not surprising to those who understand that the authentic way of Christ, even during Christendom, has always existed on the periphery of popular culture" (Pocock, et al., 2005, p. 168).

For evangelism, this means that we may no longer assume that our audience is already familiar with the Gospel narrative, nor should we presume that individuals credit the Christian Scriptures with authority for their life. Their authority structures are not based in the Christian story but may be rooted in other, often competing, narratives. In many social circles, it may be safer to assume that the Christian Scriptures are actively being discredited as sources of authority or truth by any variety of media or secular institutions. Conspiracy theories regarding the biblical text or early Christian tradition is quite marketable. Actually, when we attempt to explain the Gospel of Christ to others, while post-Christendom emerges as a prevailing cultural backdrop in Western society, one possible experience of our audience from Western contexts may be a negative rejection of what they perceive as Christianity—whether accurate or not. Clear communication of the Gospel is perhaps even more essential in contexts that may be characterized by post-Christendom because previous communication of a Christian story may be characterized as a distorted message or communicated in the context of a merely nominal faith adherence. However, a presentation of the Christian narrative embodied by the transforming power of the Gospel is necessary if the story is going to transcend a context where messages are facing constant competition for adherents and where there may be a range of presuppositions on the part of the hearer.

Addressing the need for the church in Canada to engage its North American context as a mission field, Thiessen offers five considerations for shaping missionary activity in post-Christendom. First, he advocates that leaders and church members alike must pay attention and follow the leadership of the Holy Spirit. In this regard, he offers a challenge for North American Christians: The question for missiological practitioners is how those in the Christian community can be encouraged to slow down their frenetic lives and adopt a posture that is constantly sensitive to the Holy Spirit's leading to participate in missionary efforts in Canada, and in turn, to respond in obedience regardless of the dominant cultural values that may conflict with Christ's calling on his disciples" (Thiessen, 2013, pp. 134-141). Second, he argues that Christian ministries must work to change the negative view that nonbelievers have of the church. He says, "One approach, in response to widespread perceptions that Christians are too inward looking is for churches to centre their group identity in ministry initiatives that look beyond the walls of their congregation." Third, he insists that relationships must play the key role in the ministry of the church. Studies consistently demonstrate that most people newly join a religious group because of a meaningful relationship. Evangelical believers must learn to build relationships with nonbelievers. Fourth, the church should be aware that the evangelistic charge in North America may be led by Christians who recently immigrated here from majority-world nations. Christian migrants often come with a view of evangelism that is inherently holistic and a conviction for the need of salvation to all who will listen. Finally, we must be prepared to "wipe the dust off our feet" when we encounter resistance. In North American cultural settings, there will be resistance to the Gospel, and we ought to be better prepared, when necessary, to move on in our efforts. We may keep praying for someone and not abandon the relationship entirely but continue seeking more receptive soil. "A continued dependence upon the Holy Spirit, an attentiveness and response to negative perceptions surrounding Christianity, a resurgence in building meaningful relationships with non-Christians, learning from and partnering with Christian immigrants in missionary endeavors, and knowing when to 'wipe the dust off our feet' may be effective missionary methods in Canada in the 21st century" (Thiessen, 2013, pp. 134-141). For church leaders laboring in North American cities, a reimagining of evangelism will be beneficial in the emerging cultural setting. Missiologists are facing an urban society where historical North American populations are increasingly disillusioned with the Christian narrative and simultaneously encountering increasing international diversity.

Simultaneously, as rising religious worldviews from within the historic demographics of Western cities present new challenges for the church, the persistent emergence of cultural and religious pluralism stands equal with the challenges of post-Christendom cultures. Increasing pluralism in urban society implies that many individuals we encounter have interacted with—and perhaps adopted—a variety of diverse perspectives into a religious hybrid. As an urban missionary, it is not uncommon to encounter hybrid worldviews mixing ideas that are characteristically in conflict with one another. In the city, it is quite normal to encounter individuals who merge monotheism with Buddhist concepts of reincarnation or argue for religious relativism without a real understanding of any of the particular theologies being merged together. With the numerous and varied sets of messages one may encounter in the urban-global context and the heightened role of the individual in Western urban cultural settings, any number of new hybrid belief systems may appear, both overlapping and competing with existing theological perspectives. Urban evangelists who find themselves working in multicultural contexts ought to be prepared to engage multiple worldviews rather than one seemingly monolithic people group. Even if missionaries have devoted themselves to one particular ethnic niche in the city, they will need to be prepared for their particular ethnic group to be interacting with diverse perspectives in a globally connected city. Some years ago, one of our ministry interns had recently returned to college, so I took over tutoring one of her students through our ministry's conversational English class. He was from Morocco and seemed open to discussing spiritual things, so I saw this as a great opportunity to build a friendship and share the story of Jesus with my new Muslim friend. As I initiated a dialogue about faith, I was preparing to leap into an apologetic conversation engaging an Islamic worldview and building bridges toward the hope found in Jesus Christ. I was prepared to identify the bridges from the Koran to the Gospel and discuss the unique contours of faith in the Gospel of grace, but not everything is as it appears. My new friend from Morocco told me how he had been an atheist for a short period of time, had read a number of French postmodern philosophers, and then went on to describe his worldview as, essentially, what I would describe as religious relativism. If I wanted to have a conversation about faith in Jesus, I needed to be prepared to adjust my preconceptions and dive into a discussion—quite different from the one I expected—interacting with postmodern religious relativism rather than a conservative Islamic theology. I learned that the ability to immediately switch gears in urban evangelism in a global city context is helpful at the very least, and after several years in urban ministry in New York City, these sorts of adaptive conversations no longer surprise me. On another occasion, the conversation turned out to be exactly what I expected from the beginning. I was speaking with a taxi driver from Mauritania, and after some light conversation, I shared with him that I am a follower of Isa (Jesus). This led us into discussions about Jesus in the Koran as I worked to bridge these references to the Gospel of Christ. It was a dynamic and enjoyable conversation, seemingly for both of us, as I encouraged him to consider learning more about Jesus. Often, urban evangelists in an age of globalization will need to be prepared for a variety of perspectives—addressing traditional theological belief systems, folks religions, and contemporary religious hybrids. Even focusing on a particular subculture in the city, members of that subculture are also encountering a variety of ideas, beliefs, and worldviews as actors on the new global stage. They are likely to be affected whether they adopt these new ideas as their own, integrate them into hybrid worldviews, or are repelled by them into a more conservative faith.

For the dominant culture in the West, the transition to a post-Christendom society may be seen as a generic turn in the process of modern secularization. However, it is important to remember that "the 'secular' society is not a neutral area into which we can project the Christian message. It is an area already occupied by other gods" (Newbigin, 2008 , p. 48). We are not speaking into a vacuum. We are seeking to communicate the Good News of God's grace into a crowded room of raised voices, where secular societies are rooted in historical ideologies, too. N.T. Wright has described at length the Epicurean and Deist roots embodied in the worldview of our secular society (Wright, 2014, pp. 6-25). In a global society, various stories prevail and take their place of cultural dominance even within the secular or pluralistic city. For many, evangelism in cities in North

America will require adapting to the present cultural shift as post-Christendom emerges amidst the forces of secularization mixing and mingling with the proactive presence of world religions primarily through diaspora communities—as well as Westernized hybrids—originating from around the globe. The shadow of a cultural Christendom, world religions accompanying international migration, and persistent attempts at secularization all compete as well as become entangled in contemporary global cities.

While it is debatable as to just how "Christian" our Western society ever truly was, in the past in Western cities under the canopy of a prevailing Christendom paradigm, evangelism may have primarily operated as calling stray Christians back into the flock, or it at least implied preaching repentance to sinners who were familiar with a basic narrative of the Gospel story. In the United States, in our evangelism efforts in the past we have likely related a lot more to Jesus's ministry in Galilee to call straying sinners to repentance than to the Holy Spirit setting aside Paul and Barnabas to cross-cultural barriers in a world with much less familiarity with the story of God and perhaps no news yet of Jesus the resurrected King. Yet it is the latter situation that has now come to represent simply crossing the street in our city and speaking with our neighbors from around the world.

Evangelism in an urban society calls the church to learn to function within a mosaic of cultural and religious pluralism. The story of Jesus is proclaimed in cities swirling with narratives that are both competing and merging within subcultures. Among our Sikh, Muslim, Hindu, Jewish, or Buddhist neighbors, there often may be very little actual knowledge or understanding of the message of the story of Jesus Christ, and they certainly have not viewed the Christian Scriptures as their source of authority. In order to share the hope of salvation with our neighbors from among unreached ethnic groups, we will have to learn new starting points for our communication. Equally so, when explaining the Gospel of grace to Westerners who have rejected the Christian message as their basis of authority, starting with, "Because the

Bible says..." will likely carry little weight as the starting point for evangelistic proclamation (Newbigin, 1989, p. 39). Evangelism in post-Christendom may in turn have more in common with missionary communication methods among unreached nations than it does with the Christendom age that preceded it. While we hope to bring our friends and neighbors into a relationship with Jesus and see the Christian Scriptures become a source of authority for their faith and practice, it is unlikely that simply citing the Bible will automatically represent religious authority for either native Westerners who have marginalized the Bible as any sort of authority in their lives or migrants who originate from majority-world communities who have yet to accept the message of the cross. I recall the first time a Yemeni in East Harlem responded to my attempts at evangelistic dialogue by accusing the New Testament Scriptures of being corrupted. I have learned since then that it is a common deflection. While no actual evidence supported his claims, it is quite the trump card. If he, as an orthodox Muslim, believed the Christian New Testament text was not corrupted, he likely would view them as authoritative. On the other hand, I've had countless conversations with Western skeptics who do not affirm the New Testament as authoritative for their life on completely different grounds. Despite the lack of authority given to the Scriptures in a post-Christendom world, I have found that, perhaps ironically, leading unbelievers to engage in the pages of the Bible has often had a profound and transformational impact on their lives. At the intersection of globalization and post-Christendom, we are being forced to reimagine evangelism in a world that no longer shares our assumptions. This is not to say that we ought not share the Word of God or sit down with someone with an open Bible. Just the opposite. I have personally witnessed how hearing the stories of Scripture has a profound impact on pre-believers as they encounter the God of the Bible, and in evangelistic encounters I want to see people engage the Word of God as soon as possible as they explore the claims of the Gospel. However, we cannot automatically assume that our hearers will initially value the Christian Scriptures as authoritative.

In globalized cities characterized by cultural pluralism, there is a constant tension between compromise and conflict. Traditional religious worldviews see postmodern society as a godless expression that undermines their own view of truth and morality. Without compromise, the potential for conflict is persistent in the midst of incredible diversity within multicultural cities (Esposito, et al., 2008, pp. 5-6). It ought not be a surprise when a religious fundamentalist is arrested in New York City or London for plotting mass murder. It should be heartbreaking, but not surprising. The inherent tension between conflict and compromise raises a remarkable tension for followers of Jesus. We are seeking the peace of the city, desiring to bring compassion, mercy, and justice. Living peaceful lives with our neighbors from around world in our diverse communities is a powerful incarnational embodiment of the Gospel. Our ability to sow peace with all people points to the Prince of Peace. Furthermore, we cannot compromise the Gospel of the Kingdom with any competing narrative. The Gospel stands apart from worldviews that seek to assimilate it. Following Jesus as evangelists to the city, our lives should be characterized by neither conflict nor compromise. We are defined by the Gospel of peace and salvation.

We are invited into a narrative that claims an exclusive reign over human history. The Good News that we share with our neighbors proclaims "one Lord, one faith, one baptism, one God and Father of all, who is over all and through all and in all" (Ephesians 4:5-6, ESV). The story of the one Creator's Incarnate Word dying on a cross for the redemption of sins and then being raised to life and establishing his kingship as an invasion against the principalities and powers is not a message of compromise but of the reign of God intruding on all human history. Furthermore, we are a community of peace. The instructions to Jeremiah to seek the shalom of that pagan city echoes down to us today as we find our way in a pluralistic urban society. We may work for the common good of the city and do so without laying aside the Christian commitment to evangelism. We neither compromise the claims of the Gospel narrative nor invite conflict with those who are "other," whether down the block or around the world. Nevertheless, one of our challenges for practicing evangelism among the nations may lie within ourselves as the church of God.

In the United States where there is still a large Christian community, we might assume that there is a tremendous missionary force for sharing the Gospel among diaspora communities. Our neighbors are coming from around the world and moving in next door. It is an opportunity to share our faith in Christ with unbelievers and to partner with our new Christian neighbors. However, obstacles to communicating the message of God's grace may be more resilient than we would hope. For many Americans have been conditioned to view religion as a private matter. Soong-Chan Rah explains, "A personalism and a prioritizing of the individual can be found at the sociohistorical roots of evangelicalism. Life and ministry in the local church, therefore, became the race to please the individual so that the pews might be filled" (Rah, 2009, p. 30). To make disciples in the global city, the church will require a reorientation from pleasing the individual to joining God's redemptive mission. In an age of globalization, there is a need for Western society to encounter a public Christianity that is both peaceable and unflinching. Unfortunately, the dualistic options of either compromise or conflict are too often characteristic of the Western church.

For much of the history of our world, people largely lived in societies that were shaped by a single dominant religious worldview. However, in recent decades it has become commonplace to live in proximity of any number of religious and cultural worldviews. As religious pluralism emerges in cities both big and small, the temptation for Western Christians is to retreat into the world of personal preference. We tend to join a community or ritualize a set of practices based on our personal preferences. However, evangelism is endangered in Western contexts—or perhaps more accurately in the widespread participation of Western people—if all that matters in the religious life of individuals is personal preference. Leslie Newbigin explains:

> If what matters about religious beliefs is not the factual truth of what they affirm but the sincerity with which they are held; if religious belief is a matter of personal inward experience rather than an account of what is objectively the case, then there are certainly no grounds for thinking that Christians have any right—much less duty—to seek the conversion of these neighbors to Christian faith. To try to do so would be arrogance. (Newbigin, 1989, pp. 25-26)

A missionary to Muslims once made an interesting point by asking two simple but contrasting questions, "What are two things that Americans are never supposed to discuss?" The answer, of course, is politics and religion. "What are the two things that many Muslims are eager to discuss?" The answer is the same: politics and religion. Many Christians in the United States fail to realize the potential ease of starting conversations with spiritual themes with many of their Muslim neighbors. For Western Christians to pursue evangelism among diaspora communities from around the world, one key step must be to internalize the claims of the Gospel for all nations. Our cultural tendency to place religion in the realm of private preference highlights the Gospel's counter-cultural nature when challenging Western believers. The Gospel is certainly personal, but it is not merely private.

Ministry, the City, and the Nations

During my first year in college, I went on a short-term mission trip to inner-city Houston, and we did what college students on short-term mission trips often do. We played with children from the city's poorest communities, passed out sandwiches to the homeless, we painted something, and in the evening we wrestled together over concepts of ministry, justice, poverty, and wealth in small group discussions. Whether sending groups of college students on short-term mission trips does more good than harm or does more harm than good (a debate I prefer not to enter into here), it planted a seed deep in my own heart. As a college student, I was mobilized. It propelled me on a course of missionary service that would alter the rest of my life. My encounters lit up a passion in me for urban evangelism among the most hurting, and I followed that experience with opportunities to serve in some of the most challenging neighborhoods in Houston, Memphis, and my own college town of Abilene, Texas. During my college years, I became obsessed with learning all I could about ministry in cities. I often neglected assigned readings in my rural Christian college to read unassigned texts by Roger Greenway, Ray Bakke, John Perkins, and other voices calling the church to give heed to rapid urbanization. Of course, my steady interest in learning all I could about urban mission beyond the parameters of my degree plan didn't help me bring home very strong report cards as a young undergraduate, but nevertheless, I soaked up everything I could get my hands on. Since my college years, my enthusiasm found some balance with the realities of experience and the school of hard knocks, but I've continued to focus my ministry vocation on mission in a world that is quickly urbanizing. Once I began serving as a full-time missionary, first in Houston and then in New York City, it didn't take long to begin realizing that urban mission was in many ways synonymous with global mission as cities are increasingly becoming international hubs for any variety of nations, tribes, or ethnic groups. My personal concern for evangelism in cities led me to a genuine love for ministry to diaspora communities. Many of my peers working among diaspora communities in North American cities began as missionaries in a foreign field, so, while I have spent some time in Central America, my journey into diaspora missions was a bit backwards in comparison, starting from inner-cities in the United States and then to the broader impact of globalization.

One of the key demographics impacting cities around the world—especially in the urban centers and suburbs of North America—are immigrant communities. "Immigration to the United States is providing the American church with one of the greatest evangelistic opportunities that has existed since the first century" (Rogers, 2006, p. 147). Let us pray that the church is awake to that reality. The geographic distance has narrowed between nations and people groups and between believers and the unreached. In recent years, a great deal more emphasis has been placed on evangelism among diaspora groups in cities and nearby suburbs. I have recognized a noticeable rise in the number of articles, conference themes, and books along the thematic lines of diaspora missiology. This is likely due to Christian leaders being awake to what is happening in their cities. The fact that the presence of new city dwellers from around the world has become an obvious and unavoidable presence is increasingly hard to miss. Ministry to immigrant communities points to significant evangelistic opportunities for the Gospel to make an impact in the city. Migrants in our cities are experiencing a great deal of transition, and people experiencing significant transitions may be more open to the Gospel. As newcomers struggle through a number of life transitions, believers have the opportunity to offer compassionate service and proclaim the Gospel of Jesus Christ in the midst of change (Claydon, 2004, p. 17). Migration represents an opportunity for proclamation among unreached ethnic groups that were previously difficult to access, and migrant families may represent soft soil that is ready to encounter the Good News of the cross of Christ. "The situation of being migrants from another place and, thereby, of being minority 'others' often stimulates a mode of religious change through heightened self-awareness" (Vertovec, 2009, p. 140). For instance, evangelical Christians in Central America only account for 10% of the population; however, in New York City 30% of Central American immigrants are evangelical (Clayman, March 22, 2014). While this could be accounted for by larger numbers of evangelicals immigrating from Central American countries, it is more likely that post-migration conversion is a real factor.

Evangelism among diaspora communities in the city raises new questions. For instance, do we encourage local churches to evangelize cross-culturally and invite immigrants to their church assemblies, or do we launch church-planting initiatives among new immigrant communities? Perhaps both? Do what degree does contextualization reflect forms and expressions from their homeland and to what degree does it reflect migrants' new host culture? The challenges and opportunities vary widely across urban contexts and specific diaspora communities. Even the desires for assimilation into the dominant culture versus resistance and preservation of the home culture in the new context will vary for many immigrants from household to household and from neighborhood to neighborhood. Some immigrants are eager to join churches in the dominant culture, and they bring passion and enthusiasm, as well as greater diversity, to once-homogenous communities of faith. Congregations that have long desired to step into greater multiethnicity may welcome this new opportunity to diversify and enrich their church body by increasing their membership through newcomers from other nations. It is a great opportunity for many churches in North America to experience a richer tapestry of the global church through a greater international diversity. Of course, unless many of the members learn to consider their immigrant neighbors who possess an important cultural history as equal to themselves and find relationships with people from other cultures truly enjoyable, they are not prepared for cross-cultural ministry in their city (Rogers, 2006, p. 137). Experiencing a heavenly international diversity in our earthly communities will require Christian humility.

Many new residents of Western cities desire to join churches that represent the established culture, but despite a percentage of international migrants who prefer to join with the religious expressions of the dominant culture, many other immigrants deeply desire to experience their faith in Christ in their own language and with their own cultural expressions. In addition, many nonbelievers from Hindu, Muslim, or other backgrounds will need to explore Christian faith among their more non-Western peers or through contextualization efforts of missionaries. Our history of segregation and racial discrimination in the United States often makes us leery of focusing upon specific ethnic groups for evangelism or church planting. My own research during graduate school was on multiethnic churches, so I applaud these reservations. However, I do not necessarily see this as segregation, but rather it is the desire to not be completely assimilated to the dominant culture and lose one's own culture in the process. It is often a desire to meet God through the expressions and forms that make the most sense to us rather than through foreign communication or structures. There are many different outcomes that result from working in specific ethnic communities or reaching out to unreached people groups living in our cities. Believers will join or start churches that intentionally preserve their cultural heritage. Many of these churches will continue to minister to their own diaspora community within ethnic enclaves and constantly be revitalized by new waves of immigrants moving into their community. On the other hand, other ethnic churches begin as monolingual immigrant churches but gradually begin to open up to the wider community around them and slowly add a more multiethnic presence to their church. One large multiethnic church in Brooklyn began as a Spanish-only first-generation Latino church, but after adding an English assembly in order to reach out to their second-generation Latino children, a number of Asians living in the same area have joined the church as well. It is now a bilingual multiethnic and multigenerational church. Also some immigrant churches are multiethnic from the start. For instance, they may intentionally begin a church that represents the expanse of Latin America or start one that is intentionally Pan-Asian. Such churches are often planted or led by a second-generation immigrant who already lives in a bicultural world. Dan Rodriguez at Pepperdine University has explained that these sorts of churches are becoming increasingly common in the urban landscape (Rodriguez, 2011, pp. 82-107). In some cases, the children or grandchildren of immigrants who may have been assimilated into the dominant culture sometimes return to diaspora communities within their culture of origin as a way of exploring their own cultural identity (Adeney, 2011, pp. 11-12). Many nonbelievers arriving from radically different societies from the one in which they now live are likely to only be reached through evangelism methods that are contextualized for their culture and that communicate within the framework of their worldview or by others who follow Christ from within their own cultural group. While many second-generation or multiethnic communities of faith will likely continue to emerge through the context of globalization, there is an increasing need to continue intentionally planting ethnic- or language-based churches among diaspora communities. The need to develop contextualized church planting in diaspora networks should not be overlooked.

Assuming that local churches from the dominant culture in the United States will automatically be a fit for all new immigrants is shortsighted, but assuming that established churches cannot connect with new immigrants and add some of these newcomers to their membership is equally shortsighted. There is simply not a one-size-fits-all approach when it comes to individuals and families who have immigrated to Western cities. While the majority of immigrants to the United States cluster together in order to form a supportive network when facing economic challenges, educated and wealthy immigrants are settling in Western cities from around the world much more so than in the past, and these wealthier migrants tend to settle in ethnic clusters much less often than their struggling counterparts (Scott, 2001, p. 319). These new immigrants will often actually prefer to connect with an American church, helping them gain a sense of belonging in the dominant culture. Even contextualized church-planting efforts in their ethnic communities might miss them altogether because they desire to assimilate quickly into a community of faith that represents an historical Western culture. While most ethnic communities will require contextualized church planting, some individuals will more likely gravitate to established Western or multiethnic churches. As members of the diaspora, they may provide a strategic bridge between established Western churches and ethnic churches from their communities. In addition, many individuals maintain ties to family and friends in their homeland and may create links between their new church community and relationships in their country of origin. Among many immigrants, the motivation toward greater assimilation provides a wonderful opportunity for local churches to demonstrate hospitality and friendship across any number of cultural boundaries.

However, while there are open doors for ministry and fellowship for established churches, most newer immigrants are more likely to encounter the Gospel through evangelism and church planting within their own community and culture, and there is a also a greater likelihood that they will transmit the Gospel to others back home if communication and church-planting strategies are reproducible and easily contextualized within their culture of origin. This should lead the church to placing a weightier emphasis upon contextualized evangelism and church multiplication strategies through diaspora communities. In many cases, ethnic neighborhoods emerge precisely because first-generation immigrants find clustering together within their cultural group to be to their advantage. "In general, the networked nature of immigration makes for local concentration, impeding geographic diffusion. The more dependent on networks for information and support—a characteristic usually linked to lower levels of marketable skills—the more likely are the immigrants to converge on a limited number of places" (Scott, 2001, p. 309). In some cases, migrants living in an ethnic enclave prefer to stay within their cultural community even when they have achieved an economic status that would allow them to relocate outside of their enclave (Abrahamson, 2004, p. 60). Although they have achieved the ability to live as bicultural citizens between their professional identity and their ethnic community, they may prefer to come home at night to the community that culturally feels like home.

While established churches should engage diaspora communities with hospitality and service, new contextualized church-planting efforts are needed as a primary strategy in order to address the dynamic fluidity and complexity of globally linked immigrant communities. In addition, more contextualized approaches to evangelism modeling reproducible forms of church planting are potentially more likely to result in creating bridges of ministry to migrants' countries of origin or to ethnic diasporas in other parts of the world. While established churches should eagerly embrace opportunities to reach new migrants in their communities, much of the mission efforts to diaspora populations should involve new church-planting initiatives reflecting thoughtful contextualization in global and urban society. Such new initiatives may open the door for the Gospel to penetrate the larger clusters of immigrants in a city or metropolitan region and may have an impact in countries of origin through natural connections across an ethnic or linguistic network.

In this book, there is an underlying assumption and an intentional emphasis on evangelism through contextualized church multiplication. Nevertheless, the strength of established congregations reaching out to their international neighbors shouldn't be overlooked. Instead, churches serving their ethnic neighbors ought to be encouraged. Even if we emphasize church multiplication as a primary strategy, it would be unfortunate if established churches neglected evangelism among immigrant communities as simply the job of the church planter or professional missionary. Indeed there are a number of individual immigrants in North America who quickly adapt to the dominant culture and are open to participating with a local church if they receive an invitation and feel welcomed. This is especially true for a large number of immigrants who became believers in Christ in their country of origin and were taught in a church setting that already adopted— whether through the historical influence of a foreign missionary or expatriate involvement or simply through the influence of global media —many of the cultural and structural traits of American churches.

For some migrants, they made the long journey into a new cultural setting precisely because they are already fairly individualistic in their mindset and in some cases may be on the margins of their home culture. They desire to assimilate, at least to some degree, and long for a community of peers from their host culture. This population segment provides an opportunity for established churches to reach out in the midst of dynamic and diverse populations in metropolitan areas throughout North America. For established churches, the influx of migrants from all around the globe provides a profoundly theological moment. It is an opportunity to provide hospitality to refugee and to love foreigners as themselves. This example of Christ's invitation to all people points to the Gospel of grace as the church acts as a witness in a pluralistic culture. American churches can play a valuable role in welcoming migrants and exiles in their midst. In a postmodern culture that values diversity and an ethos of acceptance, a church that welcomes brothers and sisters who have arrived from around the globe and creates space for a diverse set of global voices represents a powerful witness for the Gospel of reconciliation in this society with its particular racial and ethnic history. Yet, many churches will need to be trained in cross-cultural relationships. It is not uncommon for an international migrant to join a local church and express excitement and joy over ministry options or church programs that the congregation has to offer, but nevertheless, soon begin to experience moments of genuine discomfort and loneliness due to a lack of cultural understanding or sensitivity among those of the dominant culture making up the majority of the congregation or leadership. Missiologists may provide a valuable service to established churches in multiethnic communities by offering cross-cultural training and coaching as urban and suburban churches reach out to increasingly diverse neighborhoods.

Simultaneously, the advantage of evangelism through contextualized church planting in diaspora communities cannot be overemphasized. Fresh contextualization is needed to address diaspora populations in an age of globalization. As new immigrant populations emerge in urban and suburban neighborhoods, they represent new opportunities for the advance of the Gospel, resulting in new faith communities. Nevertheless, conventional approaches to church planting in North America are often driven by religious entrepreneurs offering events that are attractive to the religiously affiliated. Planting incarnational communities across cultural barriers or multiplying churches throughout a mosaic of subcultures in an urban area will often require a different approach than religious entrepreneurship seeking to attract adherents. Furthermore, Stuart Murray insists that continuing to pursue church planting as we've always done it will not be sufficient for addressing the new challenges confronting the church. Rather, new kinds of church planting are needed that will both catalyze evangelism and strengthen existing congregations in the process as well (Murray, 2001, p. 25).

The fabric of urban life is interwoven with overwhelming diversity, and while many evangelists and church planters simply hope to cast a wide enough net to bridge the breadth of that diversity, such an approach fails to incarnate the Gospel among the various population segments that fill the apartment buildings, housing projects, neighborhoods, and nearby suburbs of many of our cities. Cities are mosaics of subcultures. Contextualized church planting opens opportunities to engage the unique needs and worldview issues of each cultural or lingual community. Such contextualized engagement does not mean that we continue recreating a segregated Christianity. Rather, it should be quite the opposite. Contextualized church planting throughout the fabric of urban subcultures actually prevents evangelism efforts from assuming the dominance of a single culture likely to assimilate all other subcultures. "Loving others mean[s] giving them freedom to be who they are created to be without forcing them to be like us and empowering them to love God in their own ways. Loving others is about empowering them to love God with their own heart, soul, mind, and strength" (C. Kim, 2013, p. 101). Of course, every kind of church should strive for a unity of fellowship. As new believers mature in faith and continue to learn to coexist in a diverse society, new ethnic churches should learn to develop cross-cultural partnerships with congregations that are culturally different from themselves, which many do. Of course, efforts at multicultural fellowship will require intentionality and should be proactively sought through mentoring new disciples and leaders. Some assemblies will also evolve into multiethnic or bicultural congregational churches as they address the needs of the second generation who are living between the culture of their parents and the culture of the city in which they've been raised. Urban evangelism in the context of globalization will result in both multiethnic churches and monocultural churches. Both face significant challenges as they participate as communities in the one Body of Christ. Multiethnic churches represent a beautiful picture of the heavenly throne room but are also prone to only bring highly assimilated migrants under the umbrella of a dominant cultural expression. Contextualized church planting is needed to bring the Gospel into many unreached diaspora communities across the mosaic of the city, and as they mature in Christ, those churches will need to be encouraged to develop collaborative relationships beyond their own ethnic boundaries. Cross-cultural partnerships should be invaluable components of ministry in urban evangelism.

As churches launch evangelistic efforts in cities that are intended to result in new churches, approaches to church planting will need to be examined. Often the economic models incorporated in church planting undermine the vision for evangelism. Many of the entrepreneurial approaches to church planting in the United States are focused on sustaining the organization of the church as an independent institution as quickly as possible. As a result, the church planter is at risk of overlooking population segments within the city that are not predisposed to financially support the institution of the church right away nor automatically attracted to their new programs, polished preaching, or dynamic worship service. In an effort to quickly pay the bills to support a building, pastor, sound equipment, and advertising, large population segments that require a significant investment of time and thoughtful cross-cultural contextualization are often overlooked. In order to sustain the costs associated with the new church project, the missionary church planter must gather believers who are already predisposed to pay the bills. Too often our economic models for church planting undermine evangelism among resistant cultural groups, unreached people groups, and the urban poor in order to attract those who are already inclined to support the new project in short order. Most often this means gathering large numbers of Christians to form the new church. The incremental process of disciple making typically won't pay the bills quickly enough under the prevailing entrepreneurial model. While a new church may be geographically near, the cultural distance quite often keeps many immigrant households beyond arm's length from the new church's evangelistic initiatives. Reaching cross-culturally usually requires intentionality. However, researching what is already available to immigrants in their area of the city, evangelists may discover what needs remain for a diaspora community and discern how new inroads into the community may be developed (Rogers, 2006, pp. 135-136). If the Western church desires to evangelize unreached ethnic communities in the city, evangelism processes allowing persistence and patience to overlap should be considered. It is unlikely in most cases that migrants from an unreached ethnic enclave are going to pour into a nearby church no matter how effective their programs and services might be. Just a couple of blocks from Bangla Bazaar, the heart of the largest Bangladeshi community in the Bronx is one of the largest multiethnic churches in the New York City borough. The congregation has a pastor with a genuine heart for the community, and the congregation has an active ministry. It is very multiethnic and organizes a vibrant worship service. It's a wonderful community of faith in Jesus Christ. However, Bangladeshi Muslims are not rushing to attend Sunday morning services. Geographic proximity has not bridged the gap to this community. Contextualized and intentional ministry efforts are necessary for the Gospel to gain a hearing in this diaspora community. Despite close geographic proximity, evangelism that closes the cultural distance will require intentional efforts to express the Gospel within the culture of this ethnic enclave.

With the explosion of international migration over recent decades, there is an opportunity and need to pursue multiplying churches among myriad cultures and subcultures among diaspora communities through intentional evangelism. If we desire to see ethnic churches reproduce new disciples and churches among their cultural group, church planting and evangelism methods should be reproducible based on the resources already present in the immigrant community. Church-planting methods should be simple, so that evangelistic church planting may be reproduced by members of the diaspora. "As our means of teaching, developing leaders, and modeling become more and more complex, the likelihood of reproduction by the migrants decreases." Church-planting initiatives should focus on simple methods in order to lead to multiplication. Simple approaches may challenge many of our assumptions about church life in the West. "Much of the way we experience church life is extremely complex, technical, and difficult to multiply" (Payne, 2012, pp. 136-137). Methods that require the constant coordination of a religious professional will not likely reproduce easily. Church-planting missionaries should seek to understand what elements of church life are biblically essential and what optional elements are more easily reproducible in the migrant's homeland and among neighboring diaspora. If a new believer migrated from a closed country, it is highly unlikely that modeling professionally driven Western church structures will result in reproduction of church planting if the migrant either returns to the country of origin or begins sharing the Gospel with family members through phone, Internet, or short-term visits. Western churches often assimilate new migrants or international students with the hope that the ministry will expand to the new member's homeland. However, our Western forms are considered foreign to the home culture, and our American orientation around the leadership of religious professionals as well as the heavy infrastructure of church forms may create unnecessary barriers that inhibit the reproduction of evangelism and church planting in the country of origin. While local multiplication of church planting among diaspora communities remains feasible, the likelihood for a rapid spread of new church planting among the diaspora using Western forms and expensive structures remains unlikely.

Applying Multiplication Principles

Roland Allen, who labored in China more than a century ago, cast a vision for planting churches that multiply and expand through indigenous leadership rather than rely on outside control. He said "that meant that the very first groups of converts must be so fully equipped with all spiritual authority that they could multiply themselves without any necessary reference to us that, though, while we were there, they might regard us as helpful advisers, yet our removal should not at all mutilate the completeness of the church, or deprive it of anything necessary for its unlimited expansion. Only in such a way did it seem to me to be possible for churches to grow rapidly and securely over wide areas" (Allen, 1962, p. 1). It took several decades for Allen's thoughts to be accepted, but eventually his thinking became a mainstream focus for many missionary church planters.

Decades later, Donald McGavran argued that multiplication movements occur when a series of social groups within a culture or society make decisions for Christ. As social units within a cultural stream come to an active faith in Christ, momentum may build into a multiplication movement (Wagner & McGavran, 1990, pp. 221-223). David Garrison's report on church-planting movements around the globe near the end of the 20th century describes indigenous multiplication of disciples and churches among a number of different people groups on every continent. While missionaries spark these movements in their beginning, they are then characterized by lay-led indigenous house churches or cells that multiply throughout a culture (See: Garrison, 2003). By empowering indigenous leadership and keeping church structures simple and reproducible from the beginning of the missionary's ministry, the likelihood of churches being planted and multiplying throughout a cultural group becomes much more likely as the door has been opened for local contextualization.

Applying multiplication principles in global urban areas may reflect many of the same principles applied in traditional societies. As a practitioner in the environment of the global city, I believe much more pioneering work should be done in exploring the application of multiplication principles in diverse urban contexts. Urban practitioners must also intentionally adapt to the realities of urban life, ongoing globalization, and its resulting social fragmentation. For those applying church multiplication principles in an effort to evangelize a community or people group, urban realities force missionary practitioners to make adjustments. For example, rather than focusing evangelism on a geographic community, urban strategists may need to focus on multiple population segments. However, facing a different set of circumstances—perhaps even in the same city—an urban missionary may find himself or herself focused on a single neighborhood. Adaptation is a key skill for urban mission. Neighborhoods often change, even more quickly under the influence of persistent globalization. Missionaries seeking to multiply disciples and churches in a city must recognize that they may need to target different segments of the city's diverse makeup sometimes working with both geographically oriented and affinity or cultural groups for evangelistic engagement. While in traditional societies, church multiplication may move fluidly along familial lines, social groups in urban settings where church multiplication takes place may be among a group of coworkers or friends rather than merely neighbors or family (S. Smith, 2009).

A few years ago, I was conducting research on church multiplication movements, and during one of the interviews I posed a question to an experienced missionary in Asia. I asked, "What is the difference in evangelism practices between the United States and what we see happening in these rapidly multiplying movements in Asia?" His response was packed with implications. He said, "In evangelism in the United States, we win them and then try to group them. But in church-planting movements, we group them and then we try to win them." One of the key factors in multiplication movements is that evangelism takes place in groups. After developing a relationship with a key person of influence, the evangelist seeks access to the circle of influence of that initial contact. Entire households may be won to Christ by making disciples of a family or group of friends rather than an isolated individual. Of course, this raises a new set of challenges for attempts by missionaries at launching church multiplication among Westerners with a heightened sense of individualism, but even then the degree of individualism versus community will vary across the various subcultures even within the dominant American society, and many diaspora communities maintain a much more communal existence than their American neighbors. Still, among diaspora communities, such a methodology raises new complexities as well. To what degree does an immigrant maintain a strong communal worldview, or are they more assimilated into a worldview of American individualism? This may vary from family to family and community to community. I am apt to argue that multiplication principles are applicable in the global setting, but the social units that make up new groups are much smaller than in traditional societies. Still, more questions come up. Do new arrivals have many connections in the local diaspora community or in the dominant culture, or are they in need of someone to help them build a new community since they are newcomers to the city? To what degree are they seeking assimilation or are they largely tapped into their ethnic network in the city? Many immigrants will actually be a person of influence with a group of family, friends, and associates, but often those connections are maintained across borders through transnational interactions. Multiplication may occur across significant geographic distances, and this challenges traditional Western church-growth metrics. Sometimes the value of putting multiplication principles into practice will be the potential for reproduction of evangelism and church planting through the new disciple's contacts in the home country or diaspora communities in other parts of the world rather than in the immediate community. However, at other times, ministry may be reproduced through the new believers within the local diaspora community or even jump to other people groups in the city. Several years ago, I was teaching the Gospel to a single mother from the Dominican Republic. Although most of her connections were Dominican, I also met Jamaicans, Ecuadorians, and a Punjabi Indian through visiting with others who gathered to hear the Word of God in her home. As I taught her Bible stories, I encouraged her to pass them onto others through her daily encounters. I still expected that she would mostly pass on the stories she was learning to other Dominicans living in her ethnic enclave in the West Bronx, but one of the first reports I received back from her concerning her own retelling of the Gospel stories was of her sharing with a white Jewish woman she met while volunteering in a nearby community. In the global city, the Gospel may move through relationships within a diaspora, to other people groups within the same city, and to family and friends overseas. The potential for Gospel advancement through grassroots connections is multidirectional. However, a key practice is to model evangelistic methods that can easily be passed on to new believers who come from a variety of cultures. Applying multiplication movements is a viable strategy in the city; however, the implications of applying these principles in the context of globalization may lead the urban missionary to a more fluid global engagement as she works through communities that may be simultaneously experiencing both traumatic social fragmentation and dynamic global connectedness.

Reaching Diaspora Communities

Urban Christians in North America have a tremendous opportunity before them. Many of the most unreached ethnic groups on the planet now have representatives living in Western cities. They are driving cabs, working in restaurants, representing foreign consulates, cleaning houses, serving in hospitals, and starting businesses. Nevertheless, the rising tide in demographic shifts also presents a real challenge for the church. There is a need for churches throughout North America to become fully present in the midst of global diversity swirling around them. "Ironically, even though urban churches have more access to unreached people groups within their own geographic setting, they are much less directly involved with unreached ethnic groups than suburban or even rural churches—who spend billions of dollars each year on short-term mission trips around the world" (Clayman, March 22, 2014). For urban churches and missionaries in Western contexts, the geographic challenge to evangelism among the world's most unreached peoples has narrowed. However, reaching diaspora communities in North American cities requires intentionality as a cultural gap persists between local Christians and nearby ethnic communities that have sprouted up in our cities. A renewal of the church's missionary identity is needed.

Positively speaking, there are examples emerging of intentional evangelism and church planting among unreached diaspora communities in cities in the United States. I've heard accounts of Pakistani, West African, Bangladeshi, Chinese, and Somali immigrants recently becoming believers in Christ in American cities, and a ministry in the southeastern United States has witnessed a large number of Muslims in their region becoming followers of Jesus Christ. While many discussions about diaspora missiology revolve around what we ought to do, there is an increasing number of efforts taking place among diaspora communities. Indeed one of the goals of this book is to encourage us to move beyond our noble ideas of what should be done and begin standing on the shoulder of missionary practitioners, so that we may learn what has been done, learn deeply from these perspectives, and keep pressing forward as a missionary people. Certainly, we have much to learn from pioneering efforts among diaspora communities located in the West where post-Christendom is still emerging, and new stories of evangelistic breakthroughs are emerging on a regular basis.

For example, Bukharan Jews are considered an ethnic group that is resistant to the Gospel. Originating in the countries of Uzbekistan, Tajikstan, and Kyrgizstan, the Bukharan Jews have endured under conquerors and rulers ranging from Gengis Khan to Alexander the Great to the Soviet Union, and they have existed over centuries as a minority population under various Muslim dynasties. They have suffered under targeted persecution in Islamic societies in Central Asia, and share in common the Jewish experience of anti-Semitism. With the fall of the Soviet Union, many Bukharan Jews sought a new life in the United States, and today there are 50,000 Bukharan Jews clustered together in the borough of Queens in New York City. This is the only Bukharan diaspora community so closely concentrated in the world. Naturally, such a phenomenon opens a unique opportunity for missionary engagement. While the Bukharan immigrants were helped by Eastern European Jews to settle in their new home in the United States, they also are seen as entirely different from the existing Jewish communities that received them, which kept them as a unique subculture within the city. Bhukaran Jews are a distinct ethnic group within the fabric of the city's many subcultures (Ford, March 22, 2014).

Randall Ford, a missionary to Bhukaran Jews in New York City, has planted a house church in Queens among this ethnic community. They baptized a small group of new believers and are continuing to engage the community with the Gospel. Due to their Jewish heritage, this ethnic group embraces the inspiration of the Hebrew Scriptures, but they often have not read the Bible for themselves. As a missionary to Bhukaran Jews, Ford often attempts to utilize Isaiah Chapter 53 as a bridge for sharing the Gospel of Christ. The Bhukaran Jews recognize this passage as inspired, and it provides an opportunity to introduce the work of atonement in the cross of Christ. Ford has worked through relationships and direct evangelism while honoring their Central Asian and Jewish traditions. He finds that while they believe in inspiration of scripture, they are at times not even willing to read it themselves, so they often arrange to sit down and read the Bible with the individual contacts they've made. Ford explains the experience of evangelistically starting a church among the diaspora community of Bukharan Jews in New York City:

> We represent Jesus to a group who, most likely, will never wander into a church meeting. Since the congregation/church-planting in Queens was new and pioneering, we tried many different things to see what works. We found that Bukharans prefer to meet in our apartment, rather than in a rented space, even though we feel a little crowded sometimes, and our apartment suffers wear and tear. Meeting at home makes sense, because Bukharans love to hang out together, to cook, and drink tea. Meeting somewhere else doesn't make much sense to them. This family atmosphere counters one dark stain in Bukharan culture—abusive relationships. Over the years, to our horror and amazement, we discovered that every Bukharan woman we know has either personally suffered abuse or witnessed other family members abused (Ford, March 22, 2014).

Evangelism among the various nations living in our cities requires intentionality, cultural sensitivity, and patience. Evangelism has always been primarily a function of relationship. We must love others of different cultures if the Gospel is to have a lasting influence. On the one hand, evangelism should be direct. We have learned in our experience in New York City, that among Muslims if we do not share the Gospel early in a relationship, many will believe it is not very important to us if it eventually comes up later in conversation. In order to see an abundant sowing of the message of the Kingdom of God throughout our cities, evangelism should be direct, but direct does not mean pushy or overbearing. It simply means seizing opportunities and being up front in our identity and purpose. If the Gospel of Jesus Christ defines who we are as individuals and as communities, we are simply sharing ourselves when we are intentional in sharing the Gospel with new friends and neighbors from around the world. Simultaneously, our evangelism must be centered in relationship and reflect loving patience. Glen Rogers explains:

> Some believers are taught to make a short, powerful presentation of the Gospel and expect and push for a quick response. After all, eternity hangs in the balance! That is a very Western way of thinking about things. But the Gospel is not Western and neither are the immigrants who are coming here from other cultures. They do not embrace new ways quickly or easily. Many of them come from cultures considerably older than our own, cultures rooted in ancient wisdom and centuries of experience. Immigrants from those cultures will take a wait and see attitude for things that are new and different—which is what Christianity is to them, new and different. In our evangelistic zeal, justified and appropriate as it is, we need to learn to slow down and let people think. They need to observe, sometimes for a long time, to see if this Christian kindness and love is real or not. When they are convinced, they will respond (Rogers, 2006, p. 90).

Subcultural Theory

Too often we imagine cities as being united under a single story, but cities are better thought of as an anthology bringing together a collection of cultural stories and images. Urbanologist Claude Fischer, applies subcultural theory to urban life, making the case that cities are not one monoculture but a mosaic of human identity and culture. He argues that urbanism encourages the persistence of diverse subcultures, but simultaneously argues that urban ecology impacts these subcultures causing change in each one as well. With the existence of a plethora of subcultures and consistent change caused by the urban environment, new subcultures are always evolving (Fischer, 1984, pp. 35-36). Cultures and people groups in metropolitan areas are in a dynamic context of change and adaptation. Approaches to evangelism and church planting that allow the initial structures to remain fluid and organic will allow indigenous communities in the diaspora to adjust to the unique and often changing realities affecting the diaspora community. Monolithic forms and methods face a crisis in the urban world of globalization.

Cities are mosaics of subcultures. This internal diversity is probably one of the key contrasts between urban and traditional societies. Fischer has argued for an understanding of the city that applies subcultural theory. This approach challenges old ways of studying urbanization that either suggested that cities dismantle social groupings on the one hand or that the urban environment has no affect on social groups at all on the other. Fischer argues, rather, that social groupings persist in urban contexts but that urban contexts also have an impact on these social groups. Actually, he suggests that the nature of the urban setting "intensifies subcultures." The city has a profound impact on the life of urban dwellers, and the concentration and compression caused by urbanization stimulates an increase in subcultural groupings throughout the city. Cities naturally draw from varied social groups from a variety of locations, thereby generating greater diversity within their territory. In addition, not only do cities draw multiple groups and cultures from very different original locations, urbanism stimulates the proliferation of subcultures. The reality is that urban dwellers often are connected to a social world as much as rural people are, but their connections are often through subcultures with which they identify themselves. As a social group rises to a "critical mass," a subculture emerges (Fischer, 1984, pp. 35-41).

Fischer's subcultural theory for the city points to the reality that urban missionaries sense viscerally everyday as they walk the streets of their city. Cities are mosaics of numerous subcultures with the potential for spawning new cultural groups as well. Artistic networks emerge in cities like Seattle or Austin. Second-generation Koreans in Los Angeles develop into a subculture wholly distinct—yet still similar in some respects—to their first-generation immigrant parents. Bengali gangs band together in London differing significantly from lower-crime Bengali communities in New York City. The city constantly transforms the life of its residents, enhances subcultures, leads to cultural hybrids and stimulates conflicts between groups with competing interests. Cities reflect cultural collectives as various subcultures encounter one another in urban space. However, if cities are collections of subcultures, what are the implications for evangelism?

For missionaries engaging in urban evangelism and church planting, the presence of myriad subcultures refines the vision for contextualization. While contemporary Western-style multiethnic church plants will often succeed at reaching a portion of the population, it may represent only a percentage of the city's overall demographic. Planting these sorts of churches will make a positive impact on the city and should continue as they positively contribute to the expansion of God's Kingdom. However, most of the city's population will require a refined approach to contextualization with multiple evangelism streams reaching into the variety of subcultures living and working in the city. Missionaries may focus on a single ethnic diaspora, or teams of missionaries may pursue multiple streams of evangelism among different cultures living within geographic proximity but remaining culturally distant from one another. In Global City Mission Initiative, our ministry represents both focused efforts to specific ethnic communities and multiethnic ministry in diverse neighborhoods. As new believers mature, they may begin to interact with other new believers from different subcultures in the city who were reached through different evangelistic streams in order to strengthen the unity of the body as multiple church plants are developed. Seeing the city as a collection of subcultures, refined contextualization among the various cultural and social groupings will require intentional practices to engage diaspora communities who otherwise might remain culturally distant from church-planting initiatives not focused on their cultures. Often our approaches to ministry in the city reflect a perception of urban places as singular entities; however, cities are more like a collection or a mosaic of cultures and social niches compressed together in shared space. Therefore, intentional evangelism and church-planting efforts must sensitively contextualize among urban subcultures while helping new believers mature theologically toward reconciliation and unity across cultural barriers.

Continuum of Assimilation

Globalized cities, as international hubs for diaspora communities and numerous emerging subcultures, are in a constant state of assimilation. Even as third-generation immigrants constitute ethnic representatives now learning to think and act as one in the dominant culture, they are replaced by a new arrival just stepping off the plane. Internally, families experience a diversity of perspectives as first-, second-, and third-generation immigrants differ in experience and worldview. Individual migrants may drift toward greater assimilation or hold tightly to their cultural heritage, or they may fall somewhere between these cultural poles on a continuum between conflict and assimilation. Cities are in a constant state of change, and ministries addressing diaspora communities and engaging urban populations must be prepared to be adaptable across a spectrum of cultural diversity and flux.

When new immigrants arrive in a new city and culture, often their first priority is survival. They must tackle the most basic needs for themselves and perhaps a family. As they learn to function in the new society, they begin to adjust their life to the new customs that surround them. Immigrants first experience "surface level acculturation." That is, they learn their way through the essential behaviors and structures within a culture. They learn how to operate in this new world, but their worldview is unchanged. A Pakistani migrant may learn how to shop, open a bank account, get an apartment, file taxes, and enroll her children in school, but her worldview is still inherently Pakistani. Her underlying assumptions about the world and how it is supposed to work are unchanged. Rather, she has only adjusted her life structurally to the operations of the host culture (Rogers, 2006, pp. 39-43).

On the other end of the continuum are those who have acculturated into the culture at a deep level. It involves understanding the "why" of the behaviors of a culture. In reality, many people from within a culture don't understand why they think the way they do or why they do the things the way they do them. For someone to become completely assimilated to the new culture, they experience both a change in surface behaviors and a transformation of deep-level assumptions. Their own cultural behaviors and assumptions must begin to fade into the background. Across the spectrum of immigrants in a city, some embrace the process toward assimilation, but others resist it (Rogers, 2006, pp. 43-44). In reality, a deep level of cultural understanding can be difficult to grasp. Many Americans don't even truly understand their own cultural assumptions or comprehend why they think the way they think. As a result, most migrants may live somewhere between complete assimilation and complete resistance. Some are at the beginning of making adjustments to the new culture. Others have assimilated to the new host culture. Still others have grown up at least partially as a native to the culture but, due to their parents' cultural history, their household connects them to their ethnic history and the migration journey of their family. Many are somewhere in the process of assimilation to the culture or sometimes in conflict with the host culture or with neighboring diaspora communities. Others are resisting assimilation to the host culture, maintaining both behaviors and worldviews reflecting their culture of origin. Cities are increasingly populated by immigrants from around the world who may be located all across a dynamic cultural continuum. Individuals, households, neighborhoods, and people groups are in a constant state of change. "The timeframe for assimilation extends across generations" (Scott, 2001, p. 312).

Michael Laguerre argues that a key aspect of assimilation and resistance is played out in the treatment of time in diaspora communities and in relation to the mainstream or dominant culture of the city. In his "analysis of diasporic temporalities" he states that "New

York City is a multidiasporic urban landscape, each ethnic enclave attaining to the preservation of its cultural heritage while at the same time being shaped by and contributing to the mainstream." The global city becomes a place of multiple calendars, each claiming its own cultural rhythms but unavoidably being affected by the scheduling practices of the dominant culture and global demands of the city. He writes, "One must pay attention to the immigrant's time because it informs the rhythm of socialization in the new country, the speed with which adaptation occurs, group conflicts between different perceptions of time, generational conflicts among parents and children, diasporic holy days and holidays, and the recognition of different temporal perspectives within a given nation." Majority-world migrants in a Western city are faced with the need to adjust their temporal rhythms. Yet, life within their diaspora network or their interactions with their kinship network back home prompts them to move back and forth, negotiating between differing approaches to time. As migrants in the city learn to navigate the temporal demands of their host city and the natural rhythms of their culture of origin, they develop a transnational hybrid approach for the sake of their own well-being, enabling them to interact across differing expectations of time (Laguerre, 2003, pp. 6-27).

While global cities move at a rapid pace dominated by the around-the-clock exchanges of goods and services as a key urban center for the global marketplace, there remains an undercurrent of great global diversity measured in management of time and treatment of special days. New York City is a place where Muslims are keeping special days and times of prayer, Jews are closing shops early on Friday afternoons for Sabbath, Protestant Christians are vying for Sunday as their sacred day, and Catholic masses are performed throughout the week, with Sunday as the focal point. Simultaneously, the civil day of rest remains focused on Sunday, corresponding with the influence of historical Christendom (Laguerre, 2003, pp. 28-36).

A missionary moving into the global city to work among diaspora communities must locate where a particular individual, family, or community may be along a cultural continuum of temporal expectations. For instance, several years ago when I came as a young, new missionary to New York City, I was bonding with local believers who were graciously acting as my cultural informants. A couple from Puerto Rico and Trinidad invited me to enjoy Thanksgiving in their home, and I joyfully accepted. They told me 3 p.m., so I showed up at their front door at 3 p.m. After helping run an errand to the grocery store, I sat and watched the 4 p.m. football game until around 7 p.m., which is when the rest of the family began to arrive. It was a wonderful evening, and at 11 p.m. I was ready to go home. I had been in their home for eight hours, and for my own culture that is quite a long time. However, the radio was turned on, and a card game was just beginning. The night was still young. Most missionaries reading this can relate completely and laugh at my cultural miscues. Nevertheless, what is different is the new complexity for navigating cultural customs, such as time, when encountering diaspora communities. Everyone in the room on that Thanksgiving Day regularly navigate the expectations of time in the dominant culture of New York City, but simultaneously they knew when they were adhering to the diaspora calendar instead. They naturally understood when to apply the time expectations in the context of the dominant culture, and they equally understood when to apply the time expectation of the Caribbean. They are adaptive to both professional and cultural temporalities, which may contrast significantly. I have to admit, it has taken me a long time to learn to navigate between alternative time expectations. If a missionary is working within traditional Western society, there is a clear expectation of time, and if a missionary is working in many areas of Africa or rural Mexico, there is likely a single time expectation at work in that culture. However, in the global city, missionaries may need to adjust to differing time expectations depending on the impact of a dominant culture and related professional settings, the characteristics of a cultural hybrid, or alternative time expectations of a diaspora subculture. For missionaries in the city, negotiating time is not as static as in a more monocultural or traditional society. Instead, approaches to time may vary from diaspora to diaspora and result in hybrids negotiating between expectations of the marketplace and expectations of a particular ethnic culture.

Using our example of time, the demands of the city on new ethnic communities may generate new hybrid approaches as well. When a missionary to Africans in North America requested to set up a table sharing Gospel literature at an event sponsored by an ethnic association of a specific unreached people group in the city, he was told the event started at 1 a.m. He set up the table and talked to interested contacts at the event all night long. The event, sponsored by an ethnic association, began at 1 a.m. because it was scheduling around the realities of the African diaspora in the urban marketplace. Most of the members of the association are laborers in the service sector. Many work in restaurants, and most nights they don't arrive home until midnight or later. The only feasible time to gather the majority of them into a single room was in the middle of the night stretching into the earliest hours of the morning. Missionaries to diaspora communities in global cities will need to navigate between approaches to time since migrants often must negotiate between unspoken expectations in their own ethnic community, their home culture through transnational exchanges, the expectations of the dominant culture and the global marketplace, and hybrid approaches to time forced upon them by the realities of the urban market. Approaches to time is certainly one tangible example of the global city as a continuum of assimilation and the impact upon diaspora communities and the missionaries seeking to reach them. Time is one example of a cultural factor that has real implications for the lifestyle and interactions of the urban missionary, and the environment of the global city forces the need to adapt to increased complexity.

Evangelism among diaspora communities should be adaptable to a regular state of change. Transnational relationships create links to long-held cultural practices or worldviews. Many migrants adapt to the expectations and, at times, even worldview of the host culture, but some are crushed by new cultural norms to which they simply cannot adhere. Well-established migrants have adapted to the culture while maintaining their historical cultural identity, but their children live between cultures. Still, new migrants are constantly arriving, keeping the cycle of change and adaptation fresh and in a regular state of flux. "Because migration is driven by networks, it also involves a process of social reproduction, in which the current crop of workers begets a new bunch that looks very much like themselves" (Scott, 2001, p. 319). In global cities, evangelism efforts not only confront a dynamic continuum of assimilation but also a regular phenomenon of community turnover. Missionaries among diaspora communities in international urban centers must be prepared not only to contextualize among a subculture or subcultures but be ready to adapt and change as diaspora communities themselves evolve.

In addition to the regular state of change and adaptation along a cultural continuum, neighborhoods experience routine change as well. In New York City, the streets of neighborhoods that were once iconic Puerto Rican communities are now lined with Mexican shops and restaurants. A Greek neighborhood has become a Little Egypt, and Italian restaurants are now managed by Albanians. One of the largest churches in the Bronx is located in a neighborhood that first transitioned from Irish and Italian to Latino and African-American and is now rapidly becoming Bengali and African. In the city, nothing stays the same. Church leadership that assumes neighborhoods will continue as monolithic communities will need to evaluate their underlying assumptions. Ministry plans based on expectations that a neighborhood or people group will remain static will need to be reevaluated. Approaches to ministry should assume change.

Contextualization

In light of globalization, the challenges of urbanism, migration, and transnational identities, missiological contextualization is confronted with new sets of challenges. Subcultural theory informs us that contextualization remains relevant in the global environment among the various subcultures moving through urban space despite the contemporary arguments that globalization leads to a global monoculture. In the cultural compression resulting from globalized processes of urbanization, new cultural hybrids are developing, older cultures are sustained in networks of diaspora communities, and through mobility and natural shifts in demographics, cultural groups are constantly arriving and fading from the city's cultural landscape. Missiological contextualization faces new challenges, to be certain, but remains an invaluable discipline for missiologists in the city.

Our example, as followers of Christ, for the contextualization of the Gospel is the Living Word, Jesus, who took on the human condition and fully entered human reality. "Jesus entered our world, our culture, a community, and even a family. Jesus learned the languages, customs, habits, heart, and hurts of the people. He communicated up close and personal" (McRaney, 2003, p. 102). The essence of contextualization is found in the example of Jesus. "Jesus Christ Himself exemplified contextualization at the cost of His life" (Gwamzhi, 2013, p. 12). As the Word was made flesh, he entered a specific human culture and communicated in a specific language, using stories that reflected the realities of the world at the time. Although he is the King of Kings, he humbled himself to the embodiment of a blue-collar itinerate prophet. When Paul later describes his ability to "become all things for all men," he is following in the footsteps of Christ. The Gospel finds expression in different cultures and customs while remaining fixed on the Lordship of Jesus Christ.

We typically realize that different approaches are needed when sharing the Gospel with people from different parts of the world. We wouldn't necessarily assume that someone in the South Pacific requires the same communication style or church forms as someone in the Middle East—even if they were both from the same religious background. Missiologists today generally recognize the need for contextualizing our communication style, expressions of community, training models, and the like for the specific cultural context in which we are working. While globalization influences the spread of what some suggest is an apparent global monoculture with recognizable symbols proliferated through worldwide corporate marketing (Kling, 2010, pp. 107-125), simultaneously cultural pluralism is becoming the norm for cities around the world. As common images and messages—many originating from the West and moving through the private sector—are proliferated throughout cultures and societies where these same images or messages were once foreign to the local context, cultural pluralism is in the same instance constantly emerging and represents a variety of both Eastern and Western worldviews. In a global world, it is not simply missionaries journeying into the Amazon forest or hiking into the Himalayas that must bring the Gospel message into a foreign context. Contextualized communication and church-planting efforts need to be addressed from one neighborhood to another in the multicultural makeup of cities. With vast diversity in our midst, the same sensitivity of culture, tradition, or worldview is required of us among serving various diaspora communities (Claydon, 2004, p. 24).

As the media has evolved into a global communications system, a challenge for missiologists is to remain sensitive to the cultural nuances of people groups living in the tension between their traditional society and the process of globalization. As our natural default, we often assume that Western approaches to church are the best way to connect. While it's our default position, Western forms are not always embraced by other cultures. Sometimes when they are embraced by new believers, they may become a barrier inhibiting the Gospel from spontaneously expanding from those new believers throughout a given culture. However, as we contextualize our communication of the Gospel among the various ethnic subcultures in our cities, it opens up a range of possibilities. For instance, some Christians have put together a Gospel-oriented alternative to Diwali or Festival of Lights events as a way to invite their Sikh or Hindu neighbors and explain the Gospel of Jesus (Claydon, 2004, pp. 17-18). One missionary to West Africans in the

United States has utilized baby-naming ceremonies for each of his children. His family recognized that baby-naming rituals was of great importance among his Muslim neighbors, so he arranged baby-naming parties as a means for sharing the Gospel. They've conducted baby-naming ceremonies in homes and in Islamic community centers. Each of his children is named after a famous missionary, so this also has opened a gateway for sharing the Gospel message by explaining the meaning behind their names. A missionary to Albanian diaspora has organized parties celebrating national and cultural holidays, and evangelists in Mexican communities may find attending quinceañera celebrations to be an important event for building relationships with the community and acknowledging their cultural heritage.

Between migrant communities, there may be a great deal of differences even within the same city. One diaspora community may be educated and upwardly mobile while another may be struggling in poverty. One may be generally accepted by the dominant culture while another may face discrimination (Claydon, 2004, p. 50). For instance, to the outsider passing through a Chinese enclave in a Western city, it may appear that the culture is uniformly representing Chinese culture, but the reality is typically much more diverse as families from different regions, classes, religions, primary languages, and ethnic groups gravitate to the same diaspora neighborhood due to relatively greater cultural proximity than the dominant culture. They cluster around other near cultural groups, but in reality some ethnic enclaves are themselves quite diverse and even fragmented. Urban communities spotted with storefront church buildings every few blocks may not at first glance reveal that numerous Hindus—primarily from Trinidad and Guyana— reside in the same community and may require an intentional effort to reach Caribbean Hindus. Such variances across a mosaic of subcultures in metropolitan areas requires contextualization that is characterized by sensitivity to the various subcultures living side-by-side.

In urban and global contexts, there is a persistent need for contextualization. However, our approach to contextualization may require greater fluidity. From one standpoint, the processes of "assimilation, acculturation, culture loss, culture mixing, creolization" may be viewed as negative outcomes forced by globalization and large-scale international migration. However, another view is that these processes are actually "culture-building" (Rynkiewich, 2011, p. 210). In an urban and globally connected world, cultures are constantly wrestling with change. It is simply a reality, for better or for worse. In New York City, there are thousands of African immigrants. They are often interacting—usually through cell phones—with relatives or business associates in their home country. They are sending home remittances to support immediate family or extended kinship networks and, as a result of their perceived success in the United States, they are gaining social status among their peers and relatives in their homeland. They are becoming "Big Papas" and "Big Mamas." From a continent away, they are emerging as leaders of their society. They are becoming the shapers of culture. Often missionaries have traveled to an African village, located the person of influence in that community, and after sensitive negotiations receive access through that community leader to share the Gospel with the families that will gather. In a world impacted by globalization, urbanization, migration, and transnationalism, the leader or influencer of that community may in fact now be driving a taxi in downtown Chicago or be working in a warehouse in Boston. Encountering the numerous clusters of cultures in urban settings should stimulate our missiological imagination as we address issues of contextualization in growing and dynamic cities.

Citizens of the Diaspora

Missionaries begin their work as learners. When missionaries travel to foreign lands, they must learn the language, culture, customs, and social structures of the people they are serving. They seek out bridges to relationships with the local people and lay down foundations for relating to them. They don't seek to build identification with the people they are serving simply to make the people feel better or to relieve anxiety felt by the missionary. Rather, while there are natural limits to identifying with a culture that is foreign to the missionary, they seek to find ways to identify, as ambassadors of the Gospel, with the people they are serving in order to develop "communication and a communion" with those in the local culture (Reyburn, 2009, pp. 470-476). "Identification occurs on two levels—the one from the missionary identifying the people and place of mission and the other by the missionary understanding, embracing, and sharing community with the people among whom he is appointed as God's redemptive agent" (Gwamzhi, 2013, pp. 9-10). Missionaries build the bridge of identification with those they are serving in order to communicate the Gospel in word and deed in a way that makes sense across cultural barriers. Any time we are engaging another culture with the Gospel of Christ, one of our chief ethics ought to be the practice of humility.

> Inevitably the missionary realizes that to be acceptable, local community members must first find him teachable. The role of learner is an especially useful entry role. The learner's dependence and vulnerability convey in some small way the messages of identification and reconciliation that are explicit in the gospel. Entering a new community as a sincere learner (of language and culture to begin with), the missionary approaches the local residents with humility, offering dignity to the people from whom he learns. (Larson, 2009, p. 455)

Missionaries are capable of communicating the message they seek to convey when they have entered the cultural context of the community they seek to reach (Gwamzhi, 2013, p. 12). This is equally true when reaching out among a diaspora community. It may be easier to forget to enter the culture as a learner if they are a marginal subculture and if the urban missionary is a member of the dominant culture. Nevertheless, taking the posture of a learner is an essential missionary discipline. We must learn to build the bonds of fellowship with members of the diaspora community if we desire to see bridges of the Gospel expand into an ethnic enclave or diaspora network. It may be a challenge for many Westerners to enter an ethnic neighborhood or interact with a network with the same humility that is required when entering a village in a foreign land, but as the distance gap for cross-cultural missions has narrowed and cities are becoming more diverse places, the call for a missionary posture as learners resounds for those who desire to reach their neighbors from around the world. The genuine need for Christian humility and cross-cultural identification persists.

One hindrance that negatively impacts the ability of American Christians to relate to diaspora peoples among us is that we often possess a "promised land" mentality. American Christians often feel settled. We have a tendency to claim our citizenship as Americans before claiming our citizenship in heaven. This attitude can hinder the work of the Gospel among our new international neighbors. While Paul made use of his Roman citizenship, he understood that he was first a citizen of heaven. This is a hindrance for American Christians because we are called to be pilgrims. We are resident aliens and our true citizenship is with Christ as a holy nation belonging to God (Dean, March 22, 2014).

For missionaries reaching out to diaspora communities in the global city, they will need to become a "citizen of the diaspora." Just as missionaries must learn to acculturate to a new culture when working overseas, there is a need to identify with the diaspora culture in very similar ways when working in the context of global cities without ever leaving their country. "By being a citizen of the diaspora, the Christian worker can begin constructing values, schedules, and ministry plans that look completely different than typical American ministry" (Clayman, March 22, 2014). Evangelists to diaspora communities in Western cities will need to do more than take a mission trip to an ethnic enclave, but often they will need to learn to conduct ministry that is aligned with the rhythms of the diaspora community.

Immigration and Identity

"If there was ever a linear process by which immigrants assimilated to American culture, it no longer exists." Immigrants arrive in cities in North America, and they find a mosaic of cultural pluralism. Rather than being forced to assimilate into a single American cultural mold, they often find themselves fitting—or being assigned—with a cultural group already present in the city. Such categories are not neat packages but may be arbitrary, such as lumping Koreans, Chinese, and Thai as Asians in general or seeing Guatemalans or Ecuadorians as virtually the same as Mexicans (Warner & Wittner, 1998, pp. 18-19). Migration can result in discovering new identities as ethnic groups learn to relate to their own ethnic identity in relation to others. Someone emigrating from Africa may not have thought of himself as Black in the same sense that she is categorized in the West, but coming to the United States and stepping into its racial history, she learns a new identity in relationship to the larger culture. Previously, she may have identified with her tribal group or region, but by immigrating she has stepped into a new set of ethnic categories.

Being dislocated from one's culture, immigrants struggle with their cultural identity, but any degree of loss of a culture or identity may be "compensated with a strong adherence to the pilgrim reality of the Christian on earth." Immigrants struggling with their identity in a new dominant culture may learn to live between cultures. In order to do so, they will need to gain an understanding of both cultures in order to exist in the tension between them. Christian migrants are to identify with the movement of God, and their deeper identification as God's holy nation allows them to cling to an identity beyond homeland or foreign cities. The space from which they engage in ministry between cultures is based on them establishing their identity in God. As Christian migrants grapple with the tension between homeland, the new host culture, and their heavenly citizenship, an important role for Christian leaders with experience moving between cultures should be to help Christian leaders migrating to Western cities to move through their transition with sensitivity. With help, Christians settling in a new city can transition to affective ministry in the host culture. Missionaries who have returned from overseas service are ideal candidates for equipping diaspora peoples for ministry with a pilgrim identity, because the missionary herself has also moved through these same transitions. "By embracing the marginality of transition, the missionary is prepared to more fully identify with the example of Jesus Christ." Once someone has lived on the margins outside of a dominant culture, he or she is in a stronger position to serve those in diaspora communities with the journey of transitioning from their home culture to another cultural world. Those who have never experienced marginality face a much greater challenge to relate across cultural boundaries. However, "those in mission must keep in mind the continual thread throughout the Bible." We are all strangers and aliens. Each of our identities as Christians is not entirely different from the immigrant (Dean, March 22, 2014). Learning from immigrants and embracing our pilgrim identity will help us share a missionary identity. While the Western church can help immigrants adjust to their new surroundings, these same immigrants may become our teachers in leading us to recall our own identity as pilgrims, as foreigners and aliens, and as citizens of heaven, even in our homeland.

Second-Generation Faith

In a discussion on evangelism among diaspora communities, it is important to take into account the dynamics of the second generation or children of international migrants. When I served as a youth evangelist at Impact Ministries in Houston's central city, our youth group was multiethnic, multicultural, and bilingual. It was a bilingual church that met as two congregations—one in English and one in Spanish—and these two groups came together once a month for a united bilingual worship assembly. Bilingual assemblies were long and sometimes complicated, but they were symbolic for a church that desired to serve and worship together as a community unified across language and culture. Among the Hispanic youth, some were most comfortable worshipping with their families in Spanish. Usually these were teenagers who had been born outside of the United States and migrated to Houston as older children or teens. Others, however, preferred to connect with the English fellowship. Still, there were others who seemed equally comfortable in either setting.

Years later, I was invited into the home of a Dominican family in New York City where we were to start a Bible study. A group of middle-aged women gathered with open Bibles prepared to talk about God and faith and truth. They invited their teenage and twentysomething family members to join in, but the teenage daughter of the host would quietly but politely slip out during the study. One of our college interns explored her interest in learning the Christian faith, and the young woman explained that she found the discussions quite boring. We then decided on an experiment. We obtained a DVD of the movie The Gospel of John, and we played it in English with Spanish subtitles. Each week we played a different section as we worked through John's Gospel, and vibrant discussions began to emerge. Jesus's antiestablishment boldness and his gentle grace began to soften the hearts and captivate the imaginations of our small group of seekers. Discussions were vibrant, but use of language was fluid. We would switch back and forth with ease between Spanish and English, and it seemed quite natural to do so. It was not a carefully crafted multilingual meeting, but it carried on with the natural back-and-forth exchanges of Spanish and English as the two generations interacted with the Word of God, with us, and with one another because this was the natural lingual flow of their household. The fluid movement between languages was almost as though we were meeting in a third language, but it was really just the hybrid nature of an intergenerational discussion.

When I moved to New York City, I began thinking of the city in terms of layers of cultural change as well as resistance to that change. New immigrants are constantly entering the city and bringing their cultures with them. Each individual ethnic group adapts to the dominant American culture at a different pace and to varying degrees. While some preserve the culture and customs of their homelands, others seek to assimilate and blend into dominant society. While there will remain a spectrum of different patterns of adaptation among first-generation immigrants, second- or third-generation immigrants may create hybrid cultures as they live between their parents' heritage and what is perceived as mainstream society. Change does not happen first thing out of the womb. "The timeframe for assimilation extends across generations" (Scott, 2001, p. 312).

Serving diaspora communities and conceptualizing strategies for missionary engagement, these communities should be seen within the framework of a continuum of assimilation. The preservation of a home culture and transplanted customs, tensions between generations, the emergence of new hybrid cultures are all possibilities along the continuum. In addition, transnationalism keeps the flow of cultural concepts and symbols flowing both directions. Diaspora communities may influence life in their countries of origin, and keeping strong connections with their homeland encourages a more resilient cultural identity.

"A prime motivation for immigrants to found religious organizations is to pass on their heritage to their children"; however, despite these efforts at preserving a cultural and religious heritage, many children of immigrants often become disoriented with the traditions of the parents' country of origin (Warner & Wittner, 1998, p. 25). Naturally, new immigrants desire to pass on their values, faith, and way of life to the next generation, and at times this presents a real challenge for migrant communities as they begin to realize they live under the same roof with members of the dominant culture. One of the key concerns or questions for the first generation is "concerning the maintenance, modification, or discarding of religious practices among the subsequent generations born and raised in post-migration settings" (Vertovec, 2009, p. 139). For migrant parents, they often resettle in a new city with the hope that their children will progress further than they did, but ironically it is this same journey that may result in a sense of loss as they watch their children grow up in a very different world with strangely different values. As immigrant families build a life in the city, a cultural difference often sets in between generations. The children and grandchildren of first-generation immigrants often experience tension as they absorb a greater amount of influence from the dominant culture of the host country (Claydon, 2004, p. 14). However, while rapid assimilation may take place in smaller cities where diaspora communities are a clear minority, in cities like Vancouver, San Francisco, London, or Toronto populated with a dizzying number of diverse cultures and ethnic enclaves and a high degree of global connectivity, the cultural issues of the second generation in immigrant communities may be quite dynamic. "The contemporary second generation does not feel undue pressure to reject the languages, beliefs, and behaviors of its immigrant's forebears. Nor do its members feel the need to cling to them to keep the dangers of assimilation at bay" (Kasinitz, Mollenkopf, Waters, & Holdaway, 2008, p. 357). The ability to move fluidly between ethnic enclaves and a multiethnic dominant culture strengthens their bicultural identity.

Daniel Rodriguez spent five years studying church trends among second-generation Latinos, and he discovered new churches emerging that may, in general, represent a new but growing expression of the Christian church in American cities. He spoke with a number of church leaders of Spanish-speaking churches serving first-generation immigrants who were wrestling with how to connect with the second and third generations. However, he also discovered a number of churches that were both Latino- and English-speaking. He found that many second-generation Latinos did not feel welcome in the English-speaking churches of the dominant North American culture nor did they feel completely at home to continue serving in the Spanish-speaking congregations of their parents or grandparents. As a result, he discovered a number of churches that were English-speaking, led by Latino pastors, that could be categorized as culturally Latino and sometimes becoming multiethnic through the churches' outreach as well as intermarriage by the Latino members (See: Rodriguez, 2011).

Sharon Kim, addressing second-generation Korean churches, argues that these congregations "are not mere way stations en route to assimilation. Rather, they operate as spaces of creativity and hybridity and play a central role in the invention of new identities." She insists that second- generation Korean Americans are neither finding themselves at home in mainstream churches nor are they staying with the churches their parents started. "Rather, they are charting out an entirely new path, by creating and inhabiting an innovative, self-constructed third space" (S. Kim, 2010, p. 12). It's not my intention in this book to dive into the theological and cultural nuances of addressing second-generation immigrant churches. However, if we are going to take seriously the tasks that flow out of a diaspora missiology, the issues, opportunities, and challenges involving the children of immigrants must be in the minds of urban evangelists. If for no other reason, it will be an issue for the churches that are started among diaspora communities as the children of the first generation grow up between cultures. This space between cultures may perhaps form common ground for diaspora congregations and established churches of the host culture to partner with common interests in order to help assist second-generation leaders creatively pioneer new ministry initiatives. To some degree, assimilation may play a part, but a more common phenomenon seems to be cultural hybrids that neither represent the dominant Western church culture nor the churches planted by their parents. However, as these second-generation communities live between worlds, they may represent a potential missionary bridge in an age of globalization.

Conclusion

The Western church in the shadow of an emerging post-Christendom is, at times, conflicted when it comes to the concept and practice of evangelism. At the same time, one of the greatest evangelistic opportunities is unfolding in cities in North America and Europe as well as elsewhere around the world. It is truly imperative for the church to embrace her identity as a missionary community as she encounters global networks in increasingly diverse metropolitan areas.

For missiologists and evangelistic practitioners wrestling with the opportunities and challenges of diaspora missiology, adaptation will be a key skill for ministry in our urban and global world. Cultural differences emerging within multigenerational families, differences in time and religious rhythms, the challenges of pluralism in urban contexts, and migrants' relationships to the global marketplace will all provide challenges that were unseen by many in previous generations. Nevertheless, these challenges also represent new opportunities as Christian leaders and churches are forced to become more adaptive creatures. People living between worlds become bridges for faith across once distant places, and with Christians from around the world constantly on the move, regions where the church has grown lethargic share a constant potential for new members to breathe fresh perspectives and enthusiasm into their communities of faith. Missionary engagement is no longer simply a local endeavor but reflects opportunities to share the Gospel locally and globally through the same urban space. In a time when unreached peoples from a number of majority-world nations are settling in Western cities where the church can openly evangelize with few restrictions, the fields of the city are ripe for harvest.

Reflection Questions

1. When you think of evangelism, what comes to mind?
2. To what ethnic groups in your city do you feel most drawn?
3. Does your city host ethnic groups or communities that remain unengaged by the Gospel?
4. What could your church do to help start evangelistic church planting among an unreached people group in your city or region?

Chapter 6

Transnationalism and the Gospel: Mission Without Borders

In New York City there is a small Christian congregation that meets in an apartment rented for Bible classes, worship, and fellowship. When the church began meeting together, they encountered two men who were in need of help, and the church met the challenge of serving them and explaining to them the message of Jesus Christ. This small church provided for their physical needs, taught them the Gospel, and eventually baptized them. Eventually, one of the men was deported back to his home country of El Salvador, and following his return to his homeland, he started a church. The other brother grew tired of navigating the American economy, culture, and immigration laws and eventually chose to return home to the Dominican Republic ...where he also now leads a church.

By typical church-growth standards, this small Spanish-speaking church wouldn't make any headlines in Christian publications. Meeting in Spanish in an urban apartment building, they seldom gather more than 20 people on a given Sunday, so it is unlikely that their bivocational minister will be asked to speak on the stage of any Christian conferences or be invited to any leadership think tanks. Nevertheless, this church has reproduced two leaders of two churches in two different countries, and it has done so primarily by lovingly making disciples in a global city where migrants from around the world regularly come and go. This story repeats itself over and over in international cities where migrants move in and out of the city, and some have the fortune of encountering Jesus during their time in the city and becoming his disciple before moving on to life's next season and destination. Diaspora communities in cities represent an emerging mission field where local and global overlap. These communities represent pathways for evangelism that are multidirectional—within the city, to the migrant's homeland, and to new destinations beyond both the city and their homeland. As international migrants live between cultures and nations, the flows of transnationalism raise new possibilities, generate new questions, and add new dimensions to old tensions within missiology.

People and Place

As the world becomes more interconnected, even the smallest cities feel the impact of globalization and international migration. Ironically, even as technology and mobility supporting the advancement of globalization allow for increased opportunities for individuals to telecommute from remote locations, businesses to move out of an urban core to more suburban locations, and instantaneous communications to take place over vast distances, the strategic nature of place—specifically urban areas—are actually of even greater importance for world missions. When technology opened the door for communication and interpersonal exchanges to take place across wide geographic divides, it was tempting to assume that the importance of cities as centers of commerce and human activity would begin to fade into the background, but it appears that civilization has gone quite the opposite direction, with cities being more important than ever. Despite a degree of decentralization, cities play an increasingly important role in the global economy and, therefore, persist as major drivers in human activity. In an age of globalization, cities continue to play a key role in human interactions as nodes in the global network. Metropolitan areas are centers of influence, and as international ports, they support migration, commerce, and sharing of culture. The way we do ministry may now involve an intersection of local and global dynamics, and where we encounter the intersection of global and local is most often in cities.

As the world undergoes major structural changes through globalization, urbanization, international migration, and a number of other contemporary factors, missiologists are challenged to react to these changes with careful cultural and theological reflection while ministry practitioners experience the full weight of these societal shifts at the local level—whether or not they fully grasp what is swirling around them. Naturally, it should be expected that large societal shifts will have a significant impact on missiological theory and practice. Diaspora missiology may not only represent simply a ministry to migrants but may actually reflect the embodiment of a global mission field experiencing a contextual transformation as the world becomes an increasingly mobile and interconnected place. International migration is one of the most tangible expressions of globalization that is playing out in an overhaul of local communities worldwide. These cultural and demographic shifts will continue to make an impact on missiological theory and practice.

In the study and practice of world missions, there is often a strategic tension between people and place. During the last few decades, a great deal of emphasis has been focused on identifying and reaching specific people groups. The Joshua Project provides a valuable resource for profiling specific people groups that are considered unreached due to a lack of indigenous Christian witness within that population segment. A number of missionary agencies are now focused on targeting specific people groups, and some churches decide to adopt a specific people group, orienting their prayer emphasis and giving activities around that focus. As missionaries carry out this singular emphasis, they are able to contextualize evangelism, church planting, and leadership development for their adopted people. This focus on people groups is helpful in many respects. It raises our awareness to literally thousands of ethnic clusters that have not had any contact with the Gospel of Jesus Christ, and it encourages missionary practitioners to contextualize Gospel communication and church-planting practices to reach otherwise unengaged populations. This focus on specific cultural groups has made real contributions to the advance of the Gospel in the majority world. Numerous church-planting movements have emerged in recent decades throughout the majority world with testimonies emerging of real life transformation, and these Gospel movements usually find their momentum as they spread through a particular cultural group. Of course, there is a temptation for this focus on targeting the unreached to slide into a strategic accomplishment where our strategies reign supreme and we risk depersonalizing unreached people as an evangelistic target (Escobar, 2003, p. 156). In order for intentional evangelism among the least-reached peoples in the world to remain rooted in Christ, it must remain a relational endeavor. Evangelism among the unreached must be motivated by the love of God in the life of the missionary and not driven merely by "decisions" to report to institutional authorities and donors.

Other missionary practitioners focus on a given location. They are sensitive to the Gospel's call to love our neighbors, and many focus their ministry on becoming an incarnational expression of the Gospel in a specific neighborhood or region. With more of a parish approach to caring for their neighbors, they cast a wide net focused on a local community and see themselves as servants to a neighborhood or city. They seek to bring salvation and justice to a given population area, and they are concerned with the systemic injustices affecting the lives of people in their community. While targeting a specific city or neighborhood, missionary workers focus on bringing the shalom of God to their community through evangelism, development, relief, and/ or justice ministries. Naturally, urban missiology has emphasized place due to its inherent interest in the context of the city and its impact on urban dwellers. Urban missiology often seeks to bring both evangelism to the lost of the city and works of justice to the poor and marginalized trapped in the systemic injustices of the city. The urban ecology is of great importance to community workers focused on developing a specific neighborhood or section of the city. Therefore, for urban ministers an emphasis on caring for the people living in specific urban space may trump the potential focus on a population segment. This emphasis has advanced the ministry of the church especially during times of urban flight, and urban missiologists have often been key pioneers for global mission during an era of increasing urbanization.

I suggest that contemporary shifts in urban and global reality actually point to the need for a more dynamic relationship in our understanding of both people and place. Those concerned with the transformation of the city and those focused on evangelizing unreached people groups may be standing on common ground in the city. Cities are the crucial hubs of contact with ethnic groups from around the world. Cities are now nodes in a global network. As such, they are the spatial links between people groups interconnected across vast distances. Cities are becoming hubs of global activity and influence in a highly connected world (Clark, 2003, pp. 12-13). Therefore, ministry in urban communities is increasingly important not only for local neighborhood ministry or for an evangelistic movement in a city but also for its increasingly coherent connection to global missions and evangelizing the unreached. Through urban space, the binary emphasis placed on either a people or a place intersects and mingles in new ways in the new global economy. In cities, local and global impact may overlap in both major and minor ways. Being attentive to the work of the Holy Spirit in urban centers leads to an even greater strategic emphasis than any previous focus of targeting cities for their own sake.

Simultaneously, the need to focus on specific people groups with contextualized strategies and evangelistic practices continues to be crucial for the expansion of world mission into populations otherwise untouched by the Gospel. Without intentionality, it is likely that entire people groups may be overlooked despite our best of intentions and noble missionary endeavors. However, with the mobility of people groups around the world, strategies for engaging specific groups must begin to reflect this mobility as well as the interconnectedness of migrants, their diaspora communities, their countries of origin, along with the dynamic part played by urban nodes that emerge as powerful centers in a web of relationships. The homelands of many unreached people groups are located in the midst of geopolitical space that makes evangelistic access to them extremely challenging. Much energy goes into building creative access platforms to gain access to these people groups, but many of these groups have extensions through diaspora communities living in Western cities in Europe and North America as well as global cities in South America, Australia, and Asia. Evangelizing unreached people groups, reasserts the importance of cities as many of these people groups occupy urban space maintaining diaspora networks linking once-distant cities in newly formed connections. One of the key connections formed between majority-world cities and cities in the United States, Canada, and Europe is developed through the relational connections of diaspora peoples. The missiological emphasis on targeting specific ethnic groups with contextualized church planting has not diminished the importance of the city as place; rather urban space plays a more critical role than ever. Cities are now urban nodes in the global network where grassroots connections link local and global expressions of human interactions.

Often immigration chains result in new ethnic associations established as cultural networks in the city. Associations provide an avenue for adaptation from life in a traditional society or village to making the adjustment to the context of the city. These associations often represent a dynamic fleshing out of globalization. In an ethnic association, migrants know the cultural "rules." They can be comfortable in an environment where they know the language, custom, and culture of those sharing membership in the association. While ethnic associations provide a cultural safe haven for many immigrants adjusting to a foreign society, they also provide a resource for transitioning to the host culture as more experienced members of the diaspora community share their insights on living in a city that was once foreign to them as well. Missionaries may have an opportunity to share the Gospel with specific ethnic groups by developing relationships with these associations (Rynkiewich, 2011, pp. 224-225). I've worked with ministry partners in our city that have developed relationships with ethnic associations, and as a result, these relationships have opened opportunities for sharing the Gospel with the leaders of the association or even teaching Bible stories or English classes in an Islamic association or neighborhood mosque. At times, missionaries in the city have been able to set up a table for sharing the Gospel message at ethnic festivals or take the opportunity to proclaim the Gospel of grace through foreign media.

While some may join an ethnic association, other migrants utilize or create networks in the city. "A social network is not a group, but rather a series of links between people that a person may use to mobilize small groups, gather information, or obtain resources." The makeup of networks will vary from person to person, and a network may be made up of people that know each other well, or it could be a scattered collection of social connections that have very little relationship with one another. A network is essentially a web of social resources connected to an individual (Rynkiewich, 2011, p. 225). Some years ago, I was meeting with a young man who had been participating in one of our churches. He was an Albanian from Kosovo, had worked in New England until his visa expired, and then relocated to New York City where he could more easily secure work through his network of ethnic connections. Around this time, the economy had taken a drastic downturn and was beginning to be labeled "The Great Recession." Yet he seemed to have little problem finding a job. If one job didn't pay well enough or offer sufficient work hours, he seemed to find a new one almost instantly. Personally, I was amazed at the frequency with which he could switch from one job to another when the former one didn't quite meet his needs. I knew plenty of people in the city struggling to find work. However, he would utilize the ethnic network already established among his Albanian peers. He came to New York City, at least in part, because developing a network was possible. He had worked for awhile in Cape Cod, but when his visa ran out, he came to New York City where he knew his ethnic connections would likely sustain him while he worked on his permanent residency. When looking for work, he would simply visit Italian restaurants—with many now being managed or owned by Albanians—and seek work as a waiter. Some upscale Italian restaurants in New York City pay quite well in tips, so these opportunities can be quite prosperous. The Albanian-speaking community gave him priority simply because he was a member of their diaspora. He didn't belong to any ethnic associations in the city, nor did he participate in a church or mosque of his ethnic heritage. (Our house church was completely multiethnic, and he was the only Albanian-speaking member.) However, he understood how to use the natural connections of his diaspora community. If a church learns to tap into these types of networks with the influence of the Gospel, the potential impact could be quite profound.

Diaspora communities certainly make an impact on the cultural fabric of the city, and the city indeed impacts the lives and cultural rhythms of diaspora communities. In addition, diaspora communities often contribute to the ongoing shaping of the culture of their homeland both through physical remittances as well as transmitting cultural change. In some cases, migrants to Europe and North America emerge as leaders among their people. They are pioneers and entrepreneurs, so there is an opportunity, at least for some, for their status to increase among their ethnic connections specifically due to their participation as a member of the diaspora.

Evangelism and church planting in global urban settings will inevitably require evangelists to become students of culture, while concurrently realizing the impact of the city on their people group. If evangelists do not target specific people groups in the city with contextualized strategies, significant ethnic and cultural communities in the city will be neglected. Evangelists that do not take into account the impact of urbanization and globalization on the life and culture of a people group living in a local community may very well fail to effectively contextualize their mission strategies. Emphases on people and place find common ground in the new global city. In the urban arena of diverse subcultures, many diaspora communities and emerging hybrid cultures will need intentional evangelistic contextualization among them in order to sensitively address the specific needs, challenges, and opportunities within that cultural community. This is not an either-or scenario. Many multiethnic churches will need to be planted as well. However, to assume that every subculture can become immersed in the Gospel through a general outreach to a perceived urban monoculture misses the unique cultural experiences, worldviews, and sometimes relative exclusivity—even with an international city—of a particular ethnic community. Cities are mosaics of subcultures, and some groups are culturally distant from the mainstream voice of the dominant society. Simultaneously, many transnational migrants grow in leadership and influence among a global ethnic group due to their role and function on the global stage for their kinship circles back home. The need for intentional contextualization among ethnic cultures and language groups will persist, likely to varying degrees, among different people groups, and the strategic importance of cities for evangelism among these people groups is increasingly important. In an emerging transnational society, the tension for missionaries between focusing on a people or focusing on a place may in fact be forming a symbiotic and dynamic unity through the increasing strategic importance of cities for world mission. It is not difficult to imagine how ministries specializing in compassion ministries, community development, evangelism, or church planting could find common ground for partnering together as they share the same urban space.

Missiologists are now forced to engage the mobility and fluid patterns of people groups and their impact on cities as centers of international interaction and connectivity. Today, 1 out of every 35 people on the planet is a migrant. More than 60% of these sojourners are relocating to developed countries, and despite the associated political tensions with various foreign policies, the United States is the leading host country receiving more immigrants than all other host nations (Kalu, et al., 2010, pp. 71-72). Perhaps ironically, it may be that significant strides in global missions in the majority world may be possible by looking to cities in the United States. Current patterns of migration are having a transformational impact on a global scale. "Today immigrants not only move back and forth between societies but maintain social relationships and networks that transcend borders. Rather than moving out of an old society and into a new one, they participate simultaneously in several arenas located in several parts of the world" (Lessinger, 1995, pp. 87-88). Ministry to ethnic diasporas is no longer simply working among a gradually assimilating ethnic enclave. Rather ministry among diasporas has become ministry at the intersection of global and local as migrants maintain relational networks that transcend political boundaries and customs checkpoints. A struggling migrant living in cities in the United States is often more of a global citizen than his American peers living across the street. For Christians living in increasingly diverse cities, much of their ministry will be cross-cultural. Indeed we are all missionaries now.

There is certainly a continuous need to send missionaries to remote places on the planet to share the Gospel with unreached people groups. However, new strategies need to be considered for engaging unreached peoples. My friend "Bob" explains that he has done more pioneering work as a missionary to West African Muslims in New York City than he did when he lived in a town in West Africa. While living in his African neighborhood, he didn't have access to any of the leaders of that community. He didn't know a single homeowner, but when he came to New York City and sought out the same ethnic group, he met a number of homeowners from his former neighborhood in West Africa on the streets of Manhattan and the South Bronx. While they are employed near the bottom of the economic "food chain" in New York

City, they are becoming big people in their society back home. Conducting their business from across an ocean, they are now the "big papas" and "big mamas" for their home communities and kinship networks. Since coming to New York, Bob has traveled back to his old neighborhood in West Africa and stayed as a guest in the very homes that previously had afforded him no access. He has been able to share the Gospel with families in West Africa through his relationship with the heads of households who are living and working in the United States. The access that he lacked as a missionary living in a town in the country of origin for this people group, he has now gained by moving to New York City and working among the diaspora community there. Doors that were closed to him have now opened. In order to evangelize an unreached people group in West African, he had to move to New York City.

Many within this ethnic diaspora have emerged as leaders for their community. They send home remittances, build houses for their families in their country of origin, and gain status among their peers in their homeland. By networking among them, Bob has closed the gap for proclaiming the Gospel despite the perceived gap in physical distance between his home in the city and the people for whom he is pioneering to reach with the Gospel of Christ. The potential for reaching many of the most unreached nations in the world may lie within learning to serve the corresponding diaspora communities. Many of these communities are within cities that serve as global hubs, and these urban nodes are of great strategic importance for the evangelistic work of global mission.

Global Nomads: Understanding Transnationalism

Migration is not a new phenomenon. People have been moving from place to place as early as there have been human settlements. The story of our salvation history begins with Abram following God's call to migrate. Jacob escapes Esau to another region. Joseph is taken in captivity to another kingdom and rises to power within that government. The nations of Israel and Judah are taken into exile, and Daniel rises to prominence and serves as a witness for God to foreign kings. The story of the Gospel begins with Jesus's flight as an infant political refugee, and the early church spreads and grows along the waterways and Roman roads of the Empire as Jews and Gentiles alike are tossed to and fro by economic and political forces. The story of God's people in the Bible is a story of migration, relocation, and adaptation. It is the story of our salvation and our humanity. However unique each journey may be, the story of the immigrant is not a new tale.

For Americans, our folklore is enveloped by the story of migrations —both voluntary and forced. Our national narrative has highlighted the journey of religious refugees arriving in a new land for a new beginning. Each November, families in the United States travel for the Thanksgiving holiday, causing the Wednesday before to become the most traveled day of the year. Sitting around a table to a family feast at least loosely commemorates a story of migration and settlement embodying a type of American quasi-Passover. While the actual history is a complex mix of both righteousness and greed, the story of migration is deeply ingrained in the American myth. The migration story of the dominant culture is mingled with themes of forced resettlement of African slaves, Irish bondservants, dislocated Native tribes, Asian railroad workers, and other perhaps lesser known journeys. Far from the romanticism of the Mayflower, the marginalized and oppressed subcultures of this country's history reflect stories of long and often painful journeys. From nearly every perspective—whether Europeans fleeing religious persecution, Irish settlers escaping economic or political hardship, Conquistadors conquering ancient kingdoms, the cruel journeys of African slave ships, or Natives exiled to reservations—the mythic vision of American history is one of migration. Journeys have defined the nation both in the mainstream folklore and in the narratives of the marginalized. It should be no surprise that the transformation of contemporary North American cities is now also being driven, in large part, by international migration. The resistance to welcoming newcomers to American shores (or border crossings or airports) is ironic at best considering the mythic history of the United States.

Throughout generations, migration has most often signified a new beginning. It's meant dislocating from the land and people that have been home and starting over in a new season to build a new life in a new place. Being an immigrant meant leaving everything one once knew and afterwards arriving in a strange new land having very little connection to the home that was left behind. Immigration was a starting over with all of the challenges that such a new beginning entails. It's not that there weren't ties back to one's homeland, but those connections were strained by distance, enculturation, and the natural passing of time. Maintaining ongoing connections may have been through letters, infrequent visits, and eventually the occasional and quite expensive long-distance phone calls. Indeed, ". . . long-distance connections maintained by migrants 100 years ago were not truly 'transnational'—in terms of one contemporary sense of regular and sustained social contact; rather, such earlier links were just border-crossing migrant networks that were maintained in sporadic fashion as best as migrants at that time could manage" (Vertovec, 2009, p. 16). However, in the last few decades, the nature of migration has been radically altered. Some have insisted that migrants may be thought of less as immigrants who come and build a new life, but instead be thought of as "transmigrants" because even as they cross an ocean they are bringing much of their home with them. They live "in between Home and home" (Garcia-Johnson, 2012, p.116).

For generations, migrants have strived for maintaining connections to relationships and culture despite the formidable challenges to do so. Immigration patterns have often involved developing networks in order to facilitate an immigration chain for family members to follow behind the first of their kinship group to settle in a new country, and there certainly have been migrants that returned to their country of origin or made trips back and forth between their host country and homeland. Letter writing has often kept family and friends connected across borders between different countries, and it's often a common practice for immigrants to send money home for a project in the community or to provide ongoing support for family members to whatever degree possible. It has not been uncommon for immigrant-owned businesses, ethnic associations, religious institutions, or political alliances to form as embodied expressions of the culture of origin in the new city where they have settled. Such patterns are not new (Vertovec, 2009, p. 14). The basic motivations and desires of individuals who have taken the journey of immigration remain consistent.

However, now the experience of immigration is being transformed due to the emergence of a strong and persistent transnationalism. The essential desires of migrants has remain unchanged, but now their ability to actually meet those desires to a much larger degree and greatly increase sustained activity and connections within their culture and kinship network is causing a metamorphosis in immigration activities. "Enhanced transnational connections between social groups represent a key manifestation of globalization" (Vertovec, 2009, p. 2). Immigrants no longer wait for days or weeks for letters to arrive from their distant relatives. These connections can take place at the push of button. Internet, inexpensive calling cards, e-mail, satellite television, Skype, wire transfers, cell phones, and various other forms of modern communication technology have made connectivity around the globe practically instantaneous. These tools create natural links narrowing the gaps of geographic distance. The rate of exchange of communication and information makes possible consistent transnational connections where distance was once a barrier to maintaining significant dialogue and cultural exchange. Recently, I was attempting to communicate with an Indian evangelist while he was visiting California, but his Internet connection in California made our attempt at a conversation on Skype challenging, with the call frequently dropping. Frustrated, he made the comment that he would call me when he returns to India because his

Internet connection is much stronger there, and it was indeed easier to talk when he returned home. The infrastructure supporting transnational communication is being constructed in nearly every corner of the globe, connecting regional and global centers in a worldwide web of human interactions and exchanges that can take place almost instantaneously.

Cheaper modes of transportation connecting virtually every nation in the world have made the planet a much more mobile place, and this mobility has shortened the distance between host cultures and countries of origin. As a result, new migrants adapting to a host culture are now impacting life in their countries of origin to a degree unimaginable in the past, and immigrants have an increased ability to maintain cultural ties and interactions to an extent that was previously impossible. Formerly, the most significant impact on the sending society was likely not much more than the absence of the migrants that left home, job, and family, but now cultural and economic exchanges flow freely between once distant places. In fact, cycles of immigration in urban centers appear to be advancing the need for migrant entrepreneurs to maintain transnational connections between ethnic communities and countries of origin. Complete assimilation of ethnic entrepreneurs operating within diaspora networks can even become counter-productive. Maintaining transnational ties and cultural practices in a diaspora community is fundamental to the economic life of some entrepreneurial efforts. As transnational activities feed the lives of some businesses, those businesses have it in their best interest to keep channels of transnational activity open and freely flowing. Mark Abrahamson explains:

> Several studies indicate that it has become commonplace for foreign minorities living in global cities to utilize their connections to their countries of origin as a means of adapting in the countries that received them. In many nations, this involves transnational entrepreneurs whose businesses depend on the desires of co-ethnics to have cultural goods from their countries of origin (newspapers,

compact discs, foodstuffs, clothing, and so on). To be successful, the owners must maintain their networks and contacts in their countries of origin. Furthermore, these transnational entrepreneurs tend to experience upward mobility; thus, not assimilating is an effective way for them to adapt to a new economy. (Abrahamson, 2004, p. 63)

Remittances have become a major economic force with more than $300 billion being moved around the globe each year. Today, the Philippines, Egypt, and most of Central America lean heavily on remittances to sustain their national economies. It is now possible for members of diaspora communities to remain engaged in homeland politics, associations, religious organizations, or activism while diaspora associations in the host country are contributing unprecedented financial resources for projects in their homeland. Many nation-states are even developing programs for reaching out to emigrants living abroad. Indeed it is in their own national interests to do so (Vertovec, 2009, pp. 14-16). For example, in 2002 remittances became the third greatest source of revenue in the Mexican economy, and government programs even began to match remittances for specific development projects (Abrahamson, 2004, pp. 52-53). Transnationalism as a global reality creates a virtual space where the immigrant not only maintains cultural influence from her country of origin but also may contribute to forming new hybrids and expressions in the culture of her homeland as she adopts aspects of her host culture and translates those adaptations through transnational exchanges. As globalization has not resulted in a neatly ordered world, transnationalism has not led to a single social expression or activity. The variety of activities are unfolding with varying degrees and scope across a globally interconnected network of individuals, communities, religious bodies, and institutions (Vertovec, 2009). There is not a single narrative through which to explain transnationalism, but there are a large number of storylines unfolding under the canopy of globalization.

The speed, scope, and mobility of transnational connections and sustained global activity is transforming not only immigration but also the lifestyles of countless millions both interacting with and propelled by the forces of globalization. Migrant subcultures are not only impacted by the use of communication technology allowing them to maintain connections between different nations, but the transportation technology is leading to an increased mobility on a global scale. "Spurred by globalization's marginalization of third-world economies and sophisticated developments in communication and transport technology, more and more people today move from place to place at an increasingly faster pace" (Kalu, et al., 2010, p. 71). We live in a more mobile society than ever before. Missions strategies that assume people will remain static in a single location for extended periods of time may be shortsighted. People are constantly on the move, and missiological practices ought to take this new phenomenon into account. Oscar Garcia-Johnson declares "that a new transnational situation unveils a new ecclesial skin, a new type of Christian community, the glocal church." The impact of transnationalism in a global world may require a "recategorization" around our common assumptions of community and mission (Garcia-Johnson, 2012, pp. 118-123).

Traditional concepts of immigration, adaptation, and settlement are being turned on their heads. "Transnationality challenges us to go beyond modern anthropological tendencies that seek to universalize and homogenize cultural existence. Modern anthropology offers two dysfunctional extremes for immigrants to construct cultural identity: assimilation and essentialism" (Garcia-Johnson, 2012, p. 123). However, today migrants are capable of living between the extremes and bypass binary cultural options for a transnational existence. In one sense, technology is simply a tool that is extending preexisting social patterns, and simultaneously, the growth of transnational interactions through global networks is transforming these relationships (Vertovec, 2009, pp. 4-5). Contemporary advances in communication and transportation are allowing the basic desires of migrants to be realized in a way not possible in previous centuries. "Today immigrants not only move back and forth between societies but maintain social relationships and networks that transcend borders. Rather than moving out of an old society and into a new one, they participate simultaneously in several arenas located in several parts of the world" (Lessinger, 1995, pp. 87-88). Many migrants "live in constant flux." They are living between worlds and existing in the tension between differing identities (Garcia-Johnson, 2012, p. 121). Migrants today are truly global citizens maintaining relationships and activities where time and space were once virtually impassable barriers. There is little doubt that such enormous shifts in global society will be felt in missiological theory and practice. How does it impact missionary strategy when many of the heads of households from an African city live in Atlanta, Paris, or Montreal? As diaspora communities create currents of cultural exchange between homeland and host countries that are both rapid and mutual, how does this affect contextualization for missionary church planting? How does it affect the strategy for reaching a people group if nearly as many of their population live outside of the country of origin as those who live in it? How do missionary strategies adapt when church planters discover that many of the most influential people and leaders in a community are living outside the country, participating in a diaspora network and influencing community affairs from afar? How do we reshape evangelism when individuals gain influence in their cultural networks precisely because they have migrated to a global city? What if creative access really means transmitting the Gospel through natural transnational relationships from outside of the intended geographic field of evangelism? These are not questions for missiologists to consider in some moment down the road. These are not futurist predictions but represent current global trends. These are questions that must be considered now. They reflect our present-future.

As cities emerge as strategic centers in a global network of connectivity through technology, evangelism in urban space becomes increasingly important. In addition, if migrants to world-class cities are now some of the key shapers of their cultures of origin through the inevitable multidirectional flows of globalization, the importance of making disciples and developing leaders in these global cities is crucial to the advance of world mission. Many of the cultural gatekeepers are living outside of their countries of origin, and their residence in cities like New York City, Toronto, or London is often granting them increased influence among their own people living in their homeland. Furthermore, immigrant communities are often making an extraordinary impact on the culture of their host society as well. Therefore, it may be essential for missiologists and church leaders to recognize that a key demographic for world mission are the taxi drivers, shop keepers, students, dishwashers, diplomats, and entrepreneurs working countless hours in our cities. "Transnational families, networks, and communities ... strike at the heart of traditional missiological reflections on home, power, identity, and subjectivity." Transnational diaspora communities create space to embody "home" in the midst of fluid relationships and movements (Kalu, et al., 2010, p. 80). Diaspora communities function through networking. They exist as a web of relationships. In order to work effectively in this emerging social structure, missiologists will need to learn to work through relational networks in order to work effectively in and through diaspora communities (Claydon, 2004, p. 25). While the parish-oriented approach is likely still a relevant way of ministering to a local community area, especially for ministries working out of a physical space to serve a specific neighborhood regardless of demographic turnover in the area, missionaries who desire to bring the Gospel to the unreached must think in terms of networks and connections globally linked through urban space.

Many immigrants living in-between worlds embrace a transnational way of life. "Today's immigrants are afforded greater resources to maintain transnational identities or to forge multiple social networks, so that aspects of their daily lives and decision making are subject to distant influences and obligations" (Hanciles, 2008, p. 244).

I've often observed the persistence of such transnational connections. When a family member of my Liberian friend dies in West Africa, his family sets aside an evening to share in a time of mourning. They send home remittances to help with the funeral, and there is a set time when they make a call to Africa and through speakerphone sit and mourn with family members, despite an ocean standing between them. Traditional practices are not only unhindered by geographic distance but contemporary technology provides a virtual space for shared practice between distant locations. Old customs and kinship expectations are often maintained to some degree, but they also are transformed in virtual space. They are approximating shared rituals through modern advances in technology and maintaining connections to a degree that was unheard of in the experiences of previous immigrants and their families back home.

The realities of transnational identities are fluid and varied. Transnationalism is anything but monolithic. Some migrants identify primarily with their country of origin while others mainly identify with their host country, and some reject both the identities of their new land and that of their homeland, living in tension with both worlds. However, the majority identify with both their host culture and their homeland, giving shape to "co-existing identities" (Vertovec, 2009, pp. 141-142). Transnational identities are increasingly common and becoming the norm for many international migrants. For many, their daily lives are rooted in "the multi-stranded social relations, along family, economic, and political lines, that link together migrants' societies of origin and settlement" (Foner, 2001, p. 9). Most diaspora communities themselves reflect a nodal function in global networks. They are connected through a triangulation of relationships "between (1) a collectively self-identified ethnic group in one particular setting, (2) the group's co-ethnics in other parts of the world, and (3) the homeland states or local contexts whence they or their forebears came" (Vertovec, 2009, p. 133). Through technologies allowing this degree of connectivity to persist, migrant networks are no longer simply an ethnic community in a Western city maintaining connections to their homeland. Rather, migrants now living in diaspora networks may maintain relationships and interactions with local diaspora communities, people in their homeland, and with those of shared ethnic backgrounds living in other diasporas in other regions or countries. Ethnic neighborhoods and global cities are now geographic hubs in international relational networks that might link several nations and cities together through transnational interactions. Our new mission field is both local and global at the same time.

The importance for missiological study and practice to engage the processes of migration, the emergence of diaspora communities, and activities of transnationalism cannot be overstated. Migration not only impacts our local cultures but has an impact on religious life in cities in local communities and throughout the world (Kalu, et al., 2010, p. 77). Christians from French-speaking African nations living in New York City still call on French-speaking pastors in Africa to resolve problems, and Turkish Christians in the United States feel empowered by their newfound freedom of religion to begin ministering to Christian cells functioning back in Turkey (Kraus, March 22, 2014). Christians migrating from Nigeria plant churches in American cities and maintain affiliations with their denominations headquartered in Lagos. As a result, Nigerian leaders find themselves traveling between Lagos and Houston, Atlanta, or New York to provide support to new churches under the guidance of their denominations (Rynkiewich, 2013, p. 109). These affiliations are not merely rooted in geographic jurisdictions, but they are maintained through historical and cultural relationships. As a result, many diaspora churches are functioning with a much greater attentiveness to global events and trends and to international connections than their North American counterparts.

Simultaneously, embracing congregationalism allows immigrant churches to contextualize as transnational communities living between the ties with their religious and cultural home and contextualization and adaptation in the host culture. Through transnational migrants taking grassroots initiatives, many religious communities are increasingly developing forms of "self-organization." However, despite the rise in congregationalism among diaspora churches, often individual religious expressions, denominational structures in an ethnic group's homeland, and local diaspora expressions of faith are "deeply entangled" (Vertovec, 2009, p. 146). Many diaspora congregations maintain both local and international connections to distinct entities while often experiencing a degree of change themselves. Hybrids merging old and new may develop even as they remain connected to structures and leaders in their homeland while forging new ones in their local communities.

Transnationalism represents an inspiring potential stream for evangelism that challenges previous assumptions. For instance, there are 8 million Overseas Foreign Workers (OFWs) from the Philippines, and 7% of these migrant workers are evangelical. If all the Filipino Christian workers laboring overseas see themselves as missionaries and are equipped to make disciples and plant reproducible churches in their host countries, it would mean a "tent-making" missionary force of 560,000 Gospel witnesses. Filipino churches are reportedly appearing all over the world—even assembling on cruise ships (Claydon, 2004, p. 46). Many of these OFWs are employed as domestic workers in Saudi Arabia and throughout the Middle East. OFWs may be one of the most dynamic missionary forces in the global church today. Some missions organizations in the Philippines have recognized the opportunity to participate in God's mission through mobilizing this potential missionary force. They are coming alongside churches to provide predeparture training and support for Christian OFWs (Baxter, 2013, p. 121). It is likely that Filipino migrants remain off-the-radar of many Christian leaders in the United States as a missionary force, but they are in places where many Americans and Europeans simply cannot go. While Saudi Arabia and many Middle Eastern countries are some of the least accessible in the world, one strategy for evangelism among unreached people may be OFWs. What if missionaries hoping to bring the Gospel to Saudis actually located their ministry in the Philippines as one of the best possible Gospel bridges to Saudi Arabia? Or what if missionaries initiated networking among the Filipinos already on the move by reaching out to diaspora groups in Taiwan or Hong Kong, tapping into existing OFW networks? Launching a disciple-making movement among Filipinos and equipping OFWs with strategies for evangelism in closed countries may represent some of the greatest potential for sharing the Gospel in Saudi Arabia or other countries that are among the most closed to the Gospel and hardest to access by traditional Western missionaries. While many Americans in Saudi Arabia will often be closely monitored for illegal Christian activity, many Filipinos are domestic workers with unprecedented access to Saudi families. Missions strategies in our global society need to be creatively reconsidered for our mobile and internationally connected world.

Through transnational flows of influence, ideas, and capital, diaspora communities may have an influence on the religious structures, practices, and beliefs in their homelands (Vertovec, 2009, p. 134). In many cases, new immigrants are among the boldest members of their home communities. They are the ones who have demonstrated the courage to move beyond borders and endure the psychological complexities of culture shock and the logistical challenges of transitioning to a foreign culture with its strange rules and customs. As they send home remittances and elevate the economic and social status of their family members, many migrants see their influence rise as well. It is perhaps an irony of the journey of migration that by leaving their home transnational migrants may gain greater influence with their communities back home. Immigrants are living between worlds; they are no longer fully a part of their home culture nor fully a part of the host culture where they now live and work. However, as they become a source of capital for their kinship networks in their country of origin, they become shapers of their society, transcending geographic restraints. While we sometimes mourn the effects of global influences on indigenous cultures (and often rightly so), the reality of this global influence through media, travel, and interaction with diaspora communities appears to be an inevitable trend. A key question for the church is: Are we prepared to redeem these cultural shifts for the Gospel of the Kingdom? Globalization is impacting every corner of the planet, and it may well be that some of the key players in the ongoing transformation of cultural expressions, entrepreneurship, and local structures are these global nomads who have dislocated themselves from the country of their birth only to become influencers of that culture precisely because they relocated far away, laboring—sometimes on the brink of mere survival—in rich and powerful global cities rewarding them with symbolic status.

Global Evangelism: In the City and Through the City

I began my journey into a missionary vocation during my college years at Abilene Christian University. I was energized by the opportunity to make an impact in the city, and my heart was stirred for the city's poorest residents. As a college student, I often spent countless hours digesting unassigned readings that explained the world of the urban poor. I dove into urban and ethnic studies and learned all I could about evangelism in cities. I spent time serving in the inner-cities of Houston and Memphis and attempted to minister in the poorest neighborhoods of my college town as well. Stories of Viv Grigg, Bill Wilson, David Wilkerson, Ray Bakke, John Perkins, and so many others grabbed my attention, and I read or heard the vision for reaching the nations through evangelizing immigrants in our multicultural cities more times than I can remember. Yet I didn't see many examples of ministry that went beyond a local effort and translated into a transnational impact. Lots of people talked about reaching the nations through our cities, but I was eager to see practical examples. However, in the last decade or so, that's begun to change. The effects of globalization on how we do missions is beginning to emerge as missionaries pioneer evangelism strategies in global cities. As globalization gives birth to transnational networks, new missiological opportunities may, in fact, overshadow the challenges that accompany this phenomenon. Actually, these global trends will likely change much of the way we think about missions altogether.

A casual drive through neighborhoods in San Francisco, Miami, or Los Angeles makes it obvious that much of the church growth over the last decade may be attributed to the influx of Christians from the majority world. Church signs on storefronts may be in Spanish, Korean, Creole, or Chinese. Congregations spilling out into the streets following a Sunday assembly may be Ghanaian, Nigerian, Dominican, or Jamaican. With the increasing momentum of international immigration, ethnic churches dot the urban landscape of most of our cities and are expanding into suburban communities. "Migrants today arguably witness to new ways of being church and new ways of understanding and doing mission" (Kalu, et al., 2010, p. 83). We do not need to look far to discover the present-future church. The global church is just around the corner.

The impact of transnationalism on missiology is still unfolding. However, transnational missions raises the possibility of new strategies and missionary engagement along the currents of global networks. Evangelism among diaspora communities that allows the missionary to enter the global networks of an ethnic diaspora opens a new door for pioneer church planting. Indeed, engaging diaspora networks located in global urban centers may actually be shaping up to become the profile of pioneer church planting in the 21st century. Evangelism through transnational networks opens doors that might otherwise be closed due to geographic, political, or military barriers as evangelists are working through the natural flows of connectivity within ethnic and kinship networks. "Transnational missions is an integrated approach to missionary strategy. It is the recognition of the reality of international migration, the importance of social networks, and the use of travel and telecommunications to make disciples of all nations without geographical constraints" (Payne, 2012, p. 126).

Members of diaspora communities in developed nations are often seen with admiration by their peers back in their homelands. Their relative success gives them influence among the community they left behind. If migrants in diaspora networks become followers of Jesus, they have influence to carry the Gospel to those back home (Claydon, 2004, p. 19). In some cases, many of the members of an ethnic community are building retirement homes in their home countries. In reality, many migrants may never actually live in these homes themselves, but they are used by family members or utilized as investment properties. However, even if they never resettle in the houses they've built, these carry over as an economic symbol of the influence they are gaining in their homelands through transnational exchanges.

"Corey" moved to the Northeast United States in 2011 to participate in a one-year missionary apprenticeship. When he finished his year of training, he continued serving in the city for another two years. At the beginning of his internship, his team was encouraged to begin building evangelistic relationships with an unreached people group in the city, so they began reaching out to Wolof in a largely Senegalese community. The Wolof are an unreached people group from West Africa with a significant diaspora population rising in the United States. There are approximately 5 million Wolof in the world, and despite a number of missions efforts working among this ethnic group in West Africa, there are only about 200 followers of Christ worldwide.

Cory's team spent countless hours hitting the pavement of the city seeking to build relationships with Wolof people. Often they would spend two or three months reaching out to someone before coming to the conclusion that there was no receptivity in that individual. They reluctantly kept searching for people who would listen to the Gospel and invite them into meaningful relationships. Eventually, Corey met "Abdul." He helped Abdul pass his citizenship test, and they began meeting once per week for lunch. A friendship blossomed between them, and Corey was never shy about openly sharing the message of the

Gospel with his Muslim friend. Abdul, likewise, became his cultural informant, helping him learn about the culture and fall in love with the people of this largely unreached ethnic group. The bond between Abdul and Corey led to a transnational witness as well.

As their friendship grew, Abdul invited Corey to visit his home in Senegal, and Corey made this trip twice during the period of a couple of years. He went and had the opportunity to visit with Abdul's family, friends, and neighbors still living in West Africa. Abdul would tell people that Corey is a "good person," and this recommendation would open doors for him to speak with credibility and trust among Wolof in Senegal. Because he was never shy about his faith in Jesus Christ with Abdul, he was also able to speak openly about the Good News with others during his trips to Senegal. His friendship with an African in the United States led to the opportunity to openly plant many seeds of the Gospel among of the Wolof people in their home country.

When he had the opportunity to speak with American missionaries working in Senegal, they expressed to him how surprised they were at how quickly he and his team had been able to enter the homes of Wolof living in the United States. They were amazed at the level of access available in the diaspora community, and they explained how much more challenging it felt working within the homeland of the same people. In West Africa, they had to take the time to negotiate with the leader of the community in order to gain access, and it sometimes was a long and arduous process for the local missionaries. However, among Africans in the United States, Christian workers were able to spend time in the homes of these same people from West Africa with fewer barriers to sharing the Gospel of grace with their new Muslim friends. Furthermore, Corey's relationship with an African man in the diaspora community became a gateway for planting the seeds of the Gospel both in the United States and among this unreached people group in West Africa.

As Corey interacted with his friend's family and neighbors in Senegal, he openly shared the Gospel and prayed for people in need.

He was given credibility because of the relationship he had formed back in the United States that was now translating to access to relationships and ability to communicate the Gospel across an ocean. On his second trip, he was able to apply what he observed in his first trip and be creative in his evangelistic methods. He recognized that everyone owned cell phones, so on his return trip he brought with him several small 8GB chips containing Bible stories spoken in their language. He combined the contextualization of storytelling in their heart language with advances in technology now commonly used among the local people in African cities. He was able to give these stories stored in a convenient and relevant technology to his new friends as a gift and plant seeds of the Gospel among an ethnic group with almost no Christian presence among them. Corey had these doors open to him because he hit the streets and took the time to build relationships with Muslims living in their diaspora community in an American city. It not only resulted in ministry to an ethnic enclave, but opportunities to communicate the Gospel message to several others in the country of origin.

Pioneer Church Planting

Bob's original intention was to work as a missionary to an unreached people group in West Africa. His heart's desire was to serve among unreached people groups who had little to no Christian witness among them. Several years ago, he moved to a village in a Muslim country in West Africa, but after battling a life-threatening illness, he returned to the United States disappointed that his work among this unreached people group was facing a closed door. During the years that immediately followed, he worked to restore his health and kept seeking other opportunities to serve an unreached people group overseas. However, after some time, he learned of an opportunity to conduct a missiological research project in New York City, and he also was told he should explore the possibility of working among African immigrants in New York. Immediately after coming to New York City, he began meeting individuals from the same people group with whom he had previously lived in West Africa. Walking into a hair-braiding salon run by Africans, he began speaking their language to the amazement of all the workers in the shop. Immediately during his survey trip to New York City, he met a believer from this same people group who had previously fled the country as a religious refugee, first to Europe and then to the United States. It became clear to Bob and his wife that moving to New York City would be a strategic move in reaching out to the most unreached people groups.

Soon after moving to the city, Bob began to contextualize Gospel evangelism for first-generation West African Muslims. He would walk through city neighborhoods using oral storytelling—both in person and giving out audio recordings—and he began meeting Muslims who would listen to the stories he told. Gaining acceptance among his new neighbors, Bob discovered that not only was the Lord leading him into a ministry among the specific people group he once traveled overseas to reach, but now he was encountering several African people groups who remain some of the most unreached in the world. While specific ethnic groups network together and form cultural associations, they often also interact through their jobs, African markets, and as "near culture" groups who share many of the same interests. Therefore, while Bob had cultural affinity and language abilities with one particular diaspora group in the city, he would meet people from Senegal, Nigeria, Mali, Ghana, Gambia, and other African nations through networking among diaspora communities and ethnic associations in the city.

As he continued sharing Bible stories through oral storytelling, some first-generation immigrants came to believe that the biblical stories of God are true and that Jesus is Lord and more than a prophet. They were not ready to fully convert to a Christian identity, but they believed the stories from the Bible were true. Many migrants from Africa are supporting families or kinship groups in the homeland, and as a communal culture, they are more mindful of the impact of their conversion upon the whole community. For them, it is not just an individual decision but one that impacts their whole family. Living and working incarnationally in the city, Bob has become a spiritual leader among many West Africans in the surrounding community. Even many who hold to their Muslim faith identify him essentially as "their Christian pastor."

In the early years, it would have been easy by typical Western church-growth standards to proclaim his ministry a failure. A handful of Muslims believed the biblical claims about Jesus to be true, but even fewer were prepared to go so far as to convert from Islam. However, the impact of Bob's evangelistic work is not merely local. Rather, Bob's ministry in New York City has been more of a gateway for a farther-reaching global effort. Standard American church-growth measurements need not apply in order to see the true impact of his work as many in West Africa have come to believe in Christ through the relational networks flowing from New York City.

When Bob began making short-term trips to a Muslim nation in West Africa, he stayed in the homes of men he had been teaching in New York, and he gained permission to share the Gospel with their wives and families. Homes to which he previously had no access, he was now an honored guest. Now, because of his connections through the diaspora in New York City, he was not only entering these homes but was doing so with permission to share the Gospel and with the endorsement of "big men" of the community living in New York. At times, African Muslims in New York City would send home compact discs of recorded Bible stories for their families to listen to. They would send these items as gifts, and on some occasions would send a letter instructing their families to listen to what Bob had to tell them. "The things he has to tell you are true," they would say, and this opened the door wide for Bob to share the Good News among a people who had not previously heard.

The West African Muslim men working in New York City have become "big men" in their communities due at least in part to their financial contributions sent home, and with greater economic standing, these families had become largely inaccessible to the missionaries living in that area in Africa. However, because Bob had already gained access through the influence of members of the diaspora in New York City, he was in a position to stay in their homes and open a spiritual dialogue with the families. While in Africa, he was able to act as a bridge-builder for local outreach efforts, as well as connecting local missionaries with his contacts in West Africa.

Contextualizing the Gospel for West African Muslims living in a major city in the United States, Bob is sharing the Good News with the heads of households, and these local relationships in New York City's immigrant community extend back to villages in a Muslim state in West Africa. Working through the natural flows of transnational relationships, Bob is an evangelist to both a North American city and unreached communities back in Africa simultaneously. He has contextualized the communication of the Gospel for West African Muslims in the same way he would if he were living in their village across the sea, and the impact is being felt. In a recent conversation, he pointed out that virtually all of the new church planting that has taken place in this people group in West Africa has been through contacts in New York City. It is really quite amazing. Nearly all of the major gains in the expansion of the church among an unreached people group are through the efforts of a missionary evangelizing in neighborhoods an ocean away. However, this may actually be the shape of things to come. There are some important lessons to learn from Bob's story, as it provides a helpful case study in the effects of evangelism through global flows in the context of international migration and transnational identities. There are a number of factors that may be reproduced in other diaspora contexts, and there are key missiological principles worth noting.

First, he didn't assume he should evangelize first-generation immigrants from an unreached people group using traditional Western methods simply because the work was taking place on American soil. Instead, he contextualized his evangelistic approach to the culture and worldview of first-generation West African Muslims. They are coming from an oral culture, and effective evangelism among these cultures often involves sharing the stories of Scripture through oral storytelling. It will likely be important for evangelists and churches that desire to reach out to unreached ethnic groups in their cities to learn the communication and worldview characteristics of the groups they are attempting to reach. Assuming an American worldview or Western church-growth methods would likely become an adventure in missing the mark. Instead, missionaries among diaspora groups may connect with an ethnic community as learners and seek to contextualize evangelistic proclamation and church planting. Churches may seek to create a culturally friendly space outside their existing structures for connecting with an unreached community in their city.

Second, Bob knew what he was aiming for. His ambition was to see the Gospel advance among an unreached people group from West Africa. This focus led him to conduct his ministry with an entirely global worldview. It is not that he ignored the local implications, but he also looked beyond them. Determining the effectiveness of his ministry wasn't based on local church-growth standards or limited even to evangelistic outcomes solely in the city. Instead, he labored for the expansion of the Gospel through networks of relationships within an unreached ethnic group. This meant overturning traditional Western standards for measuring church growth.

Third, Bob also became aware of the importance of his strategic location. Evangelism among the diaspora community in the city and networking through transnational relationships has resulted in the expansion of the global church. The city has played a strategic role in reaching out to an unreached people group. Bob recognizes that he is doing pioneer church planting; he is simply doing it from a location that might be unconventional when we think about missionary pioneers of the past. However, living and working in New York City has been strategic for reaching into this ethnic community in West Africa. In fact, he experienced more evangelistic progress after beginning to reach out to the people in this ethnic group who were living in New York City. In one case, he describes an African believer who was severely persecuted for years due to his faith in Christ, but since resettling in New York City his newfound influence as an African member of the diaspora in New York has opened doors for others in his family to know the Lord Jesus as well. This influence was simply not there while he remained in Africa. In fact, family members attempted to kill him for his Christian faith. However, as an African man in New York, he had gained a new status among his people in his homeland, opening the door for missionary engagement in an otherwise inaccessible family network.

Finally, recognizing the bigger picture beyond the efforts of a single missionary, Bob has worked in partnership with others. I know Bob's story well, in part, because we work together in a multiagency ministry collaboration in New York City. He has worked in partnerships in the city, but he also has demonstrated the effectiveness of transnational missionary partnerships. During short-term visits to West Africa, he facilitated relational bridge-building between African households and missionaries working locally. He utilized the open access he had gained as a missionary in New York to facilitate opening doors for missionaries who had struggled to gain access to community leaders while working among this people group in the homeland.

Simultaneously, there are aspects of Bob's story that will be less reproducible. He spent more than a year living among this same people in their country in Africa while learning the language, culture, and worldview, and he received practical training in missions methods from a major missions agency as well. Many who share a burden for reaching out to the nations who reside and work in their city don't have the background that informs them about worldview, culture, communication patterns, and all the rest. Missions organizations, missionary consultants, Christian leaders in the diaspora, and others may play a key role in building training platforms to equip Christians located in the West. Although Bob said he still had much to learn when approaching a diaspora community in an American city, he nevertheless came to New York City with a fairly full missionary "tool belt." Many missionaries who have worked in overseas contexts could continue to serve this same people group among a diaspora community, but many returning missionaries don't follow this path for a variety of reasons. Nevertheless, many believers who desire to reach out to the neighbors from around the world may need further training in missionary worldviews and cultural understandings. Missionaries and missions organizations that are equipped to help local believers and churches in issues of worldview, cross-cultural communication, and contextualization may provide a key role in filling the gaps as believers seek to serve as witnesses of the Gospel among unreached people groups living in their cities.

Ministries desiring to reach out to diaspora communities, will need to consider strategies for reaching out cross-culturally. American churches that desire to pursue local ministry with global implications will need to consider the value of contextualization if their evangelism efforts are to make a further reaching impact through transnational connections and put roots in the soil of migrants' homelands. They will need to recognize who is living in their midst and learn about them, and leaders with missionary training or experience will need to have the opportunity to consult or train believers as well as engaging them with the Gospel themselves. Mutual partnerships may provide a doorway for the expansion of the church through transnational pathways as well, and global cities remain key strategic centers for world missions.

Just Passing Through: Reaching Internationals

International urban centers could be compared to train stations with scores of migrants, business peoples, tourists, and students passing through the city on a regular basis. Some settle into life in the city and remain for years to follow; however, others are just passing through on their way to something or somewhere else. Many international students study in universities in countries such as the United States, United

Kingdom, and various other destinations. While small college towns certainly host their share of international students, the majority of these academic nomads spend their time away from their countries of origin in major metropolitan areas. In the United States, New York City hosts the greatest number of international students with approximately 60,000 studying in colleges and universities across the city. Los Angeles is a temporary home for nearly 55,000, and more than 20,000 advance their academic career in Houston (See: "Where are International Students Going in the United States?"). Among the top ten sending countries are China, India, Japan, Saudi Arabia, and Vietnam which are among some of the most unreached nations in the world (See: "Where are the International students coming from?"). According to current estimates, there were 1.7 million international studies worldwide at the start of the 21st century, and the number of international students around the globe is predicted to double around 2015 and double again by 2025 (Claydon, 2004, p. 30).

While some international students will convert their student visas into permanent residency in the United States, many will return home following the completion of their studies. We hope they will multiply disciples in their nations and beyond; however, they need to be taught to feed themselves spiritually (Claydon, 2004, p. 32). Simply experiencing the wonder of a Christian congregation in the United States won't be sufficient for many internationals to make a journey home that translates into becoming ambassadors of Christ in their homelands. In fact, the professionally organized church assemblies in the United States are often difficult—and sometimes impossible—to replicate in many majority-world settings.

Kevin King moved to Manhattan as a missionary in order to plant churches among people from countries in the least-reached regions of the world, often referred to as the "10/40 Window." He realized that a number of international students from around the world come to cities in the United States and hold the potential for being reached by the Gospel of grace and being mobilized when they return to their home countries. One of the questions he asked was: What kind of church planting would result in international students returning home with a greater likelihood of multiplying churches among their own people in their homeland? He recognized that they needed to cast off many of the Western and professionalized approaches to church in order to model something for international students that was simple enough to reproduce in their own contexts and quickly be embodied within their own cultures.

When King first began planting a house church network in New York City, he wasn't a passionate supporter of North America's self-identified house church movement and had very little interaction with other leaders of house churches in the United States. Rather, he began by contemplating how to reach international students and visiting scholars studying at prestigious campuses in Manhattan. He thought about how by reaching them he might spark evangelistic church planting in their countries of origin. King wanted to strategically reach internationals so they could carry the Gospel and continue the work of church planting when they finished their studies. He recognized that conventional Western church-planting strategies would likely not be reproducible for new believers returning home to largely non-Christian settings. Generating the resources that have been poured into American church planting, maintaining the organizational infrastructure while working in a high demand vocation in government, economics, or business, and advancing a marketing approach to outreach in contexts that are either legally closed to church planting or predominantly non-Christian would all be an unwise approach if he hoped church planting would be reproduced when international students returned home. If they were to see churches multiply through the social networks of new believers, he realized that what was modeled was at least as important as what was articulated, so he knew his team would need to pursue expressions of church that were simple and reproducible where Christians are either a small minority or even heavily persecuted. Simply telling international students they could start a church while explaining that it shouldn't look at all like their experience here was not enough. So his team began a house church network in New York City. He desired to demonstrate an approach to church planting that visiting students and scholars from non-Christian societies could replicate themselves while working in the academy, government, or the corporate sector and adapt fluidly to their contexts in Asian cities.

At the beginning of each semester, King and his team began meeting new graduate and postgraduate students as well as visiting scholars and inviting them to their homes. They began Bible studies with those who were receptive, and in recent years they have begun to see emerge the vision for internationally planting new house churches. In the early years, his team kept working at it but didn't see the kind of church multiplication to overseas contexts for which they hoped. King explained to me that they kept learning even though things didn't quite take off as quickly as they would have liked. He explains that their own values as a team still didn't match their strategy for internationals. As they began to better embody the values for reproducible approaches to church planting themselves, they saw their first breakthrough of an international graduate planting a church in his home context. After a brief stay in Japan, a Taiwanese student returned to Taipei and began a new house church. This signaled the step forward of potential becoming reality.

In recent years, King and his team have begun to adapt the Discovery Bible Study method as a strategy for launching new groups on campuses and overseas. His team began to not only model simple forms of church, but demonstrate a process of reproducible church planting from the very beginning of an evangelistic relationship. Applying this strategy as the method for launching new group Bible studies with international students, some additional house churches have begun to emerge in Asian cities. New believers regularly return to positions in businesses or academic institutions in Asia, and new churches have started in officially closed nations in Asia. King regularly uses Skype to continue a mentoring and coaching relationship with converts as they share the Gospel and start house churches in their home contexts. They have begun to see transnational church planting move through second-generation evangelism as well. An international student shared the Gospel with a family member in an Asian country, and his relative gathered a group of unbelievers together, shared the Gospel of Christ, and several new disciples were baptized. They continue to meet as a house church and have some interaction with the leader of another house church started through New York City connections that meets a couple of hours away.

During the last few years, our own ministry, Global City Mission Initiative, has been working alongside King and his team in a one-year missionary training program in New York City, and other mission organizations send missionary candidates for training as well. As a result of a multiagency collaboration in New York City, more than 40 Discovery Bible Studies were started with groups of international students in one semester near the start of the program, and international students are regularly sharing what they are learning from the Word of God with their family and friends back home.

International students temporarily migrating to study in academic institutions provide one of the greatest opportunities for the followers of Christ in North America to engage global missions in their local contexts. However, King's example of missiological reflection is an important example. By keeping the end in mind, his team carefully evaluated how they should be doing ministry and evangelism among internationals if they hoped to see a far-reaching global impact result from their efforts. While many international students may enjoy their experience in an American church, there is a real need to model forms of ministry that are reproducible and equip new international believers to communicate the Gospel in their own nations and languages. By being intentional about modeling multiplicative approaches to church planting while in the United States, new evangelistic churches are emerging upon the return of international students and scholars to their homelands.

A Missionary Life Uninterrupted

Many American missionaries who return home to the United States find a ministry position in an American church. Others return to serve their mission agency in an administrative role or as part of the mobilization department or accept a new role in another ministry organization. Some accept positions as professors at Bible colleges or seminaries. Perhaps less frequently, some return to transition out of full-time ministry and begin a new vocation. In all these roles, they continue to serve the body of Christ in various capacities. These are good tasks being carried out by faithful men and women. However, it is becoming increasingly crucial to fill an additional ministry vocation as well. Missionaries who have served among a particular ethnic group will find opportunities to continue serving the same people group through the diaspora network or continue partnering with indigenous churches through transnational involvement in teaching and leadership development. Often missionaries who have already gained experience living between cultures are in a unique position to play a valuable role in ministry in and through ethnic groups in diaspora, and missionaries who continue to remain passionate about making disciples among a specific people and training leaders for indigenous churches may find a new and evolving ministry niche through transnational interactions.

"Pete" spent five years working as a missionary in Albania. During that time, he learned the language and culture. However, he eventually reflected on his experiences in Europe and questioned the inherently Western and especially American approaches he encountered when it came to planting a church in Albania. He determined that a more relational approach congruent with Albanians' emphasis on family life was needed, and Western forms might even be barriers to the expansion of the church among Albanian-speaking peoples.

After returning to the United States, Pete remained passionate about evangelism to Albanian peoples, and he intentionally moved to a metropolitan area with the largest concentrations of Albanians living in diaspora. Pete initially moved his family to Staten Island, working in partnership with a church in that part of the city and mobilizing church members to assist with outreach events to the Albanian community. He spent six years hosting cultural celebrations during Albanian holidays, building relationships, and networking within the diaspora network. Pete was aware of the deep-seated religious identities, strongly held nationalism, and the need to build deep levels of trust among Albanians in the diaspora. With the help of church volunteers, he hosted cultural events and community meetings, and he spent time building friendships among his Albanian neighbors.

After six years of personal investment and building trust, Pete started a house church among Albanians in Staten Island. A few months later, a second Albanian-speaking church began in a home in Brooklyn. At the time, these were only two of four Albanian-speaking evangelical churches in the United States, even though nearly 1 million Albanians lived in the country. Eventually, the church in Staten Island fizzled out while the church in Brooklyn continued to thrive. Pete moved across the river to New Jersey where he began working with an Albanian church meeting in a church where he also serves as a leader. Partnering with this multiethnic congregation in New Jersey, this church serves as a hub for evangelism and church planting among diaspora communities in northern New Jersey.

Pete has explained that the majority of Albanians don't live in Albania. To reach a people group that is scattered in diaspora such as Albanian-speaking nations, missionaries must adjust their worldview to reflect contemporary trends in globalization. I cannot help but admire Pete's ability to work across vast areas as he works to see evangelism and church planting unfold in the various pockets of Albanian culture across the metro area. His grasp of global realities is quintessential for the sort of perspectives needed among missionaries in our rising global society. Based in New Jersey and nurturing an Albanian congregation there, he continues to develop leadership within the church in Brooklyn, traveling there on a regular basis. Additionally, through ministry partnerships, he regularly travels to Albanian cities and to

Kosovo to conduct leadership training and encourage indigenously led churches. At one point, he estimated his team is providing nearly 90% of the leadership training for Albanian evangelical churches. He is demonstrating the role of the transnational missionary. He is not confined to a single geographic center; rather, he has dedicated his life to serving an ethnic community through transnational ministry—both here and there. He works fluidly both in their homeland and in their diaspora network. Living as a missionary in a global age, he is based in New York City while serving a scattered people across two continents.

On a number of occasions, Pete and I have met in an Albanian (Kosovar) restaurant in the Bronx to eat together, enjoy fellowship, and explore avenues for partnering together to see the Gospel penetrate and transform the largely Muslim Albanian-speaking population in the Central Bronx. During more than one conversation, Pete would tell me how he was just in Albania or Kosovo and met a new evangelistic contact. Of course, one might expect a missionary on a trip to Europe with the purpose of strengthening churches there to make new contacts for those churches. However, he would frequently explain that he made a new contact in the Bronx, Yonkers, Queens, or other New York neighborhood while in Albania or Kosovo. Talking with someone new in an Albanian city, he sometimes discovered that they lived in an apartment building in New York City in one of the neighborhoods he frequents for networking in the Albanian community. One day while we were finishing lunch together, a new friend of his joined us. It was someone he first met while working with churches in Kosovo. Pete is developing relationships across the expanse of a transnational ethnic network. Understanding the global and dislocated nature of the people he is seeking to serve, Pete is a transnational missionary working among a transnational people.

Recently, we were able to partner to mobilize a small team reaching out in the Albanian community in the Bronx, and a missionary couple working with Global City Mission Initiative is now invested in building relationships and sharing the Gospel with Albanian-speaking people in that part of the city. During the early stages of mobilizing new workers among the Albanian diaspora, Pete served as a coach for these young missionaries. There are now regular evangelistic conversations happening on a weekly basis.

Coaching and mobilizing outreach workers, traveling to build up churches in the countries of origin, evangelizing and planting among diaspora communities, and developing indigenous leaders who can lead young churches, Pete's commitment to this people group has placed him in a transnational reality, bridging diaspora and local contexts. In a global age, missionaries focused on being a Gospel ambassador to a particular people may find themselves moving between distant locations and connecting with people on the move, perhaps while even on the move themselves. Pete provides an example of adapting missiological strategies and redefining missionary roles in the context of globalization and diaspora.

Movements Without Borders

Over the last few years, I had been hearing about a disciple-making movement of new Bible study groups unfolding out of the San Francisco Bay Area that had subsequently spread and multiplied through relational networks to Central America. I took the opportunity to call Dave Hunt with City Team Ministries and heard an exciting story of transnational evangelism and church planting that has jumped from the San Francisco Bay Area to villages and cities in Nicaragua (Hunt, May 24, 2013).

City Team Ministries has served the poor and desperately broken in cities for decades. Dave Hunt explained that in recent years they made changes in their evangelism strategy as a result of significant self-evaluation by the organization's leaders. While they realized they had helped thousands of people with basic needs and that work should continue, they felt they needed to make adjustments in order to make up for a shortfall in disciple-making efforts. They took some of the strategies they had learned in disciple-making movements taking place in the majority world and began integrating them into programs that served the poor in California. In some of their outreach programs in the San Francisco Bay Area, they revamped their curriculum and began to include the Discovery Bible Study process. Discovery Bible Study is an inductive approach to Bible study and to spiritual formation. While participants are engaging the content of Scripture directly, the facilitator focuses the group on obedience-based discipleship. Many of the questions included in a Discovery Bible Study are designed to encourage group members to actively respond to the Scriptures being studied rather than merely build their knowledge of Scripture. Participants also are encouraged to serve one another, share what they are learning with others during the week, and apply the life lessons from Scripture immediately. The approach is completely inductive, utilizing open-ended questions and discussion. The goal is to nurture obedience to Christ and his Word, and the Discovery Bible Study is meant to serve as a process for discovering an active faith. Leaders are trained to facilitate through inductive learning in a discussion-based group setting rather than direct instructional teaching. Following the implementation of the Discovery Bible Study, they began to witness Bible studies multiply in a Latino diaspora community with an impact beyond not only municipal boundaries but national borders as well. Reaching out to Latino communities is a crucial demographic for impacting North American cities with the Gospel of grace. Latinos originating from every Spanish-speaking nation constitute the largest foreign-born population living within the United States (Rogers, 2006, p. 27). When City Team's efforts began impacting the Latino community in the Bay Area, it's not surprising that these efforts had a far-reaching impact beyond their local barrio.

Pedro was a drug addict who emigrated from El Salvador to California. Struggling with his addiction, he became a client in City Team's drug recovery program in San Francisco. The program is 12 to 24 months long, and there is an intentional emphasis on participants experiencing life transformation. Approximately nine years ago, City

Team revamped their drug rehabilitation program. They designed it to include Discovery Bible Study at the center of the transformation process. As a result, Pedro was participating in Discovery Bible Studies nearly every day during his time in City Team's rehabilitation facility. Eventually, as he transitioned through the program, he reached the stage of personal development where he was to be sent out, along with others, to engage in outreach to struggling neighborhoods in the Bay Area.

As he engaged the community, Pedro went seeking a person of peace. The person of peace is an individual who demonstrates receptivity to the Gospel message, hospitality toward the messenger, and gathers friends, family, and neighbors, becoming a gateway for the Gospel to a new community that has not yet committed to the Lord Jesus. Being from El Salvador, Pedro focused his attention on a predominantly Mexican and Central American section of the city. During City Team's Thanksgiving giveaway, he participated in taking food boxes to families in the Latino community. That's when he met Angela. Angela is from Nicaragua and is well-known throughout her apartment complex. Not unlike Cornelius in the book of Acts, she regularly helped others in her community and already had a strong awareness of the reality of God and the impact he could make in her life. She demonstrated openness to the Gospel and became a conduit for others to hear the message of grace.

Pedro began a Discovery Bible Study in Angela's home, and Angela, as a characteristic person of peace, invited her friends and neighbors to join them. The Discovery Bible Study method intentionally encourages participates to multiply new studies with new groups of people rather than continue growing the initial group. Instead of swelling larger and larger, they initiate new gatherings that center around the Word of God and repeat the process. New discussion groups multiplied quickly. As a result of the first study, nine more Discovery Bible Studies were started in Angela's apartment complex alone.

Eventually, Angela traveled back to Nicaragua to visit family and friends during Christmas vacation. She stayed for awhile in the home of Martha in a town in central Nicaragua. During her stay in Martha's home, Angela shared how the experience of doing a Discovery Bible Study group in San Francisco had made a difference in her life. Soon after, they began a new inductive Bible study group in Martha's home. Beginning with that Discovery Bible Study, the first group multiplied, and 30 new Bible studies started in the region around Martha's central Nicaraguan home.

Later, Martha became sick, and Rosa came to visit her. Martha shared with Rosa how much the experience of participating in a Discovery Bible Study group had been a blessing to her and invited her to participate. Rosa was moved by the experience and eager to bring the inductive Bible study concept home to her community as well. Rosa doesn't read or write. However, she has a 13-year-old grandson who reads, so he became the reader for the Bible study group that began meeting in her home. Soon after the first group began, there were 13 new Discovery Bible Study groups meeting in Rosa's surrounding area.

Rosa is from a community of sugar cane workers. The story of the community has been featured in journalistic reporting for the poor health conditions and low life expectancies of the workers in the area. Many men regularly die of kidney failure in this industry, but they keep working because there are no other options. When leaders of City Team visited Nicaragua, they asked the people in Rosa's community if this process was helping them at all. The Nicaraguan workers explained that they lived in a struggling community plagued by death, but they believed that a sense of hope had come to an otherwise devastated community without hope.

Eventually, Martha introduced the experience of the Discovery Bible Study group to Brenda who lives in Managua, the major urban center of Nicaragua. Soon there were 45 to 50 Discovery Bible Study groups started in Managua. Furthermore, another transnational expansion occurred as new Bible study groups jumped borders a second time and multiplied through natural family connections from Nicaragua to Costa Rica. New Bible study groups have started in Costa Rican neighborhoods as a result of grassroots transnational connections between the two nations. What began with an El Salvadoran recovering addict in the San Francisco Bay Area has multiplied across borders, and City Team has observed evangelism to six generations from the first participant to the latest newcomers, and across three countries. Virtually none of the people involved have come from preexisting backgrounds of church participation; it has been purely an evangelistic movement reproduced through grassroots relationships in the Bay Area to Nicaragua and from there to Costa Rica.

City Team leaders desire to support the process beyond their metro area, so they send a leader from San Francisco to Nicaragua on a quarterly basis in order to provide training and support to the indigenous leaders and groups in Central America. City Team has seen 1,000 Discovery Bible Studies begin in the United States and an estimated 300 groups begin in Central America. As Bible study groups evolve, they have seen 100, approximately 10%, of these Discovery Bible Studies evolve into churches. New churches beginning through this process typically add music and other activities that we often associate with a church's worship assembly, but their teaching format continues to reflect the Discovery Bible Study approach, involving inductive study and open discussion. Sometimes a single Discovery Bible Study becomes a house church, and occasionally a handful of Bible study groups join together to form a new Christian congregation. In my discussion with Hunt, he stressed that the movement was early in its development. He had participated in a similar strategy in East Africa when serving there as a missionary, where they saw a high percentage of Bible study groups become churches over time, and he emphasized that the emergence of churches through the Discovery Bible Study method is often a natural maturation process. Therefore, he expects not only additional groups to be reproduced through families involved, but that

Bible study groups will likely continue to mature into new churches over time.

The strategy of starting Discovery Bible Study groups through a receptive gateway person—or person of peace—in the community has resulted in numerous new Bible studies in the United States, and the reproduction of this approach across the Nicaraguan and then Costa Rican borders has taken place through the natural transnational connections between family and friends participating in grassroots global networking. The evangelistic networking that has begun to spread through Central America hasn't been led by ministry professionals. Rather, it has been a movement of immigrants and relatives passing on what they have learned to their friends and family. The natural transnational connections led to the expansion of a network of new discipleship groups. Hunt explains that their intention was to see a viral multiplication of evangelistic communities; therefore, he emphasizes that City Team's evangelism strategy depends on methods that are "simple, sustainable, and scalable." Also, the Discovery Bible Study method focuses on a process of growing in obedience to God's Word over time instead of an emphasis on learning doctrine at the start of the process or on-the-spot conversions. Not to misunderstand, Christian doctrine is learned, but orthodox understandings of doctrine develop over time through the ongoing process of the groups' inductive study as a community. Hunt explains that he has seen this process work before and expects it to continue making a positive impact. While in northeast Africa, this sort of church multiplication through Discovery Bible Studies resulted in new believers sharing their crops with one another, supporting each other in daily struggles, and leading the members of their community to faith in Jesus Christ. Indeed, it led to a vibrant multiplying witness throughout the area. While there cannot be an exact guarantee that the same trends will continue in this movement that started in San Francisco and that leaped to Central America, so far the flow of multiplication and maturation is remarkably similar to Hunt's experience in East Africa.

One of the key factors in the development of this movement across national borders has been the characteristics described by Hunt—simple, sustainable, and scalable. The Discovery Bible Study method is a format that allowed a transformed drug addict to start the first meeting, a Nicaraguan immigrant to take the process with her when visiting her home country, an illiterate woman from a struggling farm community to spread through her community to Nicaragua's urban center, and eventually to spring up in Costa Rica. The key element of reproducibility facilitates the advance of the Gospel through the transnational connections of immigrants' natural kinship networks—both local and global.

A New Kind of Short-Term Mission Trip?

When we read Paul's letters in the New Testament, he is often visiting places where he has contacts that will open a door for his work, or he is sending someone else—such as Phoebe or Timothy or Titus—to go through that same door. Paul is utilizing connections that have been generated through a first-century social network and is maintaining and nurturing connections through the pathways of migration, transportation advancements such as the Roman roads, and an astonishingly efficient use of sending mail. Much of Paul's work was built on established relationships or ethnic connections in order to open new pathways for sharing the testimony of the Gospel, and it was enhanced by the transportation and communication advancements of his day.

In recent years, short-term mission trips have been widely discussed and a subject of debate. It's not the subject of this book to fully enter that critique, but I do want to add some fresh thinking to it since the nature of transnationalism potentially leads to some creative approaches to short-term missions travel. All sorts of different types of short-term trips have developed over the latter part of the previous century. Medical missions teams travel around the world to deliver emergency medical care motivated by the Gospel's irrevocable call to care for the poor and suffering. Sponsoring agencies and churches send leaders to visit missionaries in far-off locations whether for accountability and correction or for encouragement and missionary care. Perhaps most famously, scores of teenagers and college students make short-term mission trips every year to destinations around the world. They go with a heart full of service and compassion. Critics accuse such short-term excursions of becoming a type of Christian tourism, while mission educators often cite these trips as valuable mobilization platforms. Both sides of the argument have merit. As a student, I was largely drawn into missionary service through short-term mission experiences. Spring Break trips into inner-city communities played a part in launching my missionary vocation. However, I also have observed both positive and negative effects as a host of short-term mission groups. Neither the benefits (however minor) nor the critiques (however harsh) ought to be ignored. In a world increasingly connected by modern transportation and advances in communication technology, short-term mission trips are here to stay. However, another kind of short-term mission trip seems to be emerging through modern transportation and communication advances making it possible for a Gospel witness to ride the waves of transnational flows between countries.

Bob's story provides a window into the possibility of tying short-term missionary travel to ministry in diaspora communities. Short-term mission trips by individuals or very small teams navigating through the relationships in a diaspora network may represent a new type of short-term mission trip. When Bob lived in West Africa as a missionary, he found that access to the leaders of the culture was limited. They had higher socioeconomic status and their homes were kept secure from unwelcomed outsiders. Like the elites of many societies, their lives were more insulated from those outside their circles of family, friends, or business associates. However, when he began working among this unreached people group in New York City, relationships began to develop that would lead him to the homes he previously could not enter. Due to the relationships he had developed with African Muslims in New York City, he now had the keys to open doors in communities previously closed to him and to other missionaries.

Now Bob makes regular trips to Africa. He stays in the homes built by funding from immigrants living in New York City. He stays in some of the homes in the very neighborhood in which he previously had lived as a missionary, but when he was a missionary living in that community, he had no access to these homes to teach the Gospel and demonstrate the love of Christ. Now, however, when he travels to Africa he is welcomed into these homes because many of the homeowners are the men he is reaching out to on the streets of New York City.

When Bob travels to Africa, his contacts in New York make arrangements for him to be hosted in their homes. They often send letters to family members instructing them to listen to what their friend Bob has to tell them. "The stories he will tell you are true. Listen to him," they say in these letters. They also send home CD recordings of Bible stories in their language, which they had originally received from Bob. As a result of these short-term visits, many of the families of immigrants in New York City who remain in Africa have now become followers of Jesus. The "Big Papas" and "Big Mamas" in New York have opened the doorway for the Gospel, and in some cases Bob has walked through the door as a witness of God's grace during a short-term visit. In some cases, Bob has been a bridge for other missionaries. Through his relationships with the leaders of neighborhoods and villages who have grown their influence while working in New York, Bob has traveled to African communities and opened access to these families, who are leaders in their culture, for some of the missionaries who have been laboring in the same neighborhoods and villages but were unable to gain access. Bob was not only able to directly evangelize indigenous families through his New York connections but created access for missionaries struggling to break into the mainstream culture and build relationships with community leaders in Africa.

Bob's short-term travels to Africa have resulted in new disciples and new churches, and they also have opened doors for missionaries who previously had not found a way to enter this segment of African society. The gatekeepers of that society live in New York City, and it required a missionary walking the streets of New York to open up the pathways for the Gospel in Africa. For Bob, a short-term mission trip encompasses visiting the family connections of immigrants laboring in New York City who are growing their influence and status in their place of origin.

Bob's story is unique. He speaks the tribal language and has lived in their land. When he arrived in New York, he already had a great deal of understanding of the ethnic group's homeland culture. One of the concerns I've heard him express is that his situation isn't reproducible for everyone. Nevertheless, having trained in New York City, Corey learned from Bob's story and has repeated a similar pattern. He didn't know the language or the culture, so the process of entering into the lives of the ethnic diaspora community took slightly longer. He has not yet planted any new churches but has gained numerous opportunities to communicate the Gospel in the homeland of a hard-to-reach ethnic group, making two trips to West Africa using his relationships through the diaspora network.

A number of Chinese migrants take the opportunity to visit their home communities in China and maintain their relationships with family, friends, and other contacts. This certainly provides a platform for sharing the Good News among natural connections through the Chinese diaspora (Claydon, 2004, p. 41), and Grace Church to the Fujianese also has begun to experiment with short-term mission trips through the natural flow of transnational connections. The church provides daily ministry to Chinese immigrants. Many of these immigrants are struggling to adjust to a new culture, establish themselves financially, and in many cases work to pay off the debt for their passage to the United States. As the church received a number of Chinese immigrants, many have been baptized and remain connected to the church. As a result, an idea formed in the minds of the church leaders for a creative short-term mission initiative.

One of the members of the church, herself a convert to the Christian faith and an immigrant to the United States from China, returned to her country of origin for a short-term mission trip. However, instead of planning a special program, passing out evangelism tracts on a street corner, or going as a guest speaker for a church revival, she went armed only with an iPad. She traveled from city to city and village to village, and she visited the homes of the parents of young Chinese immigrants who had connected with Grace Church to the Fujianese upon their arrival in the United States. She knocked on the doors of the homes of the parents of new believers, and she shared news from their children. She was able to report that their children were doing well and making progress in their new life, and at each home she would open up her iPad and show them pictures of their children in their life in North America. Sharing pictures of their adult children in their church and in their new community in New York, she would then take the opportunity to tell them that their children want to encourage them to listen to the message that she also has to share. With each family, she was able to report on the well-being of their adult children, and she was able to share the message of the Gospel. Through family connections more than an ocean away, she is welcomed into the homes of unreached people who are prepared to hear good news, and it is good news that she shares in more than one way. Through technology, she is able to offer comfort in the midst of the uncertainty that naturally accompanies international migration, and through a shared hospitality that has been mutually beneficial on two continents, there is no better moment to share the good news of the Gospel that has already entered the life of their family members.

Bob, Corey, and Grace Church to the Fujianese illustrate the potential for a new kind of mission trip. Trips providing emergency care and disaster relief should continue. Short-term exposure may stir teens and college students toward greater long-term involvement in the mission of God. We should be attentive to what needs to be reformed when it comes to short-term missions, and we should continue to utilize the ease of modern travel for Kingdom purposes as well. However, I propose that these stories give us a glimpse into a highly relational and much more strategic approach to short-term missions. What if churches and organizations focusing on diaspora evangelism mobilize either a missionary worker or a believer from within the diaspora to be sent out through the global flows of transnationalism? What if instead of young adults experiencing a one-off mission trip, they make a cultural exposure trip that was then followed by a year-round evangelism ministry initiative among the same diaspora community in the city in or near the church. Then resources could be directed toward sending an ambassador of the Gospel to visit the neighborhoods and villages connected back to those ethnic enclaves in North America? Mobilization and evangelism would still be primary agenda items in the short-term ministry but with application through developing a diaspora outreach. Resources would be streamlined, and year-round ministry would be fundamentally connected to the short-term ministry experience. This integration could take place while still providing an educational and cultural exposure trip to students. Some of the pitfalls of short-term mission trips could be avoided because a well-defined short-term trip could help the group avoid ministry overreach or other typical mistakes. Utilizing short-term experiences to mobilize a church or college group for working in a local diaspora, short-term exposure may translate into long-term impact among a diaspora. Of course, church leadership should still be trained in contextualization, cultural sensitivity, and the like, and one or more leaders should be appointed to oversee outreach efforts and make sure that avoidable blunders are avoided among the diaspora community as well. Then, a second mission trip may become possible, but this time by one or two individuals following the relational connections of the diaspora community. Such coordination may seem absurd in light of the usual patterns of short-term missions by Western churches. However, my proposal is that strategic approaches such as this may not only potentially fuel greater advances of the Gospel but also begin nurturing a culture of intentionality and shaping purposeful experiences in the church. Ministry in the context of globalization generates the possibilities of new ideas and new ways of thinking about mission.

Sending Development Home

Globalization is reshaping our world. International migration is certainly one of the most dynamic and challenging aspects of globalization, and the movements of peoples from one place on the planet to another is providing significant opportunities as well as challenges for Christian mission. Stories of transnational evangelism and church planting that have emerged thus far seem to be only scratching the surface of the potential missiological impact of aligning mission strategies with the reality of international movements and global networking of diasporas around the world.

War, famine, government oppression, ethnic genocide, and religious persecution force particular people groups, communities, and families to flee their homelands and everything they know in order to build a new life in a place that is strange and foreign. Often the people they leave behind will eventually rely on their assistance to survive the new challenges caused by catastrophic events in their country. Many migrants leave due to economic hardship in their country of origin, which is sometimes difficult for Westerners to understand because raising our standard of daily living often simply means a move to the suburbs. However, for many immigrants, their relocation to a Western city means real economic improvement for them and their family, and they provide a financial lifeline to their family members and community back home. Often they face hardship in their host city as they may be forced to navigate living in a high-crime neighborhood, manage difficult work hours, confront historical racism, overcome language barriers, and learn a new culture with its strange laws and customs. However, for many the economic improvement over their original conditions keeps them in their new context, overshadowing real challenges. Many migrants are working and living for more than their own personal advancement, pleasure, or life goals; they are working for their whole family. This may be for the survival of their immediate family or for the economic advancement of an entire kinship network. One day I was speaking with a friend in New York City who was from West Africa, and he said to me, "Jared, here in America you care for yourself and your wife and children, but it is different for us. We do not just work for ourselves. When we speak of our family it includes our cousins and aunts and nephews and nieces. We are working not just for ourselves. We must work for our whole family." Others may have been doing well in their country of origin, but they bring their family to a more developed nation in order to provide their children with opportunity. One of our evangelism teams in New York City was reaching out to a South Asian neighborhood, and one man that they spent considerable time with owned a small hotel back in Bangladesh. The people in this ethnic community respected him as a young businessman full of achievement and promise. Yet he was living with his family in a small city apartment because he wanted to provide the opportunity for his children to attend school in the United States. He chose a path of real difficulties and immeasurable challenges to provide an education for his children that he didn't feel he could provide for them in his home country. His move to a city a world away was for the benefit of his family and future of his children.

It is worthwhile to raise some questions for the church to ponder in an age of globalization. How does global migration impact economic development in the world's poorer communities? Do diaspora communities linking global networks open new pathways for helping struggling communities in the developing world? What impact do international migration and global diasporas have on Christian community development? While this text focuses specifically on implications for the Christian practice of evangelism, compassionate service is an essential act of Christian witness. Therefore, taking time to consider the relationship between diaspora missiology and community development is an important conversation to explore. While economic development is not the subject of this book, it is worthwhile to consider the implications of the relationship between diaspora networks and economic development, and it is important to consider the work of community development that may accompany Gospel proclamation in a number of opportunities for transnational evangelism.

Much effort by nongovernmental organizations (NGOs) has been poured into the work of assisting impoverished communities in countries with struggling economies. Are there ways that the church may partner with Christian diaspora from poorer nations to bring compassionate aid through existing networks? Where are the gaps in the economy of migrant remittances and grassroots aid programs that the church in the West may be able to fill through mutual partnerships brokered by transnational citizens? Could smaller churches or organizations utilize relational networks for providing aid to overlooked communities? What are the potential negative consequences of a heavy reliance on international remittances, and are there ways the church may help soften some of the potential negative impact resulting from remittance-based economic growth among impoverished communities? Answering all these questions is not my focus in this text, but missionary efforts working through compassionate aid and community development programs must begin to evaluate the impact of globalization and international migration in light of their ministry vocation. As the church seeks to embody the work of the Gospel through works of mercy and bring economic development to suffering communities around the world, it will be important for Christian leaders to consider the opportunities and the challenges presented by contemporary global trends.

Many American Christians have been making significant strides in bringing compassionate aid to impoverished communities around the world. A powerful wave of conviction was echoed throughout the evangelical community when Bono, of the band U2, called out the church for a lack of concern for global poverty during an interview with Bill Hybels during a Willowcreek Leadership Summit. A couple years later in a follow-up interview, Bono admitted to Hybels that the church had stepped up and responded with action to the needs of the world's poorest communities. A number of efforts have taken place both before and after the Bono interview as Christians are indeed called to respond to global poverty with proactive compassion and care. With the distance gap between followers of Christ and our global neighbors increasingly shrinking, opportunities to serve people who were once a world away increases as well. A handful of ministries have focused on digging wells in towns and villages where clean water is severely needed. Many doctors have taken time off from their local practices and traveled to serve as medical missionaries, giving emergency care where people would otherwise go untreated. A number of child sponsorship programs are making an impact on the lives of children in some of the world's poorest communities. Some years ago, I had breakfast with a Vietnamese pastor in New York City. He told me his background, and his story began by being sponsored through Compassion International while he was a young boy in Vietnam. He was eager to recommend sponsoring other children through the same program that had lifted him. Many of these efforts and so many others are making real contributions to the poor and marginalized and to struggling communities around the world. Can we identify mistakes that are made in these efforts? Of course, and we should continue to do better and improve wherever there is a need to make changes. However, many lives are saved and suffering eased as ordinary people serve "the least of these" in the name of Jesus.

Nevertheless, the sheer volume of people in desperate poverty continues to persist, and despite many of the church's truly wonderful efforts to combat the epidemic of global poverty, these economic needs continue to weigh heavy on the world stage. Right under our noses, perhaps, is one of the greatest forces of economic aid the world has ever seen—that is, struggling immigrants. Diaspora communities connected to their homelands through global networks have had a tremendous effect on world economics. Fair employment and opportunities for advancement in a North American city can mean a whole family living on the other side of an ocean is lifted economically. Alan McMahan challenges our assumptions, saying, "We're having to admit that immigration-migration patterns are probably doing more to alleviate global poverty than all the Christian charities combined in terms of flow of money going back home" (McMahan, 2013, p. 116). This reality does not negate the ongoing efforts of Christian charities or the good intentions of millions of Christian households giving generously to trustworthy organizations working on the frontlines of economic relief and development. Nevertheless, with the rise of global remittances over the last 40 years, the vast majority of that income has gone to developing countries. Remittances from immigrants around the world have indeed become a greater source of income for developing countries than the official assistance they are receiving from international development programs (Vertovec, 2009, p. 105). The realities of global migration and the enormous capital of their networks beg the question: What strategies may arise that may positively contribute to economic development and provide relief to impoverished or suffering communities through churches developing intentional diaspora partnerships?

Grassroots Economics

Immigrants laboring in cities throughout North America and Europe are making tremendous contributions to the economies of their countries of origin. Through remittances—the money sent home by migrants—many families are living at a higher economic standard than they previously had experienced. Sick relatives can afford medical care. Children are often attending better schools. Entire families are experiencing better living conditions. These strides are lifting families and communities that might otherwise have few options. There has even been research demonstrating "a direct correlation indicating that infants in migrant-sending families are less likely to suffer infant death or to be of low birth weight—a key determinant in health outcomes later in life. Remittances offset the effects of poverty by raising standards of living, improving nutrition and facilitating access to medical care" (Vertovec, 2009, p. 110). While it may be easy to critique negative aspects or potentially unhelpful outcomes resulting from global migration, families and communities are experiencing improved health, education, and living conditions due in large part to international migration.

For many churches, it may be easy to overlook the potential of an individual immigrant's contribution to alleviate global poverty. It may seem that his or her contribution is meager, and it is easy for feelings of sympathy to stop short rather than reaching a crest of missiological creativity. However, the amount these individual contributions add up to is really quite astounding. "The relatively small amounts of money which migrants transfer as remittances to their places of origin now add up to at least $300 billion worldwide" (Vertovec, 2009, p. 8). The amount of money moving between nations through the grassroots support of international laborers rivals virtually any international aid program in operation today. As a result, it appears that the greatest economic force combating global poverty is international migration.

As an American, I have to admit it is difficult for me to fully grasp the creative and efficient means many migrants employ to advance their families living back home. Several years ago, I was sitting with a friend from The Gambia. I was listening intently as he described his contributions to his family. He only worked in a coffee shop in Midtown Manhattan. He shared rent with two or three African roommates. He had to buy food, and he was paying an immigration lawyer as he was working on his immigration status in the United States. Yet, from his job at the coffee shop, he was able to coordinate with his brother in The Gambia to build a five-bedroom house. Similarly, a couple of years ago my friend from Liberia came to my apartment to get help typing up a lease. He had saved over five years and slowly built a house in Monrovia that he was about to rent to a high-ranking government official. The entrepreneurial spirit of immigrants utilizing their diasporic networks is impressive. They represent some of the most battle-tested and skilled entrepreneurs in our midst. While a good deal of money is used for creating an opportunity toward upward mobility into the middle or upper classes, the majority of remittances sent home by international migrants goes to basic needs such as housing, food, education, and medical care. These contributions lift the overall health and productivity of their homelands (Vertovec, 2009, p. 105). The growth of communication and information technologies has opened the door for everyday business, such as work, shopping, and education to carry on irrespective of geographic proximity (Susser, 2002, p. 329). It is difficult to imagine trends in global migration reversing anytime soon if this sort of economic empowerment continues through grassroots networks. The challenge for the church is to envision how she might be attentive to these global currents as she participates with God in his mission among the world's poorest communities.

As a result of international migration, new industries have emerged to meet the needs of a global network, connecting homeland with ethnic diasporas. Industries focused on global migration have seen significant growth over the last couple of decades. Companies providing long-distance phone calls, air travel, money transfers, shipping abroad, and similar products and services are seeing commercial growth within their sectors as they ride the waves of globalization and the vast movements of people around the planet (Vertovec, 2009, p. 102). The surge of commercial growth among these industries really points to the powerful economic engine that global migration represents.

From a missiological standpoint, one of the more interesting developments in the economic impact of global migration has been the development of "hometown associations." These associations are diaspora networks that engage in philanthropic work in their home country or community. Hometown associations contribute to their communities back home doing such things as "donating clothes, goods for religious festivals and construction materials for repairing the town church. They raise money for improving infrastructure such as sewage treatment plants and healthcare facilities. They support educational institutions, such as providing scholarships and library books." They even invest in projects that are "income-generating" and have shared management between members of the diaspora and personnel back in the home community (Vertovec, 2009-14). Such hometown associations are intentional about providing support and development to their communities of origin. They represent a grassroots community organizing on a global scale, and they illustrate the raw potential for global partnerships that provide compassionate support and economic lift to communities in developing nations.

For instance, "Mexicans have emerged as one of the newest and fastest-growing immigrant groups in New York City." For the last couple of decades, they have been arriving predominantly from the south-central region of Mexico and continue to maintain connections between villages back home and their lives in New York City. Some municipalities in the Puebla area of Mexico lost as many as 30 or 40% of their population to migration to New York City. Therefore, it is natural for significant networks among Mexicans to emerge in New York and build connections between their host city and hometown as well as form symbolic expressions of their cultural origins. Building networks and community among Mexicans, the Mexican Sports Federation of the Northeastern United States connects Mexican migrants through sporting events. Soccer teams form by gathering a group of friends who originate from the same town or village in Mexico, so each team may represent a different homeland village or neighborhood. The soccer field becomes a place for renewing community ties linked to their nation of origin. Former elementary school classmates or neighbors may reunite on a soccer field in Queens or the Bronx. Upon arriving in New York City, migrant families from Mexico naturally settle in neighborhoods that have characteristically been known for demographics reflecting a Latino flavor, such as Puerto Rican or Dominican communities in The Bronx, Brooklyn, Queens, and East Harlem. While these communities originally embodied a different culture, they operate largely in Spanish, making for a more natural transition for Mexican immigrants. Interestingly, migrants from Mexico have become a favored group for hire in the city. They have attained a reputation for hard work, and other ethnic business owners have realized they can hire Mexican workers for cheaper labor and without cultural obligations attached that may imply common commitments or social pressures among those of the same ethnic network. While there may be a negative "brain-drain" on the Mexican economy in communities where large percentages are emigrating to the United States, Mexicans in New York City are providing a powerful source of financing and infrastructure support back to their communities of origin in Mexico. Demonstrating a global perspective, many Mexicans who have migrated to New York measure their income by what they can buy in Mexico instead of comparing their income to the earnings of others working in the United States. Their economic consciousness is largely linked to their transnational identities rather than local comparisons to their counterparts in the United States. Their global connection to home remains at the center of their consciousness and takes precedence over local standards. For Mexican municipalities such as Ticuani, where nearly half of its citizens live in New York, Mexican leaders in New York City may participate in town hall meetings with local leaders in Mexico through conference calls, and Mexican New Yorkers make trips to Mexico to check on community projects they are financially supporting. Since the 1970s, numerous projects have been funded in the Ticuani municipality by Mexicans working in New York City. Mexicans in New York have funded the building of two schools, provided for repairs to the town church, paid for installation of a lighting system, and raised more than $100,000 for a portable water system to be installed. The New York contribution to the installation of the water system in Ticuani was greater than the amounts provided by the local, state, and federal governments in Mexico combined (R. C. Smith, 1996, pp. 57-79). Examining transnational activity of Mexican communities linked between hometowns in the Puebla area and networks in New York City points to a dynamic grassroots global economy empowered by international migration as well as modern technology enabling communication, travel, and the ease of transferring funds across national borders. Grassroots associations and international networks have emerged as major engines in the global economy and in local community development through global flows.

With the rise of transnational activity as a major manifestation of globalization, many nations depend on remittances from their citizens laboring overseas in order to support their national economy. Nations such as the Philippines, Pakistan, and a number of countries in Latin America rely on their citizens pumping foreign capital back into their economy. Remittances have become a substantial portion of their national economy. As a result, many national governments have begun to develop economic policies to integrate remittances into their government's financial structures (Vertovec, 2009, pp. 8-9). Hometown associations are demonstrating intentionality as they provide grassroots support for developing their homeland communities, and commercial enterprises focused on patterns and activities of global migration are growing. Simultaneously, immigrants in American cities are often entrepreneurial and intuitively in touch with global currents. They often bring an entrepreneurial drive to the marketplace in their new city while lifting economic conditions for their family residing in their homeland. Christian leaders would do well to pay attention to these global currents. What potential may be discovered by the church when imaginative thinking and creative planning is matched with transparent, mutual partnering with transnational citizens?

Linking Communities at Home: Angel Reyes's Story

At age 10, Angel Reyes moved from the Caribbean coast of Honduras to live in the South Bronx in New York City. Growing up in the city, he actually dreamed of going back to his childhood home of Honduras, so he wanted to study agriculture in a university in the United States to prepare himself for his return to his home country. To pay for college, he took advantage of the opportunity that military service provided and joined the United States Army. Following his time in the military, he began attending a college with an agriculture program in upstate New York, but something deeper was stirring within Angel as well. He was searching for spiritual direction and wanted to pursue opportunities to find spiritual guidance and discover faith in something more. He began researching Christian colleges that offered an agriculture major, and in 1982 he drove to west Texas to attend Abilene Christian University. It was the first college he found, due primarily to its place at the front of the alphabet. It was a Christian college, and it offered an agriculture major. He determined to address his desire to study agriculture and his spiritual searching with the same move. With Texas's reputation for agriculture, he assumed he had found the right match.

Naturally, Angel experienced a great deal of culture shock. If moving from the villages along the Caribbean coast in Central America to the South Bronx as a 10-year-old boy wasn't culture shock enough, moving from New York City to a private Christian college in west Texas provided another round of cultural whiplash. He was surprised to find that many of his classes were about the Bible. Also, being Black and Spanish-speaking made Angel feel completely out of place. He was neither African-American nor Mexican-American, and in a predominantly White student body in a private university in Texas there wasn't a cultural group where he naturally fit. Despite large populations of African ancestry throughout the Spanish-speaking Caribbean and Latin America, many in that west Texas setting had never conceived of a culture where someone was both Black and

Hispanic. Nevertheless, he continued his spiritual seeking, and during his studies at Abilene Christian University was baptized in Jesus Christ.

After one and a half years there, he went home to Honduras and lived with his family and childhood neighbors for a year. As a new follower of Jesus, he started a church in his grandmother's house in the town of Travesia. About 15 to 20 people gathered in his family's home, and his father, grandmother, and others in the community turned their hearts to Jesus and were baptized. After a year of living in Honduras, he left 20 to 30 people regularly meeting as a church, and he partnered with a church leader in a nearby town who would commute to the coastal town and help teach the new church each week. Angel returned to the United States, but his heart stayed connected to the family of God that had come together in Travesia. After some time back in New York City, he returned to Abilene Christian University and completed his studies. Still, he continued caring for the small church that he had planted in Honduras. While studying in Abilene, three times he drove from the dusty plains of west Texas, across the Rio Grande, through Mexico, and on to the tropical coast of Honduras.

In 1986, he graduated from college and returned to New York City. He eventually became the Spanish ministry leader and an elder in Manhattan Church of Christ, but his heart continued to pound for the community in Honduras. For several years, he financially supported a preacher, from his own income, to serve the church in Travesia. Angel began recruiting members of the church in Manhattan to go on week-long mission trips to Honduras, and that exposure led to the church in New York getting heavily involved in the ministry to Travesia. One of the elders of Manhattan Church of Christ began making trips to Honduras, was moved by the experience, and even stayed in the town for a month on his own. Despite being an English-only Brooklyn native, he was overwhelmed with love for the Honduran community. Other leaders from the Manhattan Church of Christ eventually made trips to Honduras as well, and with the relief efforts following

Hurricane Mitch, a new phase in the Honduras-New York partnership began.

After the punishing blow that Hurricane Mitch delivered to Honduras in 1998, numerous churches got involved in helping with relief efforts. I was part of a church in the central city of Houston that helped coordinate a united effort involving dozens of churches across metropolitan Houston. The devastation of the storm motivated believers to respond with urgency, and Manhattan Church of Christ was no exception. With connections to a specific community in Honduras through a member of the Honduran diaspora, they began seeking how they might help with the community's physical concerns. Angel developed a partnership with a medical ministry, which had connections to a faculty member at Abilene Christian University, that was located on the Caribbean coast. They opened a dental clinic in Travesia and sponsored an annual medical mission trip. A computer class was offered in the town for three years, and his church continued to seek ways they could help their new sister community.

When one member of Manhattan Church of Christ accompanied Angel on a week-long trip to Honduras, he returned and started a child sponsorship program providing school supplies for a group of children over an eight-year period. They called the program Giver of Dreams, and many of the sponsors were members of Angel's church in Manhattan. The vision for Giver of Dreams has now evolved into plans for a new Christian school in the community, starting with kindergarten and first grade. As numerous efforts have flowed from his church community in New York to offer help to his first home in Honduras, Angel read a book that began to reshape his strategy for helping his hometown. He read through the pages of When Helping Hurts (Corbett & Fikkert, 2009), and it began to transform the way he thought about his ministry to his Central American home. He said he realized this could no longer be simply an American project in Honduras. It needed to be a mutual partnership. While maintaining U.S. involvement, he began recruiting more Hondurans to become partners in the project. Some of the American Christians, motivated by sincere love for the people, sometimes gave extravagantly to families to whom they had grown close in their relationships. Therefore, Angel counseled Americans involved in being discerning in their generosity to include the wider community, and he began shifting the focus of how development was taking place. Giving would continue but needed to be distributed more throughout the village rather than New Yorkers giving to a single family. Previously, much of the development work was through annual mission trips made up almost entirely of North Americans. Now Angel, while still leading mission trips from New York City to his hometown, has shifted the work of economic development in the community from almost entirely an annual infusion of resources to longer-term and more sustainable development projects based on mutual partnerships between local Hondurans, American volunteers, and transnational Honduran migrants who identify with New York City and Honduras simultaneously.

As they start the new school in Honduras, Angel is strategically recruiting sponsors for the project from differing spheres of influence and backgrounds. He is not only involving members of his church in Manhattan, but he is also partnering with Hondurans both in New York and in Central America. He is recruiting local Hondurans near the coast from middle-class backgrounds to contribute $25 per month, and he is getting Hondurans living in New York City involved as well. Many of them also travel to Honduras to visit family or conduct business and can have even more direct involvement in the education project. He is networking with fellow transnational Hondurans to mobilize them for the project. Realizing the need for cross-cultural and mutual partnerships, he is joining members of his diverse community of faith in Manhattan, Honduran professionals in Central America, and transnational migrants from Honduras living in the boroughs of New York City.

Recognizing that mutual partnership was needed for medical care in the community as well, Angel began building relationships with doctors in cities in the larger region near the Caribbean coast. Angel recruited doctors from Honduras to serve Travesia during annual medical mission trips, and now the church in Manhattan sponsors eight Honduran doctors to spend a week each year serving the people in his home community. Angel also arranged for recent medical school graduates in Honduras to spend a year of their residency program serving the Travesia community. As members of Angel's church in Manhattan continued to get involved in serving his hometown in Honduras, another member who works in New York City's fashion industry decided to start a sewing class. Today, the sewing class is a shared venture between the Honduran government and the church. The government provides the teachers, and the church provides the sewing machines, fabric, and a physical space for the class.

Angel's story is one motivated by love for his family and for his childhood home, and his strategy has been refined through experience and a continued posture toward learning. During my interview with him, I was moved by Angel's willingness to continue learning and making adjustments to improve his work in Honduras. He's one example of a transnational urban dweller creating a bridge between his faith community in New York City and his community in his country of origin, and now he is drawing in other transnational migrants. The first steps that led to his ministry to this Central American town began with his desire to share his newfound faith in Christ with his family members, and as a church emerged in his childhood home, transnational flows of ministry continued to evolve. While neither his background nor that of the leadership or members of Manhattan Church of Christ were well-versed in economic development or schooled in cross-cultural church planting, they were motivated by a sincere desire to help, and they were prepared to keep learning how they might improve their methods to benefit the community in the long term. Angel would be the first to admit there were things that needed improvement in order to better serve his home community, but I can't help but wonder what other potential projects could be born out of transnational partnerships where a migrant has connections in a church in the United States and an underserved community in the majority world. There will always be potential for mistakes. However, with a learning spirit, we might imagine what other transnational migrants could spearhead church-planting and community development projects in areas of need.

The Church in Transnationalism

Transnationalism presents a challenge for the church. New ways of thinking about missiology and practicing evangelism will need to come into play. Existing paradigms are being confronted by a world constantly on the move. Garcia-Johnson offers three ways of being church that have particular relevance in a "polycentric and transnational context." First, he explains, the church must be a "eucharistic community," a community that welcomes others who are culturally different and calls them brother. Christ's table must be a safe space where each one may maintain individual cultural identity while sharing a common identity in Jesus with others around the table. Second, the church must be "a community of proclamation." In a pluralistic society, cities are intersections where a variety of individuals and communities meet Jesus's story. Third, we must be a "pastoral community." In a world in constant flux, individuals are in need of grace. "The pastoral practice points to a capacity for seeing people and their stories, embodying a new social reality, and becoming a restorative-healing community" (Garcia-Johnson, 2012, p. 125).

Conclusion

Encountering a transnational world may be challenging as communities are less static and cultural practices and identities are in flux. However, missiological strategies are beginning to emerge to pioneer new evangelism opportunities through dynamic pathways of global flows. It is likely that these stories of transnational evangelism and church planting are only the beginning of a new platform for Christian mission. Transnational citizens linking cities in a global network provide new avenues for Gospel witness. Church multiplication strategies have led to making disciples and planting new churches in the homelands of transnational migrants, but to see these sorts of stories increase, conventional church-growth paradigms will be confronted with new global realties of mobility and fluidity. Expecting local communities to remain monolithic is shortsighted in light of current global realities, and individual believers are more mobile than ever before. Church models and structures will need to take such mobility and fluidity into account while grasping opportunities for a more expansive global witness. Change is a constant, and urban contexts are regularly being reconstructed. Challenges faced by missionaries are dizzying; however, opportunities for global evangelism shaped by transnationalism are unprecedented.

Reflection Questions

1. Are there transnational citizens in your church congregation who are active in their home countries?
2. Where do you see transnational businesses operating in your city?
3. What role is your church taking in addressing global poverty? Could creative solutions present themselves for mutual partnerships through transnational networks?
4. Has your church evaluated its approach to short-term mission trips?
5. How might the presence of diaspora communities in your community impact your church's mission involvement?

Chapter 7
The New Context for Missions and Ministry Implications

The Church at Global Intersections

Urban missionaries are standing at the global crossroads, and with the rise of international migration, the increasing tide of urbanization, and the complex and dynamic movement of diaspora communities from around the planet, new thinking needs to go into missions philosophies and practical evangelism strategies. While the shifts in the cultural makeup of the global village is increasingly obvious to Christian leaders and a great deal more attention is shifting to diaspora missiology, mission leaders are faced with the task of thinking through the practical missiological implications for the new world in which we now live. "The global reality of the church poses challenges to some of the assumed patterns of engagement. ... Reimagining current models will involve sensitivity and tenacity, alongside well-researched analysis of the connections, networks, and movements already touching or present in the local Christian community" (Davey, 2002, p. 106). The global movement of ethnic diasporas represents the mobility, connectivity, and constant flux of today's global mission field.

With the rise of a multitude of diaspora networks and ethnic enclaves throughout many of the world's postindustrial cities, mission leaders are challenged to take on key tasks to stimulate missionary engagement with the nations residing in our cities. Paul Kraus points out three areas of needed development for the church to serve evangelistically among the nations within North American cities in order to facilitate a missiological impact in and through diaspora communities.

First, he emphasizes that mission training is needed for existing churches in American cities. The renewal of the North American landscape as a mission field is long overdue. While there has been a growing awareness of the need to reenvision evangelistic engagement within Western society, the arrival of a host of ethnic groups and unreached peoples from a number of different nations is stimulating an increased recognition of North American cities as a mission field. Many well-established churches in Western cities lack a missiological vision for strategic engagement with the diaspora communities in their midst. Therefore, missiologists should be challenged to bring cross-cultural training to churches that have a heart for reaching their ethnic neighbors but lack key insights or understanding of cross-cultural evangelism principles. Second, there is a need for training for ethnic churches populating American cities. Often new churches are formed as a result of gathering immigrants from the same ethnic background, and these new congregations represent a vibrant and dynamic potential for a new missionary force. However, training is often needed in order to help ethnic churches become an effective evangelistic force within their new host culture and to other nearby diaspora groups. These ethnic communities are experiencing culture shock and face tremendous challenges as they seek to adjust to a foreign culture. Despite many diaspora churches having the desire to be a missionary presence, many will need help navigating the strange terrain of Western cities. Third, there is a need to evangelize diaspora communities. Many new immigrants are not Christians when they arrive, and evangelism among diaspora populations may result in finding open doors for the Gospel among an unreached ethnic group. Often, this cross-cultural evangelism will require taking intentional steps to build bridges into ethnic communities and pursue purposeful Gospel sharing (Kraus, March 22, 2014). Building bridges to diaspora communities that are dotting the landscape of Western cities may strengthen the church's renewal as a missionary community. While the American church needs to be equipped in missionary practice, there are indeed many opportunities for engagement in global missions through local contexts.

There is a need for evangelistic efforts to engage global networks as well as new church-planting initiatives among local diaspora communities, and established churches in Western cities may play a key role. Clayton Milano offers six suggestions for American congregations to join God's mission among diaspora communities. First, he explains, American churches must stop engaging only those who look and sound like them. They must move beyond their own cultural profile to embrace others. This will require Christians to take intentional steps to build relationships outside their normal cultural world. Second, American churches must put aside their old missions paradigms. Many churches still think of missions involvement in terms of a single direction. That is, financing a missionary to go overseas. While churches should continue sponsoring overseas missionaries, they must begin to recognize a more dynamic set of demographics and engage diaspora communities within reach of their congregation. Third, local churches in Western cities need to begin exploring what people groups live and work in their city. They need to begin seeking to find out who their neighbors are and what ethnic communities are emerging in their area. There is clearly a need for ethnography to emerge as a pastoral practice as leaders relearn how to care for their community that is gradually becoming increasingly international. Fourth, ministries will need to intentionally focus on an ethnic culture in their city. In order to effectively contextualize the communication of the Gospel and focus their church-planting efforts on the unreached in their communities, they need to concentrate on learning the culture of the ethnic group they are adopting for missionary engagement. Fifth, outreach ministries must "create new structures where unreached people groups can flourish before and after they come to Christ." We often assume we will simply invite new migrants to our large American church, but at times, these spaces—associated with Western forms and structures—can become a barrier for some diaspora communities. New structures can still operate under the leadership of the sponsoring church, but should facilitate the opportunity to develop Gospel-centered community in a cultural space where seekers and new believers from unreached people groups can thrive and grow outside of the potential constraints of Western culture. Finally, they should develop a plan. Once they identify an ethnic community in their area and begin learning the cultural traits and worldview of the people group, they should begin putting next steps into action for engaging their diaspora neighbors with the Gospel (Milano, 2014).

While there is a need to focus time, energy, and resources toward contextualized evangelism and church planting among diaspora communities, there is much that existing churches can do. Churches in the dominant Western culture can sponsor missionary efforts among migrant networks, and they can foster hospitality among new arrivals in their community. They can offer services to immigrants in need of English, education, legal help, and assistance in adapting to a new foreign culture. Existing churches can help facilitate a culturally appropriate space outside of their church building for non-Western migrants to explore spiritual conversations or for developing a contextualized church assembly in a neutral space that removes many of the barriers present in the host culture. Many churches and mission organizations have several connections to missionary efforts overseas and may facilitate collaborative relationships between those ministries and evangelists working through ethnic diaspora networks in North America or Europe. As the realities of globalization continue to emerge and are increasingly felt by urban evangelists, virtually everyone is still in a learning and pioneering mode while addressing this new global context for mission. It is important that churches, agencies, missionaries, and Christian leaders from within the diaspora engage in robust conversations to enhance mutual learning and potential partnerships. Through collaboration and open channels of dialogue, the whole church can grow in her ability to serve as Christ's ambassadors among an array of diaspora communities.

As local churches and ministry organizations operating in Western cities engage diaspora communities in their midst, there are significant steps they can take to enhance their evangelism strategy. Church planting should develop or adopt strategies that lead to potential multiplication as often as possible. This increases the potential reach—both locally and globally—of new evangelism initiatives. Local churches desiring to engage nearby unreached communities should continue developing hospitable space for reaching out to the least reached in their city. Finally, many churches are populated by a significant number of entrepreneurs. Much thinking remains for how business-as-mission may act as a platform for diaspora missiology.

Church Multiplication

The flood of international migrants to North American cities presents an opportunity to the church in the United States and other Western countries. As a church largely represented by homogeneous communities in a nation stressed by a tense racial history, the opportunity to integrate Christians from around the world into our existing churches is a welcome opportunity. Many years ago, my graduate research was on multiethnic churches in urban contexts, and this sort of Christian unity and cultural reconciliation has long been close to my heart. Many individual migrants—especially those who come to the United States already as believers—will gravitate to well-established American churches, and this is an opportunity we should celebrate. Nevertheless, a strategy that will likely have a more far-reaching impact on evangelism among the nations will be to focus significant energies on church multiplication.

In many cases, the intentional professionalism of the contemporary church in the United States will only be reproducible by only the most talented entrepreneurs, in nations legally open to Christian expansion, and where the same sort of resources that contribute to American church planting can be made available in that context. In other words, we really must rethink our church-planting strategies. When church planting is based on organic structures that are simple, reproducible, and scalable, they have potential to multiply throughout the city and jump borders into hard-to-reach places because any believer can become the conduit for a new community of faith. Existing churches can sponsor missionaries to the diaspora, partner with missions organizations already pursuing this strategy, or seek training for their members to spark the beginning of church multiplication through evangelism in one or more diaspora communities. As we started Global City Mission Initiative, we desired partnerships to advance the Gospel through mutual evangelism efforts, and we have seen other missions organizations actively partner with existing ministries and churches, too, for the sake of the shared mission to advance the Kingdom of God.

It is tempting for local churches to focus all their energy on their own institutional growth as a local body, and for many churches, the opportunity to transition into a more multiethnic community is thrilling. While applauding these efforts, it is important that existing churches also seek opportunities to leverage their resources to advance the Gospel beyond their walls. By prayerfully seeking opportunities to spark church multiplication through evangelistic engagement in diaspora communities, their reach as a missionary force may extend further than they might even have imagined.

Creating Hospitable Space

In some neighborhoods, churches may find themselves surrounded by an emerging community of Hindus, Muslims, Sikhs or other once-unfamiliar cultural groups. Church members may deeply desire to engage unreached people groups living in the same area of the city, but they discover that they must move beyond one significant barrier. For many of these least-reached people to enter fellowship with the church they must overcome the barrier of entering the foreign space of the church building. For some, this represents a foreign entity and creates a barrier that is difficult to overcome prior to entering into a maturing Christian faith.

As a result, existing churches may consider ways of creating hospitable spaces outside of their church facility for interacting with unreached peoples. They may use an existing community space in the city where new immigrants from unreached people groups are already comfortable visiting, like a tearoom or library. The church may rent a nonreligious space for providing English classes, tutoring for citizenship tests, or other services. One ministry in a city in the southeastern United States provides a welcome center for new migrants where they offer English classes for a fee. New migrants who come to the center for its services are treated with extravagant hospitality. As a result, they have started a number of Bible study groups among Muslims that meet in private homes throughout the city.

Exploring Business-as-Mission in Diaspora Communities

In New York City it is not unusual to walk into a Pakistani restaurant and read an announcement posted for a new mosque starting in the neighborhood or to walk into a shop run by West African Muslims and find that virtually everyone in the store is from the same country and shares the same Muslim faith. Walking along a Bangladeshi street in a New York City neighborhood at sunset, it is not surprising to find a grocery store converted into a place to conduct evening prayers, as neighborhood residents gather together facing east to Mecca. Many urban neighborhoods populated by unreached people groups are communities where businesses connect to religious institutions or become platforms for advancing the faith. However, it would be worthwhile for Christian missiologists to explore the same sort of opportunity among diaspora communities.

In our own organization, we've discussed the potential for mobilizing new migrants as missionaries to unreached people groups in the city. What if Christian entrepreneurs developed their businesses into intentional platforms for employing Christian migrants who could serve as "tent-making" missionaries to the community? What if owners of coffee shops or restaurants opened their space for English classes or other services? What if Christian business owners intentionally located in Muslim, Hindu, or Buddhist communities in order to provide an intentional Christian witness in the business sector of that community? More missiological reflection and strategic thought should go into profitable business-as-mission enterprises and entrepreneurial endeavors as platforms for sponsoring bivocational missionaries through migration streams, reaching out in unreached communities, providing an inroads for hospitable space among unreached people groups, and other creative ideas for engaging diaspora networks.

The New Playing Field: The Importance of Cities as Global Nodes

Cities everywhere are the new mission field. Therefore, nearly everything we do in missiological education, leadership training, scholarship, conference themes, and the like must become reoriented around this present reality. This is our present-future. Urban space is the new geography of missiology, and while missionaries are still needed in remote areas, many of the new missionary pioneers will carry a Metro pass for the subway rather than a machete for the jungle. Our new world revolves around the city, and when we speak about the global context, we are essentially talking about a worldwide web of cities.

For some time, missions were focused on a particular geographic region. For many missions-related ministries, the focus on a geographic region remains a consistent focus. Nevertheless, over the last few decades there has been an increased emphasis in targeting particular cultural groups for church planting and evangelism. While this approach should continue to be subjected to thoughtful critiques within missiological debates, especially when a more holistic ministry perspective is missing from the presentation of the Gospel, this intentionality in the area of evangelism has led to numerous advances for the Gospel. This emphasis has opened the door for specific cultural contextualization, and much frontier missions work has focused on carrying the Gospel to unreached people groups with a contextualized focus on a particular ethnic population or worldview. These moves toward indigenous church multiplication have not been without tension and debate between missiologists. The need for an indigenous expansion of the church on the one hand and a holistic perspective of Christian mission on the other provides for a healthy tension. However, while the church plays a prophetic and priestly role in addressing systemic injustice, the evangelistic efforts toward the vision for a more "spontaneous expansion of the church" (Allen, 1962) have helped advance the global church through the rise—both intentional and circumstantial—of indigenous leadership and church multiplication, and intentional evangelism efforts among specific ethnic networks need to continue. Planting a church to reach the general population in a specific region or city may result in much good work, but while bridging geographic barriers to the Gospel, cultural or linguistic distance may continue even within close geographic proximity if an urban area is highly pluralistic. Many populations in the city require intentional contextualization in order to make a missiological impact within an ethnic community. Still, to reach the diversity of the city, both multiethnic churches and culturally contextualized or language-specific church planting is needed. Cross-cultural partnerships may open opportunities for helping first-generation churches bridge new avenues of ministry among their second-generation children and their multiethnic world. The city is a mosaic of cultures, languages, and customs. In the continuum of assimilation running across the cultural streams of the city, both approaches should be applauded. Finding ways for ethnic churches worshipping in their heart language and multiethnic churches speaking the language of the dominant culture to partner in order to facilitate ministry gains among the second generation will go far in advancing both the evangelistic and the pastoral mission of the church in the global city.

One evangelistic effort associated with Global City Mission Initiative, as well as our ministry partners, is to people originating from Albania and Kosovo living in communities in New York City. The evangelist reaching out to this population group purposefully visits their cafes and shops and builds bridges for relationships within the community. Dozens of people have heard the Gospel—many for the first time—from his mouth. Despite a variety of churches scattered about their neighborhoods and throughout New York City, there was virtually no evangelism engagement with this ethnic community in this part of the city until recently. Additionally, many West African groups in the city are from unreached people groups with little to no church presence anywhere in the world. Simply assuming they will walk into a large assembly gathering people from the dominant culture is shortsighted. Intentionality is a key component in reaching a variety of ethnic communities across the city. Even a large multiethnic church may be overlooked by the majority of the members of a monocultural ethnic enclave or a more exclusive ethnic network.

Chris Clayman recalls a pastor of a large church in New York telling him, "We thought if we had a large, influential church in New York City that the influence would naturally trickle down and reach all people groups. We have realized we were wrong in our assumption and we have hardly touched the unreached people groups of our city" (Clayman, March 22, 2014). There remains a persistent need to recognize cultural and linguistic groups within the international and pluralistic mosaic of our cities and the need for intentional and contextualized evangelism. As new believers mature, a key role that missionaries can play is to help them work through the specifics of cross-cultural fellowship and ministry partnerships in a diverse city. Greater unity across cultural barriers should increase with greater spiritual maturity, and Christian leaders should model a cross-cultural embrace for their congregations. Simultaneously, our love for all peoples compels us to meet people from any variety of backgrounds or worldviews right where they are culturally. Overall, the intentional focus on specific peoples makes a missiological contribution to the church. Even when we have closed the gap geographically, there often remains a cultural distance still needing to be bridged through intentional ministry. However, to what extent does an ethnic or linguistic focus diminish the importance of a geographic emphasis as well?

It would seem that geographic emphases are of decreasing importance in a world constantly on the move and connected instantaneously through modern communications. That would be the logical assumption, but the evidence points toward the opposite conclusion. In a global society linked through international and regional networks, the multicentered geography of cities emerges as a key function in the movement and mobility of people from around the world. In reality, global cities demonstrate that within the global network through the "space of flows," there is still a "place-based orientation" (Susser, 2002, p. 347). There is a new spatial orientation of urban nodes connected across international networks. The new geography is both concentrated in urban space and scattered through well-connected networks. Missiologists ought not dismiss a geographic emphasis of mission, but rather what is needed in the world that is now rising is a strategic reorientation of geography around urban nodes that operate as links in a global network. That is, the geography of world missions is now urban centers connected as a global network. Such a shift requires new thinking in contextualization, mutual partnerships, and church planting. Our mission field is now regional and global urban centers, where we encounter indigenous urban dwellers struggling through an emerging post-Christendom culture, international diaspora communities adjusting to new contexts, and cultural hybrids marking out new identities in the city. Cities are of strategic importance not only because they contain massive amounts of people—though that would be enough to warrant a strong urban focus for Christian mission—but also because they are the strategic centers for reaching numerous ethnic communities and unreached people groups living and working and moving through the city. This does not mean rural or remote mission fields are unimportant. To the contrary, these sorts of efforts should continue, and in many cases a strategic focus on urban-global nodes may create links for the Gospel into more rural locations as well. When I began meeting with a new believer who had migrated from Mexico to the Bronx, he began sharing the Gospel through phone conversations with his relatives back in small rural villages of only 100 people in Mexico. Through his encounter with the Gospel in New York City, he was now becoming a conduit for the Gospel to a small village in rural Mexico. The city has become a gateway for evangelism far beyond the streets of the original city alone. In addition to local engagement, missions strategies that keep the global network in view may simultaneously coordinate missionary efforts between evangelism in globally connected urban areas and ministries in distant fields where transnational flows will enhance ministry opportunities. Cities as nodes of global influence are demonstrating real importance as the key contexts for global mission.

With the growth of information technology, many assumed that the increase in home-based electronic communication would lead to the demise of cities. Some thought interaction based on shared proximity would diminish in importance and begin to trigger a reversal in dense urbanization, but the evidence of the present state of urbanization leads to an entirely different conclusion. Rather, it appears that services and processes performed by humans in a global network have experienced both "simultaneous dispersion and concentration." Sociologist, Manuel Castells, informs us that "what is significant about this spatial system of advanced services activities is neither their concentration nor decentralization, since both processes are indeed taking place at the same time throughout countries and continents" (Susser, 2002, pp. 314-322). With the growth of the Internet and related technologies, there was, in recent years, much chatter about a flat world. However, it appears that speculation was only half right. Decentralization of services and processes is indeed occurring, but so is intense and purposeful concentration in strategic urban centers. The world is not as flat as we thought after all. Instead it is now multicentered. Cities hailed as the world's global cities—specifically New York City, London, Paris, and Tokyo—resting on top of an urban hierarchy, continue to function as powerful centers in the global network. However, with the rise of a network society, they are major urban nodes connecting to other global and regional nodes in a worldwide urban network (Susser, 2002, p. 317). The rise of communication technology and the ability of people with low resources to communicate instantaneously across oceans hasn't stopped the acceleration of urbanization. If anything, it seems to have accelerated the process. Instead, the world now looks like a network or web—or perhaps more like a series of overlapping networks. Cities are the nodes connecting the networks of human activity that play out on both global and local platforms. "So the city functions to create transmission and distribution networks that span large regions where the footprint of the city stretches out over a lot of other places" (McMahan, 2013, p. 117). For missiology, the strategic importance of cities is increasing not only as population centers but as nodal centers of global exchanges as well. There is a new geography of missiology, and it is urban-centered and network-oriented.

It might seem obvious that the strategic emphasis of Christian missions should focus on urban areas simply for the sake of the massive numbers of people living within metropolitan regions. Certainly, Christian mission is to occur where people are, and our world is increasingly a place of cities. However, the overwhelming concentration of people is only one of the key factors that strategically pushes evangelism toward urban centers. As followers of Jesus Christ, we are drawn toward compassionate ministry to people, and cities are quite full of people. This fact alone would be enough to maintain the importance of cities to world missions because our labors as missionaries are ultimately about the redemptive work of God in the lives of people. Cities around the world are growing and experiencing unprecedented migration while the numbers of urban poor living in and around vast urban areas is staggering. If our only rationale for focusing significant resources of the church to target missionary activity to cities were the sheer size of urban populations, that would be sufficient enough rationale. Nevertheless, there is more to the importance of cities than the mere enormity of their populations. Missiologists focused on indigenous church multiplication among unreached peoples should be attentive to the increasing importance of urban space for world mission and strategic evangelism. Cities are both hosts to massive numbers of people and centers of connection between cultural communities and homelands.

Cities are nodes in the global network. Urban centers—both as players deeply impacted by globalization and as agents stimulating the acceleration of global connectivity—behave as concentrations of global interaction. Global cities, while real places, may be thought of more as processes for powering and resourcing the global network (Susser, 2002, p. 322). The practice of global mission implies urban engagement in a world of cities. While the functions of cities are most often discussed in sociological analysis as related to the processes of the global economy, metropolitan areas act also as hubs for international networks of various ethnic groups as well. These connections make it possible for a new arrival to find immediate support from within his or her ethnic community residing in the host culture. New arrivals that maintain a transnational identity will become a link between home and their host city and possibly between near culture groups within the city as well. Due to the ethnic networks that already exist in a metropolitan area, many cities become magnets for particular ethnic groups who prefer to see a familiar face when they arrive in a strange new city. A large Persian population in Los Angeles, Bangladeshi communities in London, Japanese in Sao Paulo, Ethiopians in Washington, D.C., and so many other examples easily illustrate the power of cities as points of connection in international networks. Simultaneously, these cities become launching pads for new immigrants who may eventually relocate to smaller cities or rural or suburban areas within their new host country but outside of the city where they first arrived. Metropolitan areas become a hotspot for evangelistic engagement. Most people experience religious conversion when they have gone through some sort of dramatic change, and this pattern illustrates the opportunities for evangelism latent among diaspora communities. Usually there is a window of a year or two during the early transition of the immigrant to his new society when he is open to new ideas (Clayman, March 22, 2014). There is a need for agencies and churches to become capable of responding quickly when a new wave of immigrants begins to arrive in a city. Often migration takes place in waves as clusters of ethnic groups arrive in a city almost simultaneously. This implies that a new window of evangelistic opportunity opens as a new wave of immigrants relocates to an urban area, and the church may seize the opportunity to serve and proclaim the Good News of the Kingdom while the window of receptivity remains open. In a highly mobile and global culture, evangelism and service ministries in churches and organizations will need to be prepared to move quickly in response to new opportunities. In our urban world, change is a constant.

Many migrants will relocate to North American cities and then move on to another region, smaller city, or suburb. There is a need for agencies, missionaries, and churches to focus on newly arrived immigrants when they first come to highly globalized cities while there is still a window open for evangelism opportunities. Reaching these new arrivals should be accompanied by equipping them to represent the Gospel when they go to the next stop in their journey. Often, these immigrants will relocate outside of the city to a regional center or suburb only to be replaced by additional new arrivals from around the world. In order to engage emerging populations spreading out across North America, a key mission strategy will be to evangelize migrants in cities when they are likely most receptive to considering faith. Finally, there is a strategic opportunity to focus missionary resources on cities where diaspora communities are established because these urban centers act as international hubs for ethnic networks. A Nigerian diaspora in Houston may form a cultural linkage with Lagos, or a Japanese community in Sao Paulo may represent a link to Osaka. Cities become hubs of activity for specific ethnic networks, and diaspora communities often concentrate in specific urban areas. In the United States, 45% of the country's Asian populations are concentrated in three urban areas: New York City, San Francisco, and Los Angeles (Rogers, 2006, p. 19). Any missions strategy to reach Asian diasporas in North America will need to give consideration to these metropolitan centers as Asian hubs for the global networks connecting metropolitan areas in the United States to Asian cities. This framework implies that mission strategies seeking to evangelize an ethnic group would likely benefit from including intentional networking in an urban center where a diaspora is concentrated. As members of a diaspora network move between international urban nodes, relational evangelism strategies may follow these global flows. Missiological strategies for reaching the nations ought to think in terms of globally connected networks where relational styles of evangelism may ride the waves of these transnational connections.

"With the world becoming deeply urban and connected, the pioneer missionary of the 21st century will look much different than previous centuries. They will focus on reaching busy, hidden, influential unreached peoples who have migrated to cities and will spread the gospel through these migrants' networks throughout the world" (Clayman, March 22, 2014). In the past, pioneering missionaries were those who charged through an Asian jungle to take the Gospel to a remote community or navigated across an African plain to proclaim the message of grace to an African village. These were the missionary heroes of our past, and certainly there will continue to be a need for these types of missionary laborers in remote locations that continue in virtual seclusion in various locations around the world. However, many of the pioneer missionaries in the coming decades will be traveling by subway, working in urban slums, or living in city high-rises. Missions at the edge will be an urban phenomenon, and missionaries who are pioneer church planters will be riding the waves of transnationalism and global connectivity.

Ironically, as technology has made it possible to connect to even some of the most remote places on our planet, cities have become more important than ever. Global missions will require an urban concentration. Cities are where the collections of humanity live and work on a daily basis, and cities are the hubs of human activity in the global network. For missiology, this implies a reorientation toward an urban world and a networked society. We will need to adapt our skills, our worldviews, and our structures to carry out God's mission in a worldwide network of cities.

Evangelism in the Space of Global Flows: Transnationalism and a Mobile World

Global mission is now taking place in networked society where connections flow between cities once separated by time and space. Modern technology has facilitated bridges between once distant locations. Manuel Castells has argued that "our society is constructed around flows: flows of capital, flows of information, flows of technology, flows of organizational interaction, flows of images, sounds, and symbols. ... The space of flows is the material organization of time-sharing social practices that work through flows" (Susser, 2002, p. 344). When Paul of Tarsus traveled throughout the Mediterranean world, he and his teams utilized the Roman roads and waterways, and as a result of letter writing, we have many of those correspondences in our Bibles today. The global flows of transportation and information provided an opportunity for transmitting the Gospel to a variety of cultures and far-off places, but these global flows connecting cities and colonies of the Roman Empire moved much more slowly than the pathways constructed for today's world. Now communication can move through global flows instantaneously, and transportation that a century ago would have taken days, now takes hours. In addition, today's global context is being transformed in ways that are seemingly unprecedented. "The 'global flows' of persons, products, and ideas are not simply a continuation of what we have seen in the past, but ... the number, speed, and force of the flows has overwhelmed local and regional systems to the point that new economic regimes, peoples, and histories are being shaped" (Rynkiewich, 2013, p. 195).

History is full of the stories of migration movements, but people are on the move today at a global scale unlike anything we've previously experienced. As people migrate both between cities within their nation and across borders into other nations, they become more equipped to move again. Migration and travel becomes a self-perpetuating cycle. Once someone has become mobile, his or her ability to continue to move becomes more likely. While there are factors that keep numerous families stationary, a portion of the migrant population is likely to continue to stay on the move. Today, many departments and organizations—both governmental and nongovernmental—are crafting policy that seeks to leverage global migration for economic development. Because of the economic opportunities accompanying global migration, "many policy-focused agencies are promoting the creation of managed circular migration systems." They are seeking ways to encourage movement from the receiving nation back to the sending nation and often back again. Movement back and forth across borders is becoming increasingly common as grassroots expertise and capital increases enabling individuals to remain mobile (Vertovec, 2009, pp. 119-125). As many countries remain politically "closed" to the Gospel and missionaries seek to develop creative access platforms for evangelistic purposes, international migrants moving back and forth between nations may provide one of the most dynamic pathways for the Gospel in our world. As economic and political institutions are adapting to these circular migratory patterns, so should the church as well.

Sending churches and agencies will need to consider the opportunities and challenges involved in a world of global flows where transnational connections are becoming commonplace through grassroots exchanges of culture, religion, politics, and economics. Individuals may move across borders on either an occasional or a regular basis, and even when they become stationary in one location, they are likely remaining connected to family, friends, or business associates in their countries of origin or throughout diaspora networks in various parts of the world. For missionaries, learning to integrate these realities into strategies for evangelism, church planting, or development will be a necessary component for contemporary contextualization. "Most church and mission organization paradigms in North America have not adjusted to the reality that the frontier of reaching unreached peoples is not necessarily geographicly distant but is sometimes available through relational networks in their own homeland through influential immigrants." For example, all of the first churches that have started among a specific unreached people group in West Africa in the last few years have started without an on-the-ground missionary presence, but instead were started through connections with immigrants from this people group in New York City (Clayman, March 22, 2014). Learning from the stories of ministry unfolding in the context of global flows, I believe there are practical ways missionaries, churches, and agencies can act intentionally through transnationalism as global flows connect individuals and communities, narrowing the gaps between time and space.

First, evangelists among diaspora communities should seek opportunities for transmitting the Gospel through the relationships of their migrant friends. For example, when missionary workers facilitate Discovery Bible Studies with international students and scholars in New York City, the students often pass on the stories from Scripture to family or friends back in Asia. This replication is an intentional aspect of the Bible study process. When an international scholar has become a follower of Christ and returns home, he or she is encouraged to gather friends and family and begin facilitating a Bible discussion. On some occasions, this has resulted in new churches meeting in homes or offices in Asian countries. Also, when Bob works on the streets of the city sharing oral Bible stories with West Africans, some of the African Muslims receive compact discs with recordings of Bible stories in their own language, and they mail them home to their family to listen to as well. I suspect there are numerous avenues for the Gospel to impact once-distant people through migrant networks. For transnational migrants, maintaining connections with family, friends, or business associates in their relationship network is a natural part of their life rhythms. Utilizing Skype, e-mail, phone, modern travel, and other mediums, opportunities to see the Gospel advance internationally through global flows exist to a much greater degree than in decades past. Evangelists laboring in diaspora communities should be attentive to pathways for the Gospel through these relational networks.

In addition, building bridges through short-term missions based on transnational relationships may result in evangelistic gains. Stories like those from Bob, Corey, and Grace Church to the Fujianese have demonstrated the dynamic potential for short-term travel through relationships in diaspora communities. Recently, a new missionary working with South Asians living in the United States announced to supporters and friends that he is traveling to a South Asian country to connect with family of friends of his contacts living in diaspora in the United States. Utilizing relationships in the diaspora community as a springboard, missionaries are able to travel to distant lands with significant influence and receive a warm welcome by their hosts. By moving through the global flows of transnational relationships, missionaries have seen doors open for the Word of God that might have been more difficult to open with traditional missionary methods. While venues and circumstances for more traditional short-term missions will continue to provide a platform for worthwhile projects— mobilization, missions education, delivering disaster relief, accomplishing special projects, and the like—churches and missions organizations should seek opportunities to invest in missionary leaders serving diaspora communities who may find opportunities to evangelize globally through local relationships with transnational migrants. Sending one or two workers or a worker with family to visit the homeland of evangelistic contacts from the diaspora will often provide a more economic and under-the-radar approach to short-term evangelism than sending large groups of untrained volunteers with no local credibility. When creative access platforms are increasingly important for providing a Christian witness to unreached people groups, connecting through the global flows of transnational relationships may be one of the most effective ways for Westerners to serve as witnesses among least-reached groups in a postcolonial age. In most cases, all that is needed is transportation due to the extraordinary hospitality of many ethnic communities hosting a Western guest who is visiting as a friend with their son, daughter, cousin, nephew, or neighbor. As a matter of fact, the missionary worker should, as often as possible, not stay in hotels or other Western accommodations since being fully dependent on the hospitality of the host community will provide more opportunities for sharing the gift of the Good News of God's grace with his or her hosts.

Also, in a world that is constantly on the move, reproducible and relational methods of church planting should be encouraged. When Discovery Bible Study groups started by City Team Ministries multiplied from San Jose, California, to Nicaragua and again from Nicaragua to Costa Rica, a major contributor to this sort of multiplication was the simple, scalable approach to evangelism and church planting utilized by the City Team workers and volunteers. In another example of transnational multiplication, New York City International Project, led by Kevin King, has seen new evangelistic house churches started in cities in Asia. When Kevin King and his team began reaching out to internationals living temporarily in New York City, he asked himself: What would be most reproducible for temporary internationals to carry the Gospel to their homes and result in new churches in nations still hostile to Christianity? They realized that they needed to model a way of being church that was both biblical as well as simple and reproducible. Expecting the entrepreneurial model of North American church planting to move freely through the global flows of transnational networks is quite unrealistic in many cases. However, when disciple-making methods are simple and relational, there is an increased likelihood for evangelistic initiatives to move through the global flows of transnational connections.

Finally, there may be opportunities to work with transnational migrants for developing mutual partnerships toward the holistic care of economically challenged communities. Angel Reyes's story is one that paints a picture of mutual partnership for holistic ministry to a poor community in a developing nation. He is the first to admit there have been mistakes made and valuable lessons learned along the way; however, today he is forging mutual partnerships that include local Hondurans, transnational migrants in New York City who remain involved in local affairs in Honduras, and an American congregation in Manhattan. This triangulation of involved parties represents a dynamic picture of ministry partnerships in the global network. Individuals have been won to Christ, a church has been planted, evangelism is ongoing, community development has built the capital of skills and education into a poor community, and aid is provided to the sick and suffering. All of these works came about through the initiative of a transnational migrant who built bridges across national boundaries and linked diverse parties in mutual partnerships. Is Reyes's story unique? Is it just the right combination of personalities and circumstances that came together at the right time? I believe additional partnerships such as this one are possible. Much of what Angel has learned through trial and error could be implemented intentionally from the start as transnational migrants and church partnerships navigate the context of global networks. There are likely countless opportunities to labor alongside transnational citizens able to bridge the gulf between once distant places. In a networked world, transnational migrants may be the most ideal leaders for developing mutual partnership for caring for poor communities in the name of Christ on a global scale.

Adapting to a New World: Rethinking Structures

International migration, globalization, and the expanding presence of diaspora communities raise the need for missionary organizations to evaluate their structures that were mostly built in a different period in our history to address a very different global context. "While American cities are increasingly immigrant-infused and globalized in nature, our American mission organizations are largely structured for a bygone era that have not adapted to globalization and the world's transnational relationships" (Clayman, March 22, 2014).

Many missions structures have historically maintained an organizational and cultural distinction between foreign and domestic missions. When Paul Kraus, an Assembly of God missionary, came to New York City, he transferred from 20 years of service in the World Missions department of his denomination and became a cross-cultural missionary with the US Missions department. He came to New York to work among African immigrants. Since transferring to the US Missions department, he no longer had an official organizational connection to the churches in Africa, but the Africans with whom he is working in New York maintain connections with their churches and leaders in African nations on a consistent basis. Many missions organizations are faced with the challenge of aligning their structures with the present realities of globally connected relationships. With the help of the New York district for the Assemblies of God, Kraus developed a new role as an intercultural missionary in the city in order to help facilitate ministry to unreached people groups among his denomination. As global mobility and connectivity increases through the activity of diaspora networks, missions organizations must evaluate their structural restraints in this new context of global mission. A strict dichotomy of foreign and domestic no longer reflects the concrete realities of global networks and daily life in the global city.

Diaspora communities represent the forward momentum of American Christianity. Missionary engagement to cultures in North America will contain a strategic gap if they fail to take into account both unreached and Christian diaspora communities. While mainstream North American culture may reflect an emerging post-Christendom paradigm, the cultural context of Western cities is becoming anything but wholly secular. (Although secularization is certainly taking place too as a concurrent—although seemingly contradictory—process.) In fact, some may argue that New York City is a "post-secular" city due to increased immigration and the associated importation of religious practices from around the world—both Christian and non-Christian. Evidence indicates that the evangelical population of New York City has been significantly underestimated. This is due, in part, to the majority of the growth of the Christian presence coming from the majority-world migration to the city (Clayman, March 22, 2014). These ethnic communities may be undercounted in mainstream religious studies since they remain on the margins of much of academia or the institutions of the dominant culture. While the church representing the established North American culture is struggling to maintain its position, migrant churches are popping up throughout American cities on a regular basis. As post-Christendom emerges and the Christian movement finds itself potentially being pushed toward the margins of mainstream culture, it may find itself at the margins in the missionary movement of the church as well if it does not recognize the work of the Spirit among ethnic communities just a few miles, or perhaps even a few blocks, away. "The growing edge of the church in North America is no longer Anglo. If we do not learn how to mobilize and empower this 'growing edge' for cross-cultural missions, we may find ourselves out of the game" (Baxter, 2013, p. 122).

Mission agencies and sending churches are challenged to discern their structures in order to align their missiological strategies for a world that functions as a global network. This evaluation raises a question: Should they adopt a structure that is hierarchical or decentralized in order to be effective in global networks (Rynkiewich, 2013, p. 110)? It may be far more congruent with the global context for missions organizations, church-planting initiatives, and various evangelism efforts to adopt a network structure. For many missions agencies, the shape of our contemporary global context may prove challenging. They were simply organized during a far different age. "The world is connected in ways that were not possible decades ago when many of our largest mission organizations were founded" (Clayman, March 22, 2014). While many agencies will successfully update their structures and processes, new agencies will be needed to take a full-bodied approach to organizing in a way that reflects current global contexts.

Leaders are often aware of the need to reevaluate structures established in a very different cultural setting. James Engel and William Dyrness suggest four key points for missions organizations to consider as they adapt to contemporary realities. Missionary efforts should be:

> (1) sensitive to the initiative of God, (2) motivated by a vision of the reign of Christ as refracted through the multiple cultures of the world, (3) characterized by mutual sharing from multiple centers of influence and (4) committed to partnership and collaboration. For this to happen among agencies, nothing short of a top-down, bottom-up organizational transformation is necessary. (Engel & Dyrness, 2000, p. 147)

In light of the world's current rate of mobility and cultural exchange, organizations must think through creating malleable structures for mission in a world constantly on the move. When a new diaspora emerges, there is often a window of evangelistic opportunity, and missionary responses are needed to meet these opportunities when the harvest is most ripe. Just as disaster relief organizations seek to mobilize quickly to meet an immediate need, windows of opportunity for evangelism are opened by new shifts in diaspora from one place to another, and church-planting agencies should be prepared to mobilize quickly to meet particular needs and opportunities as they arise. Transnational networks represent a new missiological context where local ministry may no longer be limited to a local impact. Supporting divisions of labor between domestic and foreign missions may have been well intentioned at one time, but today this same compartmentalization may prove to be a barrier to contemporary global missions. Agencies will need to reconsider organizational structures and divisions in labor, and new organizations should strongly consider organizing themselves around the new cultural and contextual dynamics.

In many cases, agencies must rethink how to conduct training. Many missionary training programs do not locate students in urban areas, and students of missions will need to be prepared to be adaptive to a much more fluid and urban culture than in the past. It is difficult to imagine this sort of adaptability being learned outside the realm of experience. Cultural and religious pluralism is a key characteristic of cities in a global age, and yet many institutions offering missiological education are rooted in a more homogeneous cultural history in rural contexts. Agencies also will need to consider nontraditional missionaries if they are to take part in a grassroots movement of diaspora Christians participating in God's mission. They are challenged to consider who the missionary workers are to be, where or how to gain access to them, and how to resource them as a missionary force. They must discover new ways to mobilize and equip emerging leaders in diaspora communities, and they must find ways to deliver training that leads to effective ministry. Divisions of labor may be reoriented around nodal functions or in dynamics rooted in migration, urbanization, and global flows rather than monolithic geographic divides. Finally, missions organizations will need to become skilled at developing partnerships characterized by mutuality. Developing partnerships with indigenous congregations carrying on ministry in the country of origin and maintaining mutual partnerships with diaspora churches may provide access to potential missionary workers within the global diaspora (Baxter, 2013, pp. 120-121).

Rediscovering Mutuality: Global Partnerships

Often missionaries work overseas conducting evangelism, church planting, and development work, and to accomplish the larger goals of their mission, they often partner with others in order to combine their efforts and see the work accomplished. When missionaries from different backgrounds arrive in the same city in North Africa, Asia, or the Middle East, learning to work together is a natural fit in the face of what is often an overwhelming mission field before them. Missionaries whose churches or denominations might never associate in the United States find themselves functioning as colaborers in a foreign field. Usually, "in pioneering mission efforts there tend to be much more cooperation and partnership between missionaries, mission agencies, and churches from different evangelical streams than normally takes place between American Christians" (Clayman, March 22, 2014).

In New York City, I've shared in a collaborative effort to train missionaries in the city while mobilizing them among unreached people groups living in New York. When New York City International Project initiated a missionary training program, it partnered with sending agencies outside of New York City as well as Global City Mission Initiative and Global Gates. Together, this is a collaborative effort to form missionaries and evangelize diaspora communities, sharing in training, coaching, and additional leadership. At least three mission agencies with headquarters in other parts of the United States are sending missionary candidates to New York City for hands-on training in cross-cultural evangelism among unreached people groups living in diaspora communities. We've mobilized teams working with different ethnic neighborhoods in the city, and we've provided a set of training opportunities that a single organization in New York would have struggled to facilitate if doing such a program completely on their own. If we added up all of the Hindus, Jews, Muslims, Sikhs, and Buddhists in New York City, the number of unreached peoples from around the world would amount to the second largest city in the United States. Such an estimate is without even considering the huge need for ministry to the millions of secular Westerners who have not bowed their knee to Jesus. With such an overwhelming need for missionary engagement, working collaboratively is a key element for an effective evangelism effort in the city. One key aspect for reaching diverse populations in cities located along a continuum of assimilation is to facilitate a unified effort to make disciples and develop churches among diaspora communities. Often, multiethnic communities will be needed to meaningfully connect with second-generation members of the diaspora while missionaries intentionally initiate evangelism to first-generation diaspora networks and ethnic enclaves in the city.

In addition to citywide partnerships, diaspora evangelism points to an increased need for global partnerships characterized by mutuality. An important partnership in diaspora missions is to facilitate connections between the nodes through the transnational flows between geographically distant places. In other words, a global mission strategy among diaspora peoples should, whenever possible, bridge ministry efforts between the immigrant community and their homeland connections. "Global partnership of churches will be indispensable for mission in the twenty-first century" (Escobar, 2003, p. 164). Missionary workers laboring among diaspora communities may benefit from connections with Christian leaders in the diaspora's sending nation. Insight into cultural worldview, new mission-minded migrants connecting to the diaspora ministry upon arrival in the new city, and similar contributions might flow from the homeland to the diaspora ministry. At the same time, ministries laboring in the sending nation may benefit greatly from partnering with missionaries among a diaspora community. Doors for evangelism may open due to the capital —both relational and material—provided by influential members of the diaspora. In some stories of recent transnational evangelism efforts, doors were opened for sharing the Gospel and planting new churches in the sending nation through the relationships with migrants in the diaspora network. At times, missionaries laboring in the homeland of a particular unreached group have observed that evangelistic access among a diaspora community was achieved much more efficiently than their own efforts in the country of origin. Naturally, this won't be the case in every comparison; however, missionaries among a diaspora community may help open new relationships and opportunities for a missionary laboring overseas.

In an age when the global church is multicentered and the church of the majority world is in the majority within the Christian faith worldwide, it will be important for Western Christians to approach international partnerships with mutual respect and love. Humility will indeed be a key characteristic. Mutual partnership will be a new experience for Western leaders who are used to exclusively holding the reins of leadership and managing nearly every aspect of ministry. Even when Western churches may be providing the bulk of the physical resources for a development project or evangelistic initiative, paternalistic attitudes must not accompany that same assistance. Throughout the history of Christendom and colonialism, Western mission structures, denominations, and churches have been accustomed to holding the position of power. However, global partnerships should be maintained with a spirit of mutuality. Western mission agencies "must adopt the posture of a servant as we work in partnership with these majority world churches" (Baxter, 2013, p. 122). As the world becomes more connected, mutual partnerships are more accessible and likely to become common. Transnational citizens will become important ambassadors as representatives who have a degree of understanding of—or at least experience in—both cultures. Indeed transnational leaders should be key players in helping to facilitate mutual partnerships for evangelism, church planting, and development. As the church of the majority world increases in strength and in numbers, the Western church faces decline while maintaining sufficient resources, and diaspora networks manifest grassroots pathways linking cities and villages around the globe, mutual partnerships represent a key response to the new global context of world missions.

Mission at Cultural Intersections: Western Cities, Post-Secular and Post-Christendom

In global cities in Western contexts, we are experiencing the emergence of a cultural post-Christendom with the simultaneous rise of a post-secular religious vigor on the margins of society due in large part to international migration. These are seemingly contradictory processes occurring simultaneously in urban space. As North American evangelists seek to uncover pathways for making disciples in Western contexts, missiologists are recontextualizing evangelistic practices among unreached migrants in many of the same Western cities containing large populations of secular-minded unbelievers. Evangelism practices are converging at cultural intersections. Deeply contrasting populations are being engaged by evangelists in the same neighborhoods and cities, and many of the strategic themes in reaching both post-Christendom secular people and unreached ethnic groups arriving from majority-world nations are ironically similar. While each cultural setting requires its own sensitivity to the specific contexts and worldviews encountering the Gospel, there may be common factors shared between strategies applied to post-Christendom contexts and among diaspora communities in global contexts.

Adaptable & Relational

Engaging postmodernity in the 21st century and missions to people groups from the majority world both require a relational approach (Wan, 2010, p. 2). The medium for ministry at this cultural intersection is relationships. In Western cities where the cultural worldviews of post-Christendom and postmodernity set the tone for rising tensions with—and sometimes an outright reject of—existing religious institutions, it will be important for approaches to evangelism and church planting to be relational. Such tensions are complex, but a relational approach to ministry represents a clear point of convergence in these dynamic and global environments. The Gospel has always advanced through the pathways of relationships, and this may be even more true today in secular and pluralistic cities where the shadow of Christendom is straining to maintain its previous influence. At the same time, a missionary response to diaspora communities equally requires relationships to be a primary medium for passing on the Gospel.

God has always worked in and through people. If we ignore the human role in God's mission, we are overlooking God's primary means for redemption as well as its relational outcome. However, if we disregard the active part God is playing in his mission to the world, we have lost our compass and are without direction (Escobar, 2003, p. 29). Ministry in and through diaspora networks will be based on building relationships across cultural boundaries, and transnational evangelism becomes possible as the Gospel moves through the global flows of relationships maintained through transnational networks. Numerous opportunities for communicating the Gospel of Christ may be discovered through relational ministry among migrant communities. Our challenge is to recognize what God is doing and to participate with him (Baxter, 2013, p. 122).

Many people structure their lives in a way that reflects the reality of global networks. They organize their interpersonal interactions as "a social network—with many nodes but no center" (Rynkiewich, 2013, p. 110). Even as cities make up nodal points connecting a global network, people develop networks made up of relational nodes. Evangelistic work among diaspora communities will require adaptability in moving between nodal relationships where key influence lies. As populations become increasingly mobile and societal instability wreaks havoc around the planet, constant change is evitable. As urbanization stimulates shifts from rural to urban, globalization drives the reality of constant shifting between urban centers. With this mobility, people create grassroots networks through relational ties that connect regional and global centers. Evangelism strategies in this global network will need to emphasize relationship and focus on the movement of the Gospel through relational connections. Missiological engagement must take into account the need to adapt to constant change. Relationships—at times even transcending geographic constraints—appear to be the only constant. Ministry that makes sense in the 21st century will be rooted in relationship and adaptable to constantly shifting realities in an urban world.

Becoming Aliens and Foreigners

Followers of Christ in Western societies have much to learn from their immigrant brothers and sisters arriving in their cities and neighborhoods. Members of diaspora communities are living outside of their homelands, displaced from the culture and country they know and outsiders to the new culture. In the same way, in a society that may be characterized as post-Christendom, even Christians who claim a particular country as their homeland are equally foreigners in a strange society. "Today the Christian stance in the West has to become a missionary stance." Being Christian is much like being a foreigner in a strange land (Escobar, 2003, p. 73). One of the most valuable lessons that immigrants can teach to North American Christians is to renew their identities as foreigners even in their homeland. While a theological positioning for members of the global diaspora as aliens and foreigners is reinforced by the reality of actually being immigrants to a new place, the same theological positioning is important for natives of secular society to embrace as followers of Christ. As post-Christendom emerges and presents new challenges to historic Western churches, the body of Christ is challenged to rediscover its theological identity as aliens in a strange land. Indeed, Christians ought to have much in common with the experience of the international migrant. At the intersection of international diaspora and a newly unfolding post-

Christendom West, there is a great opportunity to rediscover our Christian identity as citizens of heaven.

Encountering Nonbiblical Authority Structures

Post-Christendom culture represents a move away from a dominant Christian influence on the culture. It is important to make the distinction that many attributes of Christendom may not be expressly Christian or actually reflect the heart of the Gospel; however, the Christian narrative and, to some degree, Christian ethics have had a dominant role in Christendom cultures. In the context of post-Christendom, there is an outright rejection of biblical authority structures. The church, the clergy, and the Bible no longer carry the same influence as sources of authority for the culture. In post-Christendom, there is an increasing resistance to allowing the Bible to influence worldviews or set the stage for a common set of ethics. In a society that is equally pluralistic, the Christian narrative is competing with any number of voices to be heard above the imposed restraints of a secular post-Christendom. In secular societies, a more humanist vision sets the ethical standards and vision for civilization. "Because the Bible told me so" carries little weight with a post-Christendom worldview, and in some subcultures may even be met with a degree of hostility.

Encountering nonbiblical authority structures is nothing new for a missionary church in the majority world. For centuries, evangelists have traveled into cultures that adhere to the authority of Islamic law, Hindu worldviews, animistic rituals, and other authoritative frameworks. When evangelists in New York City begin evangelistic conversations with Muslims or Buddhists, they attempt to contextualize their communication to meet individuals or family members where they are regarding worldview and authority structures. Cross-cultural missionaries in pre-Christian contexts around the world realize they cannot assume a worldview based on biblical authority when they encounter people open to spiritual conversations. Evangelism in many global cities, specifically in the West, should begin to assume that many individuals are shaped by different sources of authority outside of the Christian faith. Both secular Westerners embodying a post-Christendom worldview and migrants who have come from a pre-Christian cultural setting or represent an unreached people group are rooted in authority structures—of various types—outside the foundation of the Christian Scriptures. While there will still be many individuals who hold the Christian narrative in high regard and see the Bible as God's Word, it will be safe to assume that many of the encounters in the city will be with people who hold to an authority other than the biblical witness. While it is important to note that Western culture has never completely reflected a New Testament moral ethic, it is true that Western culture has been informed by the Bible as an authoritative voice.

The implications of a Western context no longer informed by biblical authority is that the Western church must not only recognize she is a missionary community, but she also must learn the tools of missionary practice. As evangelists, we desire to see spiritual seekers and new believers shaped by the biblical narrative, but in order to do so, we often must build bridges between their starting worldview and a new vision for life in God's Kingdom informed by the foundation of the Scriptures. When we work with Muslims in New York City, it is not unusual to build bridges from the Koran, or when we speak with a secular atheist, we may be faced with the need to bring clarity to common misperceptions of the Christian story in order to open the door to discussing the Bible. At this missiological intersection, evangelism efforts within the dominant culture and among diaspora communities both encounter nonbiblical authority structures. As a result, both contexts dictate that evangelists must share intentional practices in cross-cultural communication.

Direct Evangelism

Working with diverse international populations in New York City, we have learned the importance of direct evangelism. For example, when building a friendship with a Muslim, if I do not communicate my faith in Jesus early in the relationship, my Muslim friend will often assume that faith in Jesus is not very important to me. Direct evangelism need not be equated with approaches considered obnoxious, rude, overly aggressive, or arrogant. Rather, forms of direct evangelism should be conversational as well as humble and respectful. Direct evangelism is simply the practice of sharing our faith in Christ early and often, and we do so through conversation as we share life with others and serve those in need. At the intersection of diaspora communities and the dominant culture in Western cities, many individuals representing a more postmodern worldview desire authenticity in their relationships. While the popularizing of "friendship evangelism" in previous decades was rooted in good intentions and served as a corrective against overbearing evangelism tactics, contemporary generations do not seem interested in what appears as a bait-and-switch approach to evangelism. Delaying the articulation of a Christian identity often results in a decreased prioritization of this central aspect of our lives even as a friendship progresses in other areas. As missionaries move between encounters in the dominant culture and ministry among diaspora communities, authentic faith and direct communication of the Gospel will be important relational practices as ambassadors of Christ in a strange land.

If disciples of Christ are committed to rediscovering their identity as aliens and foreigners as a missionary people, sharing the Good News through direct evangelism, orienting ministry around approaches that are relational and adaptable, and contextualizing communication for encountering nonbiblical authority structures in everyday conversations, evangelism practice in North America may be both effective and vibrant as a Christian activity. Such evangelism practices may prove effective and sincere in cities where members of the global diaspora and secular citizens of the dominant culture walk the same streets and sometimes inhabit the same neighborhoods.

Conclusion

The church is presently confronted with the challenge of reimagining ministry in a mobile world in constant flux driven by the twin forces of globalization and urbanization. However, these shifts have led to a movement of international migration that represents one of the greatest evangelistic opportunities of our time. Individuals and families from some of the most unreached groups in the world are moving in next door. Some of the nations that allow the least access to the Gospel are represented in urban neighborhoods where evangelism can be openly practiced. The political opposition to the church in the post-Christendom West cannot be compared to the aggressive oppression of Christian voices in some nations where access to the Gospel is violently suppressed. However, diaspora communities and networks point to fresh opportunities for Gospel contextualization, evangelism, and church planting among people coming from hard-to-reach places.

Cities as the new frontier of missions ought to be recognized as urban nodes in a global network. These centers of regional and global influence are international hubs for migrants from many nations, and they are centers of cultural influence as media propagates messages, images, and new cultural expressions through modern communications technology. As numerous populations shift and move across national boundaries and form relational and transactional networks that transcend borders, missionaries are confronted with a new global context for world missions. As a result, sponsoring organizations such as missions agencies and sending churches must evaluate existing structures and policies and need to be adaptive to constantly changing urban environments. Sending agencies and missionaries are encountering a world that may be defined by its connections. Evangelism strategies will need to take into account the opportunities and challenges of a networked society, and cities are the nodes in grassroots global networks.

In Western cities receiving large numbers of international migrants, evangelists wrestling with the realities of post-Christendom may find much in common with the missiological principles applied to reaching unreached ethnic groups. Incorporating direct evangelism with a high relational orientation may represent principles and strategies at a missiological intersection. While the church certainly faces significant challenges and is being forced to become highly adaptable in light of cultural flux and global mobility, there is great potential for a robust urban evangelism to take root in the church.

Reflection Questions

1. What steps might you or your church take to plant the Gospel in a diaspora network located in your city?
2. If cities are now urban nodes in a global network, how does that impact the missiological strategies of the church?
3. What structural changes might be necessary for your church or organization to make in order to work effectively as a sending agency in the context of globalization?

Conclusion

Some years ago, I was attempting to help a young man from New York City grow in his Christian faith and overcome significant challenges facing him at that time. During the course of our friendship, he moved to Florida, and we kept in touch by phone talking nearly every week for a couple of months. Despite working through real obstacles, he possessed a strong desire to share his hope in Christ with others, and he began seeking outlets to do so. He quickly met a man who had long ago abandoned a previous commitment to follow Jesus but desired to renew his faith and learn to embrace Christian discipleship. They began opening the Bible together and sharing a friendship while discussing what they were learning from the Gospel. However, not long after they began meeting together, his new friend returned to his home in the Bahamas. In summary, I was mentoring a young man who moved from New York to Florida who met a man living in Florida but was from the Bahamas who, soon after they had met, returned to the Bahamas, his country of origin.

Our world is rapidly becoming a global society that is mobile, connected, and always changing. In writing this book, I hoped to add to the conversation revolving around the themes of diaspora missiology. Much of the conversation in missiological circles has been oriented around the societal shifts happening in our world and the opportunities, as well as the challenges, for the global church. I have attempted to draw attention to examples of real practices taking place in our contemporary context of world missions. There are trailblazers riding the waves of globalization and migration as missionary agents in our world. Through the stories flowing out of new ministry practices in and through diaspora networks, I hope we will continue to develop practices aligned with our new contexts for global missions and adjust the way we think about Christian missions.

Globalization and urbanization are twin forces impacting the way we do missions and think about church. The need for adaptability, courageous evangelism, and mutual partnering is evident in the world. International migration is a global phenomenon presenting the church with unprecedented opportunities and systemic challenges. Yet, while it is easy to frame these present realities in dramatic terms, a beautiful picture begins to come into focus as we reflect on the implications for ministry.

Local churches have the opportunity to mobilize their memberships to become personally active in the kind of evangelism they only thought possible for missionaries thousands of miles away. Church leaders can begin dreaming of multiethnic congregations where violent segregation once set the cultural tone. Church planters may enter cities with a vision for reaching unreached peoples once far out of reach. The missionary imagination for Gospel contextualization begins to emerge in numerous local communities. Church multiplication strategies may not be restricted solely to a local vision but intentionally step into global connections. Missionaries reeling from the stress of returning to a home that feels as foreign as anywhere they have ever been can discover a vital role as bridges of partnership and discernment in bringing together culturally different leaders and communities. The relational nature of missions practices is renewed as missionaries learn to navigate networks through local communities and through globally connected relationships. Ministry in the global network can bring us into a closer experience of the picture of the throne room of God with the nations gathered before him. The portrait of ministry in our world today should be characterized by relationships giving the church a renewed sense of being an international family as ambassadors of Christ in a global network. There is immeasurable potential for renewal in our churches and in impoverished communities as majority-world Christians bring hearts full of revival seeking the peace of our cities. Although the challenges ahead are real, the ministry in our present-future is a beautiful portrait of every culture, language, and people serving as ambassadors of what they have seen and heard in Jesus, the King of all Kings.

Crossroads of the Nations

References

Abrahamson, M. (2004). *Global Cities*. New York: Oxford University Press.

Adeney, M. (2011). Colorful Initiatives: North American Diasporas in Mission. *Missiology: An International Review*, 39(1), 5-23.

Allen, R. (1962). *The Spontaneous Expansion of the Church: And the Causes Which Hinder It*. Grand Rapids, MI: William B. Eerdmans Publishing Company.

Bakke, R. (1999). Urbanization and Evangelism: A Global View. *Word & World, 19*(3).

Barrett, D., & Johnson, T. (2001). *World Christian Trends AD 30 - AD 2200: Interpreting the Annual Christian Megacensus*. Pasadena, CA: William Carey Library.

Baxter, J. (2013). Western Agency, Meet the Diaspora. *International Journal of Frontier Missiology, 30:3*(Fall 2013), 119-122.

Borja, J., & Castells, M. (1997). *Local and Global: Management of Cities in the Information Age*. London: Earthscan Publications.

Bosch, D. (2008). Evangelism: Theological Currents and Cross-Currents Today. In P. Chilcote & L. Warner (Eds.), *The Study of Evangelism: Exploring Missional Practice of the Church* (pp. 4-17). Grand Rapids, MI: William B. Eerdmans Publishing Company.

Brown, R. (1997). *An Introduction to the New Testament*. New York: Doubleday.

Bruce, F. F. (1966). *The Book of Acts*. Grand Rapids, MI: William B. Eerdmans Publishing Company.

Bruce, F. F. (1983). *The Gospel of John*. Grand Rapids, MI: William B. Eerdmans Publishing Company.

Brueggemann, W. (2008). Evangelism and Discipleship: The God Who Calls, the God Who Sends. In P. Chilcote & L. Warner (Eds.), *The Study of Evangelism: Exploring a Missional Practice of the Church* (pp. 219-234). Grand Rapids, MI: William B. Eerdmans Publishing Company.

Carnes, T. (2001). Religions in the City: An Overview. In T. Carnes & A. Karpathakis (Eds.), *New York glory: Religions in the City* (pp. 3-25). New York: New York University Press.

Chilcote, P., & Warner, L. (Eds.). (2008). *The Study of Evangelism: Exploring a Missional Practice of the Church*. Grand Rapids, MI: William B. Eerdmans Publishing Company.

Clark, D. (2003). *Urban World / Global City* (2nd ed.). London: Routledge.

Claydon, D. (Ed.). (2004). *The New People Next Door*. Paper presented at the Lausanne Committee for World Evangelization.

Clayman, C. (March 22, 2014). *Reaching the Nations Through Our Cities*. Paper presented at the Evangelical Missiological Society Northeast Regional Meeting.

Cohen, R. (1997). *Global Diasporas: An Introduction*. Seattle, WA: University of Washington Press.

Common English Bible. (2013). Pasadena, CA: Fuller Theological Seminary.

Conn, H., & Ortiz, M. (2001). *Urban Ministry: The Kingdom, the City, and the People of God*. Downers Grove, IL: InterVarsity Press.

Corbett, S., & Fikkert, B. (2009). *When Helping Hurts: Alleviating Poverty Without Hurting the Poor and Yourself*. Chicago: Moody Publishers.

Crabtree, V. (2012). Religion in the United Kingdom: Diversity, trends and Decline. Retrieved January 13, 2015, from http://www.vexen.co.uk/UK/religion.html.

Davey, A. (2002). *Urban Christianity and the Global Order: Theological Resources for an Urban Future*. Peabody, MA: Hendrickson Publishers.

Dean, M. (March 22, 2014). *Doing Missions as Participants in Diaspora*. Paper presented at the Evangelical Missiological Society Northeast Regional Meeting.

Engel, J., & Dyrness, W. (2000). *Changing the Mind of Missions: Where Have We Gone Wrong?* Downers Grove, IL: InterVarsity Press.

Escobar, S. (2002). *Changing Tides: Latin America and World Mission Today*. Maryknoll, NY: Orbis Books.

Escobar, S. (2003). *The New Global Mission: The Gospel from Everywhere to Everyone*. Downers Grove, IL: InterVarsity Press.

Esposito, J. L., Fasching, D. J., & Lewis, T. V. (2008). *Religion and Globalization: World Religions in Historical Perspective*. New York: Oxford University Press.

Fischer, C. (1984). *The Urban Experience*. Fort Worth, TX: Harcourt Brace Jovanovich College Publishers.

Florida, R. (2004). *Cities and the Creative Class*. London: Routledge.

Foner, N. (Ed.). (2001). *New Immigrants in New York*. New York: Columbia University Press.

Ford, R. (March 22, 2014). *Bukharan Jews from the Old Silk Road in Queens, NY*. Paper presented at the Evangelical Missiological Society Northeast Regional Meeting.

Friedman, T. L. (2006). *The World is Flat [Updated and Expanded]: A Brief History of the 21st Century*. New York: Macmillan Publishers.

Garcia-Johnson, O. (2012). Mission Within Hybrid Cultures: Transnationality and the Global Church. In R. Bolger (Ed.), *The Gospel after Christendom: New Voices, New Cultures, New Expressions* (pp. 113-126). Grand Rapids, MI: Baker Academic.

Garrison, V. D. (2003). *Church Planting Movements: How God is Redeeming a Lost World*. Monument, CO: WIGTake Resources.

Gehring, R. (2004). *House Church and Mission: The Importance of Household Structures in Early Christianity*. Peabody, MA: Hendrickson Publishers.

Geromel, R. (2013). All You Need to Know About Sao Paulo, Brazil's Largest City. Retrieved January 13, 2014, from http://www.forbes.com/sites/ricardogeromel/2013/07/12/all-you-need-to-know-about-sao-paulo-brazils-largest-city.

Gornik, M. (2011). *Word Made Global: Stories of African Christianity in New York City*. Grand Rapids, MI: William B. Eerdmans Publishing Company.

Gwamzhi, L. N. (2013). Contextualization in Diaspora Mission: An African Christian's Perspective of the Mission Agenda in the US. *Global Missiology English, 4*(10).

Hanciles, J. (2008). *Beyond Christendom: Globalization, African Migration, and the Transformation of the West*. Maryknoll, NY: Orbis Books.

Haslip-Viera, G. (1996). The Evolution of the Latino Community in New York City. In G. Haslip-Viera & S. L. Baver (Eds.), *Latinos in New York: Communities in Transition* (pp. 3-29). Notre Dame, IN: University of Notre Dame Press.

Holy Bible: English Standard Version. (2001). Wheaton, IL: Crossway Bibles.

Hunt, D. (May 24, 2013). Phone Interview. In J. Looney (Ed.).

Johnson, T. (June 2013). *Christianity in its Global Context, 1970-2020: Society, Religion, and Mission*. South Hamilton, MA: Center for the Study of Global Christianity.

Kalu, O., Vethanayagamony, P., & Chia, E. K.-F. (Eds.). (2010). *Mission after Christendom: Emergent Trends in Contemporary Mission*. Louisville, KY: Westminster John Knox Press.

Kasinitz, P., Mollenkopf, J., Waters, M., & Holdaway, J. (2008). *Inheriting the City: The Children of Immigrants Come of Age*. Cambridge MA: Harvard University Press.

Kim, C. (2013). Mission from the Diaspora. *International Journal of Frontier Missiology 30:3*(Fall 2013), 97-101.

Kim, S. (2010). *A Faith of Our Own: Second-Generation Spirituality in Korean American Churches.* New Brunswick, NJ: Rutgers University Press.

Kling, F. (2010). *The Meeting of the Waters: 7 Global Currents That Will Propel the Future Church.* Colorado Springs, CO: David Cook.

Kraus, P. (March 22, 2014). *Foundations for Diaspora Missiology.* Paper presented at the Evangelical Missiological Society Northeast Regional Meeting.

Laguerre, M. S. (2003). *Urban Multiculturalism and Globalization in New York City: An Analysis of Diasporic Temporalities.* New York: Palgrave MacMillan.

Larson, D. N. (2009). Closing the Gap. In R. Winter & S. C. Hawthorne (Eds.), *Perspectives in the World Christian Movement* (4th ed.). Pasadena, CA:William Carey Library.

Lessinger, J. (1995). *From the Ganges to the Hudson: Indian Immigrants in New York City.* Boston, MA: Allyn and Bacon.

Marshall, I. H. (1992). *Acts.* Leicester, UK: InterVarsity Press.

Martin, C. G. (2014). *Missions in Our Backyard: Evangelism Among Newly Arrived Hispanics in the United States.* Paper presented at the Evangelical Missiological Society Southeast Regional Meeting.

McKenzie, G. (2011). Glocalization: The New Context of the Missio Dei. *Missio Dei: A Journal of Missional Theology and Praxis, 2*(August 2011).

McMahan, A. (2013). Looking for the "Social Glue": A Response to Michael Rynkiewich. *International Journal of Frontier Missiology, 30:3*(Fall 2013), 115-118.

McRaney, W. (2003). *The Art of Personal Evangelism.* Nashville, TN: B&H Publishing.

Milano, C. (2014). Embracing the Emerged Frontier of Missions. Retrieved on May 21, 2014, http://www.thetwocities.com/practical-theology/missiology/embracing-the-emerged-frontier-of-missions.

Murray, S. (2001). *Church Planting: Laying Foundations.* Scottsdale, AZ: Herald Press.

Murray, S. (2004). *Church After Christendom.* Milton Keynes, UK: Paternoster Press.

Newbigin, L. (1989). *The Gospel in a Pluralistic Society.* Grand Rapids, MI: William B. Eerdmans Publishing Company.

Newbigin, L. (2008). Evangelism in the Context of Secularization. In P. Chilcote & L. Warner (Eds.), *The Study of Evangelism: Exploring a Missional Practice of the Church* (pp. 46-54). Grand Rapids, MI: William B. Eerdmans Publishing Company.

"Nones" on the Rise: One in Five Adults Have No Religious Affiliation (2012). Washington, D.C.: Pew Research Forum.

NYC Department of City Planning (2014). *Population Facts.* Retrieved February 12, 2014, from http://www.nyc.gov/html/dcp/html/census/pop_facts.shtml.

NYC Mayor's Office for International Affairs (February 12, 2014). *International Business: Choose New York City,* from http://www.nyc.gov/html/ia/html/business/business.shtml.

Oh, M. E. (1988). *Cultural Pluralism and Multiethnic Congregation as a Ministry Model in Urban Society.* Fuller Theological Seminary, Pasadena, CA.

Olson, D. (2008). *The American Church in Crisis.* Grand Rapids, MI: Zondervan.

Palen, J. (1992). *The Urban World* (4th ed.). New York: McGraw-Hill, Inc.

Payne, J. D. (2012). *Strangers Next Door: Immigration, Migration, and Mission.* Downers Grove, IL: InterVarsity Press.

Payne, J. D. (2013). *Pressure Points: Twelve Global Issues Shaping the Face of the Church.* Nashville, TN: Thomas Nelson.

Perspectives on the World Christian Movement. www.perspectives.org.

Pocock, M., Rheenen, G. V., & McConnell, D. (2005). *The Changing Face of World Missions.* Grand Rapids, MI: Baker Academic.

Rah, S.C. (2009). *The Next Evangelicalism: Freeing the Church from Western Cultural Captivity.* Downers Grove, IL: InterVarsity Press.

Reyburn, W. D. (2009). Identification in the Missionary Task. In R. Winter & S. C. Hawthorne (Eds.), *Perspectives on the World Christian Movement* (4th ed.). Pasadena, CA: William Carey Library.

Rodriguez, D. A. (2011). *A Future for the Latino Church: Models for Multilingual, Multigenerational Hispanic Congregations.* Downers Grove, IL: InterVarsity Press.

Rogers, G. (2006). *Evangelizing Immigrants: Outreach and Ministry Among Immigrants and their Children.* Mission and Ministry Resources.

Rynkiewich, M. (2011). *Soul, Self, and Society: A Postmodern Anthropology for Mission in a Postcolonial World.* Eugene, OR: Wipf and Stock.

Rynkiewich, M. (2013). Mission in "The Present Time": What About the People in Diaspora? *International Journal of Frontier Missiology, 30:3*(Fall 2013), 103-114.

Sassen, S. (2001). *The Global City: New York, London, Tokyo.* Princeton, NJ: Princeton University Press.

Scott, A. J. (2001). *Global City-Regions.* Oxford, UK: Oxford University Press.

Smith, R. C. (1996). Mexicans in New York: Memberships and Incorporation in a New Immigrant Community. In G. Haslip-Viera & S. L. Baver (Eds.), *Latinos in New York: Communities in Transition* (pp. 57-103). Notre Dame, IN: University of Notre Dame Press.

Smith, S. (2009). Real Lessons From Real Urban CPMs. *Church Planting Movements: Best Practices from Across the Globe.* Retrieved November 21, 2013, from http://www.churchplantingmovements.com/index.php?option=com_content&view=article&id=82%3Areal-lessons-from-real-urban-cpms&catid=36%3Athe-big-picture&Itemid=78.

Snider, R. (2008). Evangelism, Salvation, and Social Justice. In P. Chilcote & L. Warner (Eds.), *The Study of Evangelism: Exploring a Missional Practice of the Church* (pp. 185-204). Grand Rapids, MI: William B. Eerdmans Publishing Company.

Susser, I. (Ed.). (2002). *The Castells Reader on Cities and Social Theory.* Malden, MA: Blackwell Publishers.

Thiessen, J. (2013). Missionaries in our Own Backyard: The Canadian Context. In C. Ott & J. D. Payne (Eds.), *Missionary Methods: Research, Reflection, and Realities* (pp. 127-144). Pasadena, CA: William Carey Library.

Tira, S. J. (2011). Diaspora Missiology. *Global Missiology, 2*(8).

Tira, S. J., & Wan, E. (2009).The Filipino Experience in Diaspora Missions: A Case Study of Christian Communities in Contemporary Contexts. Edinburgh.

Udall, J. (March 29, 2014). *Ethiopian Immigrants as Cross-Cultural Missionaries: Activating the Diaspora for Great Commission Impact.* Paper presented at the Evangelical Missiological Society Southeast Regional Conference.

Vertovec, S. (2009). *Transnationalism.* London: Routledge.

Veselinovic, M. (2013). Mixing Sushi and Samba: Meet the Japanese Brazilians. Retrieved January 8, 2014, from http://www.cnn.com/2013/06/11/world/brazil-japanese-community.

Wagner, C. P., & McGavran, D. (1990). *Understanding Church Growth.* Grand Rapids, MI: William B. Eerdmans Publishing Company.

Wan, E. (2012). The Phenomenon of Diaspora: Missiological Implications for Christian Missions. *Global Missiology English, 4*(9).

Wan, E. (2003). Mission Among the Chinese Diaspora: A Case Study of Migration and Mission. *Missiology, 31*(1), 35-44.

Wan, E. (2010). Rethinking Missiology in the Context of the 21st Century: Global Demographic Trends and Diaspora Missiology. *Great Commission Research Journal, 2,* 7-20.

Wan, E. (2011). *Diaspora Missiology: Theory, Methodology, and Practice.* Portland, OR: Institute of Diaspora Studies.

Warner, R. S., & Wittner, J. G. (1998). *Gatherings in Diaspora: Religious Communities and the New Immigration.* Philadelphia: Temple University Press.

Where are International Students Going in the United States? Retrieved September 7, 2013, from http://www.isionline.org/ChurchPartners/Whatarethetopcitiesforstudents.aspx.

Where are the International Students Coming From? Retrieved September 7, 2013, from http://www.isionline.org/ChurchPartners/Whatarethetopsendingcountries.aspx.

Winter, R. D., & Koch, B. A. (2009). Finishing the Task. *Key Readings,* 531.

Wright, N. T. (2014). *Surprised by Scripture: Engaging Contemporary Issues.* New York: HarperCollins.

www.joshuaproject.net. Retrieved June 18, 2013.

Zapata-Thomack, H. (March 22, 2014). *Tentative Diasporic Christology for Latino Global South Missionaries in the Midst of American Liminal Context.* Paper presented at the Evangelical Missiological Society Northeast Regional Meeting.

About the Author

Jared Looney (DMiss, Fuller Theological Seminary) is the executive director of Global City Mission Initiative (www.globalcitymission.org). He teaches seminary courses in practical theology as an adjunct professor, and he often teaches and consults on missiological themes.

About ULP

Urban Loft Publishers focuses on ideas, topics, themes, and conversations about all things urban. Renewing the city is the central theme and focus of what we publish. It is our intention to blend urban ministry, theology, urban planning, architecture, urbanism, stories, and the social sciences, as ways to drive the conversation. While we lean towards scholarly and academic works, we explore the fun and lighter sides of cities as well. We publish a wide variety of urban perspectives, from books by the experts about the city to personal stories and personal accounts of urbanites who live in the city.

www.urbanloftpublishers.com
@the_urban_loft

Made in the USA
San Bernardino, CA
24 July 2018